MW00781613

ADOPTING MISSION COMMAND

An Association of the U.S. Army Book

ADOPTING
MISSION
COMMAND

Developing Leaders for a Superior Command Culture

Donald E. Vandergriff

Naval Institute Press
Annapolis, Maryland

Naval Institute Press
291 Wood Road
Annapolis, MD 21402

Library of Congress Cataloging-in-Publication Data

Names: Vandergriff, Donald E., author.
Title: Adopting mission command : developing leaders for a superior command
    culture / Donald E. Vandergriff.
Other titles: Developing leaders for a superior command culture
Description: Annapolis, Maryland : Naval Institute Press, [2019] | Includes
    bibliographical references and index. |
Identifiers: LCCN 2019005813 (print) | LCCN 2019006634 (ebook) | ISBN
    9781682471043 (ePDF) | ISBN 9781682471043 (ePub) | ISBN 9781682471050
    (hardcover : alk. paper) | ISBN 9781682471043 (ebook)
Subjects: LCSH: Command of troops. | Leadership—Study and teaching—United
    States. | United States—Army—Officers—Training of. | Military
    education—United States.
Classification: LCC UB210 (ebook) | LCC UB210 .V364 2019 (print) | DDC
    355.3/30410973—dc23
LC record available at https://lccn.loc.gov/2019005813

∞ Print editions meet the requirements of ANSI/NISO z39.48-1992
(Permanence of Paper).

Printed in the United States of America.

27 26 25 24 23 22 21 20 19   9 8 7 6 5 4 3 2 1
First printing

This book is dedicated to my father, Virgil Malcolm Vandergriff, who taught me that truth is right, and to let it take you as far as it can. It is also to those officers, noncommissioned officers, soldiers, Marines, and cops who have moral courage to tell it like it is in the pursuit of effective Army, Marine Corps, and law enforcement agencies, despite the impact such candor may have had on their own careers. Finally, I would like to thank my wife, Lorraine, who stood by me through all the pain of deployments, thousands of hours away for research and writing, traveling nonstop after retirement—yet she still encouraged me to do more and do better.

Disclaimer

We would like to thank the following organizations for allowing reprinting of parts or whole of previous articles into chapters or sections in this book. They include The Association of the United States Army (AUSA) and the Institute of Land Warfare (ILW) for the introduction and chapter 6: "What is OBT&E (ASLTE)?"; the book *Raising the Bar: Creating and Nurturing Adaptive Leaders for the Changing Face of War* (originally published by the Project of Government Oversight, but turned over the rights of the author in January 2009, becoming the 2nd edition by May 2012) spread throughout the book, specifically parts of chapter 3: "Barriers to Mission Command," chapter 4: "Institutionalizing the Process: TRADOC," chapter 5: "The Result: What Happens Today?," chapter 7: "Who Teaches (Facilitates)?," chapter 9: "Tactical Decision Games or Exercises," chapter 12: "Combat Physical Fitness," and chapter 13: "Evaluations"; Armor Magazine, U.S. Army Maneuver Center of Excellence, Fort Benning, GA, for chapter 15: "J. S. Wood, the 4th Armored Division, and Mission Command." The author would also like to thank the following individuals for assisting him in writing parts of the book—Dr. Chet Richards and CPT Brett Friedman, USMCR, for chapter 1: "John Boyd, the OODA Loop, and Auftragstaktik?"; Dr. Jorg Muth for chapter 2: "The German Way of Command"; Lt. Col. Kevin McEnery (Ret.) on chapter 3: "Barriers to Mission Command"; CPT Joseph Bernard for chapter 10: "War-Gaming"; and finally Maj. P. J. Tremblay for assisting with the conclusion.

Contents

List of Illustrations   viii

Preface   ix

Acknowledgments   xi

Introduction   1

1   John Boyd, the OODA Loop, and Auftragstaktik   5

2   The German Way of Command   18

3   Barriers to Mission Command   41

4   Institutionalizing the Process: TRADOC   54

5   The Result: What Happens Today?   67

6   What is OBT&E (ASLT&E)?   78

7   Who Teaches (Facilitates)?   101

8   Creating Outcomes and Measures   122

9   Tactical Decision Games or Exercises   142

10   War-Gaming   169

11   Free-Play Force-on-Force Exercises   186

12   Combat Physical Fitness   196

13   Evaluations   214

14   Army Reconnaissance Course (ARC):   224

    What Right Looks Like

15   J. S. Wood, the 4th Armored Division, and   241

    Mission Command

16   Conclusion: It Is Not Easy, but the Payoff Will Be Great!   259

Notes   265

Selected Bibliography   291

Index   297

Illustrations

Boyd's OODA Loop   6

Heinz Guderian at Sedan   9

Field Marshal Erwin Rommel   13

Frederick the Great   27

Moltke, the "Father of Auftragstaktik"   28

The author teaching a map exercise   146

The Germans playing a Kriegsspiel (war game)   171

Prussian officers playing a Kriegsspiel   182

Students conducting reconnaissance   225

Maj. Gen. John S. Wood confers with a Frenchman   244

Lt. Col. Creighton Abrams   251

Preface

In September 2010, Dr. James G. Pierce, a retired U.S. Army colonel with the Strategic Studies Institute at the U.S. Army War College in Carlisle Barracks, Pennsylvania, published a study on Army organizational culture. Pierce postulated that "the ability of a professional organization to develop future leaders in a manner that perpetuates readiness to cope with future environmental and internal uncertainty depends on organizational culture."[1] This hypothesis was based on the assumption that organizational culture enables organizational adaptation; organizational culture perpetuates adaptability and promotes relevance and continued existence. Pierce's conclusion was alarming. He found that today's U.S. Army leadership "may be inadequately prepared to lead the profession toward future success."

This book is my recommendation for how to adapt a superior command culture through education and training. I also believe that by implementing these recommendations across the Army, other necessary and long-awaited reforms will finally take place.

This book reflects the evolution of my thoughts over the last sixteen years of research and writing. It is the latest in a series of books on the subject (*Path to Victory: America's Army and the Revolution in Human Affairs*, *Raising the Bar*, and *Manning the Legions of the United States*). I have personally experienced the power of these ideas by implementing them in the numerous organizations that I have led or served with. The results were incredible, and all because people were empowered to achieve excellence without being told how to do it in an environment conducive to learning and personal growth. On the other hand, over the last few years, the Army has plastered the term "mission command" all over documents, briefings, and in speeches by generals and high-level civilians. But what has changed?

I remember how excited I was to even see the word in Army Doctrine Reference Publication (ADRP) 6-0, *Mission Command*. Then I read it, and was disappointed in the lack of diagnosis, prognosis, and motivation. This book is how I would have written the ADRP 6-0.

Donald E. Vandergriff, MA, FRSA
MAJOR, USA (RET.)
DECEMBER 2014

Acknowledgments

A lot of great people at some point in the writing of this book helped me with it, and without them, I could not have done it. This book began in 2005 after I spent a couple of years learning to read German (at an elementary level) in order to enhance what I had discovered while writing my second book, *Path to Victory: America's Army and the Revolution in Human Affairs*. At this time, I became obsessed with how the Germans practiced *Auftragstaktik* in both peace and war. While writing my third book, *Raising the Bar: Creating and Nurturing Leaders to Deal with the Changing Face of War*, I grew interested in how the Germans created leaders and enabled them to operate under Auftragstaktik. I wanted to pass the lessons learned on to our military and other organizations. I prepared a four-week "Sergeant Leader's Course" for all sergeants of the Baltimore Police Department from August 2010 to March 2011 based on how the Germans developed their own cadets and officers using problem-solving games. The results were incredible (according to the police sergeant students who attended the course).

Many of my sources are available only in the original German *General der Panzertruppe Hermann Balck's Ordnung im Chaos*, from which I have gleaned many insights. It presents Balck's experiences as a soldier from a historical viewpoint and is also an enjoyable autobiography. This valuable work has been translated into English and I highly recommend it.

The war records I relied upon were taken from Germany at the end of the war and photo-filmed by the U.S. National Archives and Records Administration (NARA). These sources are located at the NARA College Park, Maryland, site (the staff there were extremely helpful). The originals have recently been returned to Germany. Many of these photocopied documents are written records of radio messages, transcribed by radio operators as they received calls. I appreciate the help I received from the NARA staff, particularly Timothy Nenninger, Robin Cookson, Larry MacDonald, and Less Waffen.

I am sincerely indebted to the following individuals for their time to explain, teach, and mentor me in the "German way of war" and Auftragstaktik, in helping me make the comparison with our "American way of war." While they are all authors of numerous books, I list here those most influential to my thinking: Jörg Muth, *Command Culture: Officer Education in the U.S. Army and the German Armed Forces, 1901–1940, in the Consequences for World War II.* Jörg has become a great friend and has never hesitated in helping translate or figure out German words and their meaning. He is also a man of great character, pushing the true version of U.S. leader development prior to World War II. There are also other good friends, including Bruce I. Gudmundsson, author of *Storm Troop Tactics: Innovation in the German Army 1914–1918,* who has mentored me on the details of Auftragstaktik over the years; Eitan Shamir, author of *Transforming Command: The Pursuit of Mission Command in the U.S., British, and Israeli Armies*; William S. Lind, author of *Maneuver Warfare Handbook*; Martin van Creveld, author of *Fighting Power: German and U.S. Army Performance, 1939–1945*; James Corum, author of *Roots of Blitzkrieg: Hans von Seeckt and German Military Reform* (whom I finally got to meet while speaking at the Baltic Defense College in Targa, Estonia, in October 2011); and Ola Kjoerstad, who penned "German Officer Education in the Interwar Years."

Robert M. Citino's work on the German army and military history, particularly leadership, was instrumental in my work (we indulged in frequent discussions on my Facebook page, "Developing for Mission Command," after this manuscript was submitted to the USNI Press). His books were invaluable to understanding the "German way of war." They include: *The German Way of War*; *The Path to Blitzkrieg*; *Blitzkrieg to Desert Storm*; *The Evolution of Blitzkrieg Tactics*; and *Quest for Decisive Victory*.

Also invaluable was Dr. Steven Stewart, who spent years discussing the concepts of individuals and organizational adaptability with me. His work is the basis for this book, as well as an understanding of how the Germans developed this adaptability in their forces. Finally, Lt. Col. John Sayen, USMC (Ret.), a brilliant expert on organization and force structure. His input on officer corps size and structure, as well as the history of the U.S. Army was invaluable in writing chapter 3: "Barriers to Mission Command." Without their guidance and insight, I could not have put this jigsaw puzzle together.

I cannot thank my friends and mentors enough for their input and insights: Col. Mike Wyly, USMC (Ret.); Col. G. I. Wilson, USMC (Ret.); Pierre Sprey; Winslow Wheeler; Lt. Col. Greg Wilcox, USA (Ret.); Dr. Chet Richards, USAF (Ret.); and Franklin "Chuck" Spinney. They have contributed to my understanding and appreciation of Col. John Boyd and his work over the last sixteen years, never failing to help me consider Boyd's meaning and intent. I must also mention Col. Douglas Macgregor, PhD, USA (Ret.), who made me think about how to develop a more effective Army. His work complements the developmental methods mentioned later in this book.

With regard to Army training and education as well as the latest and most innovative approaches, I owe much to Col. Casey Haskins, USA (Ret.). I consider Casey one of the best trainers in the U.S. Army. Casey is a man of incredible character, who had the moral courage and intelligence to push Outcomes-Based Training and Education (OBT&E) across the Army. But Casey is such a good teacher and leader that OBT&E continues to reside in the minds of thousands of officers and NCOs, and is still the basis for Programs of Instruction (POI) in many courses despite great bureaucratic resistance.

I would also like to thank CSM Morgan Darwin, USA (Ret.), who is a great trainer and leader. After retiring from the Army, he worked alongside Casey and me trying to reform Army leadership development. Morgan is one of the finest soldiers and gentlemen I have had the honor to know. Also, Lt. Col. Kevin McEnery, USA (Ret.), and Lt. Col. Blaise Cornell-d'Echert, USA (Ret.), who worked tirelessly to implement OBT&E and ASLT&E into Army courses over the last few years. Their efforts were significant in the development of the Army Reconnaissance Course (ARC). Their work also contributed to the chapter on Barriers to Mission Command. There are also soldiers and Marines such as Lt. Col. Chad Foster, who led the way at the Department of Military Instruction (DMI) at the United States Military Academy at West Point (USMA) in reforming how it teaches its cadets. Chad made it happen even before Casey Haskins took over as director of DMI. Once there, Casey simply accelerated the process Chad had begun. From the start Casey provided the all-important top cover from the bureaucracy and their antiquated way of developing cadets at the USMA.

I must mention Lt. Col. Scott Halter, who applied OBT&E and the Adaptive Course Model (ACM) in his battalion (Task Force Lift), while deployed to Afghanistan, and proved that OBT&E is applicable in aviation units as well. He shared these experiences in an excellent article, "Developing Adaptive Air Mission Commanders" (*Aviation Journal*, June 2014). I am grateful to Lt. Col. Ernest Coleman, USA (Ret.), of the Potawatomi Family of Companies, who worked hard to get me down to Fort Benning in the summer of 2014; and then my former employer, Yorktown Services Group, particularly Maj. Nick Fuller, USA (Ret.), and Maj. Vern Tubbs, USA (Ret.), who got me back to Fort Benning to teach my adaptability course to the Armor School in 2015. Finally, I also appreciate Capt. Joseph Bernard, whose input on chapter 10: "War-Gaming" was enlightening and Lt. Col. Andrew Dziengeleski, USA, who has been a great friend and supporter.

There is also Baltimore City Police Commissioner Frederick Bealefeld, who took a chance and allowed me to assist in implementing the ideas in this book in the development of his police officers from 2009–11. I would also like to mention my good friend Lt. Fred Leland of the Walpole Police Department in Walpole, Massachusetts, and owner of Law Enforcement and Security Consulting, who, as soon as he read my book, *Raising the Bar: Creating and Nurturing Adaptive Leaders to Deal with the Changing Face of War* in 2006, started implementing its concepts in the training of his officers, as well as consulting with other agencies. We also worked together over a year to write *The Adaptability Handbook for Law Enforcement* (Amazon, January 2014) for how to apply adaptability specifically to the law enforcement community. Finally, there is Lt. Stephen Webber, USN, who, while serving with the Ministry of Interior Advisors in Kabul, Afghanistan, during Operation Resolute Support, assisted me greatly with trimming the draft from 110,000 words down to 99,000 words, as well as making it better.

Numerous Marines at Quantico implemented the ideas of the Adaptive Course Model outlined later in this book at the Expeditionary Warfare School and the Infantry Officer Course. Thanks in particular to Lt. Col. Greg Thiele, Lt. Col. Marcus Mainz (both battalion commanders implementing these ideas), and Maj. P. J. Tremblay. P. J. also used the ideas outlined herein when he was a security forces advisor to the Afghanistan National Army in 2013–14, as well as during his time as a Marine rifle company commander in 2010–11. A big thank you to Capt. Brett Friedman, USMCR, who made some great recommendations for a better final manuscript, as well as his support of its ideas. Semper Fi to all you guys!

There are also several general officers who continue to offer inspiration to innovation and adaptability as the Army evolves in the twenty-first century after our long, costly, and frustrating wars in the Middle East. Maj. Gen. Jefforey Smith implemented several ideas against a sea of resistance while serving as commanding general at Cadet Command. Fortunately, he was followed by Maj. Gen. Peggy Combs, who, as deputy commander of Cadet Command in May 2012, first introduced my work and me to Major General Smith when he took command in April 2012. Major General Combs became commanding general of Cadet Command in April 2014 and continued to push OBT&E while revising the ROTC POI for the twenty-first century. I would also like to acknowledge my friend, Lt. Gen. H. R. McMaster, who took over Army Capabilities Integration Center (ARCIC, formally the Future's Center) of the Training and Doctrine Command (TRADOC); the Center is directly concerned with the future of the U.S. Army. No better leader could have been picked to lead ARCIC and influence the shape of the Army of the future. Lieutenant General McMaster also brought several historians into the Army's Maneuver Center of Excellence at Fort Benning, Georgia, to talk about mission command with students and cadre while he was commander from 2012–14.

I would like to thank the Association of the United States Army (AUSA) and the Institute of Land Warfare (ILW) for allowing the use of my previous articles (or portions thereof) in this book. Similarly, I am grateful to the folks at *Armor* magazine and the US Army

Maneuver Center of Excellence at Fort Benning, Georgia, for permitting the reuse of material in chapter 15.

Finally, to my wife Lorraine, who was not only patient and supportive while I spent a lot of time researching and writing, but also the rock while I was constantly deployed. She is the strength that kept the house steady while I have been away. She took care of everything, especially my "children" (four dogs and three parrots). Without her ability to help me translate mounds of German documents, I could not have gotten it done. She also constantly encouraged me to do more and push my ideas. She is truly my better half. I love you, Lorraine.

Introduction

This book is a guide to developing personnel to perform in an Auftragstaktik culture (or "mission command," as the U.S. military calls it). Today's highly complex operational environment highlights the importance of quality decision-making at junior levels for the U.S. Army. I do not address the situation as it applies to the Navy or the Air Force; while the mission command concept is of value to them, my own service and research only qualifies me to address it in the Army context.

Even with modern command, control, communications, computer, intelligence, surveillance, and reconnaissance (C4ISR) capabilities, the noncommissioned officer or junior officer on the ground has the best situational awareness (more often than not) and thus is likely to make the best decision—but only if he or she is equipped, intellectually and culturally, to properly assess the situation and creatively arrive at the best solution. The only way to gain these skills is to prepare professionally, and it is not easy.

Rote learning is no longer sufficient to produce the kind of soldiers needed for today's complicated challenges. Even now, Army courses continue to use true–false and multiple-choice exams to evaluate leaders. This will not do. Adaptability, critical thinking, and creativity have become critical skills for modern soldiers. While Army leaders may claim that they are changing the way they train and educate to ensure that those skills are instilled in their people, I say they are not. They are buying the latest digital learning devices, video equipment, sound systems, and training simulators to be sure, but the way they approach the classroom, how they develop the student's mind—especially early on—is lacking.

In this book I make the case for advancing the Army culture toward Auftragstaktik. I explain what this is and how to develop leaders who can operate within this doctrinal concept. The centralized governance within the Army—that is, top-to-bottom control—is outdated; a system such as Auftragstaktik, which gives more freedom for creativity, adaptability, and innovation, would better prepare the Army for future demands. It also encourages retention of soldiers who thrive on this type of freedom and flexibility. Additionally, Auftragstaktik would inevitably lead to reduction in undue competition between officers and noncommissioned officers. With this shift in focus, trust and flexibility become more widespread throughout the institution.

I have previously argued that the centralized personnel system currently entrenched in the Army can only be applied effectively in a stable environment. However, war is turbulent and unpredictable—particularly the type of asymmetric wars the U.S. is currently fighting—it does not lend itself to successful outcomes when prosecuted by an army that uses a centralized personnel system for recruitment, education, training, deployment, and retention of its soldiers. This also applies to the selection and promotion of its leaders. Under this system, the Army is less able to adapt to the often fast and unpredictable changes in the environment. This book addresses the cultural ramifications that render current approaches to leader development inadequate for the adoption of Auftragstaktik; the Army's members are not managed or treated as professionals. In support of Auftragstaktik, I pose many questions that must be addressed to develop a feasible and effective personnel system to support the U.S. Army in the twenty-first century.

In discussing the complexities and nuances of Auftragstaktik, I guide readers through a historical survey of the development of the military theory behind this term, highlighting specific examples of particular battles and notable military leaders relevant to the concept of mission command, addressing its failures as well as its successes. It is rooted in the German idea of Auftragstaktik, which implies that once one understands the commander's intent, he or she is responsible for using creativity and initiative to adapt to changing circumstances and accomplish the mission.

In detailing my argument, I will only touch upon the current force structure and personnel systems. These systems are legacies of the twentieth century, although certain elements can be traced back to our Civil War and even the Napoleonic era. As I have addressed the issue of personnel reform in my previous work, I will focus mainly on leader development. With the onset of advanced communications technology there is the recurring tendency for senior officers to micromanage their subordinates, rather than trusting them to accomplish the mission—and the mission is becoming increasingly ambiguous and difficult.

The question arises: Can the Army integrate the latest twenty-first-century information technologies and adhere to the philosophy of Auftragstaktik while its personnel system and force structure remain stuck in the twentieth century? Through my historical review of the last fifteen years, I have tried to show that this cannot be done without seriously examining changes to Army force structure, education, and personnel systems. We must start somewhere, and I feel strongly that we should begin by preparing leaders to operate under Auftragstaktik.

There is an answer to this conundrum and fortunately the Army is slowly moving in the right direction. Many junior and middle-grade officers, and a few senior officers, care. They see the foolishness of the current out-of-date learning methodologies employed by U.S. Army Training and Doctrine Command (TRADOC), as well as barriers to the mission command concept created by an archaic and horrible personnel system. But there is much work to be done.

Outcomes-Based Training and Education (OBT&E) and one of its learning methodologies, the Adaptive Course Model (ACM), have been implemented in several Centers of Excellence across the Army; they provide practical examples for how to teach Auftragstaktik in our twenty-first-century world. Implementing OBT&E and ACM to enable Auftragstaktik will allow the Army to take the time it needs to reform its personnel system and force structure and to support true mission command as an Army-wide doctrine.

Once we have a generation of young leaders that understands what it takes to successfully operate under Auftragstaktik, we can begin to evolve toward flatter and more adaptive organizations. This is what I will attempt to explain in detail in the pages of this book: how to develop these leaders (in every aspect of the term "how to")—including the latest data on learning science, our conceptions of adaptability, and the numerous tools available for developing our leaders. I will also provide an example of a course that is currently implementing most of the Auftragstaktik techniques, just as the Germans did more than a hundred years ago. Finally, I will also reveal the numerous barriers to innovation in today's Army, as well as the moves that can be taken to block the effective implementation of Auftragstaktik if we don't have the moral courage to address them head-on. The time is now to adopt new methods of leader development.

1

John Boyd, the OODA Loop, and Auftragstaktik

Give lower-level commanders wide freedom, *within an overall mind–time–space scheme*, to shape/direct their own activities so that they can exploit faster tempo/rhythm at tactical levels yet be in harmony with the larger pattern/slower rhythm associated with the more general aim and larger effort at the strategic level.

—COL. JOHN R. BOYD, "Patterns of Conflict"

John Boyd demonstrated the power of making sound decisions in a timely manner in his theory of decision-making. Boyd contended that human behavior follows a specific decision-making cycle. The four steps of the cycle are *Observation, Orientation, Decision*, and *Action*—abbreviated as the "OODA loop."

The side in a conflict that executes this decision-making process more rapidly and more effectively gains an advantage over his opponent because the opponent will constantly react to his actions. These continued reactions eventually result in poor decisions followed by paralysis of the entire opposition decision-making process. The common expression of the successful execution of this procedure is getting inside the enemy's decision-making cycle. The German approach to achieve this was innovative and progressive educational and training methodologies (the intangible solution), while the Western Allies, particularly the United States, have relied on technology to gain the edge over the enemy's OODA loop (the tangible solution).

The critical step in the OODA loop is orientation. In this step, analysis and synthesis of the observations take place; the process consists of taking many different disparate nuggets of data and information and translating them into a mental picture that the decision-maker can then use to make a decision. Boyd refers to this as "examining of the world from a number of perspectives so that we can generate mental images or impressions that correspond to the world."[1]

Boyd's OODA Loop

The OODA loop gains its power from the ability of a leader to form mental constructs. Timeliness and accuracy of decisions and actions relate directly to the decision-maker's ability to orient and reorient to rapidly changing and uncertain situations. Personal experiences, education, and training (which imparts knowledge) empower the leader to form these mental constructs.[2]

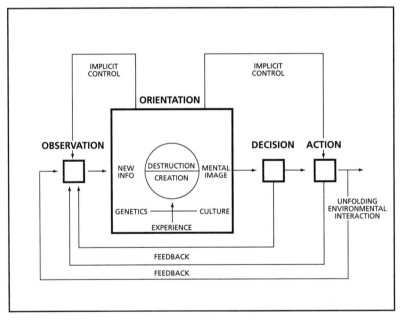

Boyd's OODA Loop

Dr. Chet Richards, "Conflict in the Years Ahead" (Atlanta, GA: J. Addams and Partners, Inc., August 2006), p.2, slide 46, "Unfortunately, it is not as simple as 'observe, then orient, then decide, then act.' In fact such a sequential model would be very ponderous and would not well describe how successful competitors operate."

Boyd's theory emphasizes the importance of the ability of leaders to think. By-the-book answers to specific well-known situations are not good enough. It is the ability to think that allows a leader to take the knowledge from personal experiences, education, and training and adapt it to the imperfect information of the present situation to arrive at a timely, sound, and workable solution to that situation.[3]

Applying the OODA loop faster than the opposition is the essence of situational or intuitive decision-making. It is the means of quantifying a mental process into a mechanistic action that your personnel can understand and apply. Decision-making superiority is merely creating a tactical decision-making base in the operating environment, but to get there takes a unique development, and it does not happen overnight or even in a few weeks.[4] As Dr. Chet Richards acknowledged, "Unfortunately, it is not as simple as 'observe, then orient, then decide, then act.' In fact, such a sequential model would be very ponderous and would not well describe how successful competitors operate."[5]

When Boyd talks about "faster OODA loop speed," he means the entire loop—all thirty-three or so arrows in Boyd's diagram. The key to quickness turns out to be the two "implicit guidance and control" arrows at the top. It is up to the subordinate to make the decision without waiting for permission; rather, he or she is guided by the "commander's intent." In other words, people and groups generally do not employ the explicit, sequential OODA mechanism. In *Sources of Power*, Gary Klein offers data suggesting that most of the time people simply observe and act.[6]

The question is, "What action?" A thinking opponent doesn't helpfully provide us with a laundry list of his tactics so we can work out our responses in advance. The mechanism that handles this uncertainty and makes the loop function in a real-world situation is *Orientation*.

As we take in information via the *Observe* gateway, and particularly when we spot mismatches between what we predict and what actually happens, we have to change our orientation (hence the implicit guidance and control flowing from orientation). New actions flow from new orientations, if we have the proper training to "meet the exigencies of the world."[7]

A leader who is prepared to operate successfully in an Auftragstaktik culture understands all the components that comprise timely (not rapid) decision-making, while understanding or explaining *why* they made the decision they made under those unique circumstances. Auftragstaktik is a "broad concept . . . embracing aspects of . . . a theory of the nature of war, character and leadership traits, tactics, command and control, senior subordinate relationships, and training and education. It . . . [is] a comprehensive approach to warfighting."[8] We will explore this foundational concept in depth in the next chapter.

Dr. Chet Richards uses the acronym EBFAS to describe the ideal company or military culture, based on German cultural concepts. An organization that has all of these elements in place is one that actually cares about having a sound "blitzkrieg culture." EBFAS stands for *Einheit, Behändigkeit, Fingerspitzengefühl, Auftragstaktik,* and *Schwerpunkt.*[9]

Fingerspitzengefühl: How Long Does It Take?[10]

Fingerspitzengefühl is one of the core concepts of Boyd's organizational climate, yet he only uses the term once in his *Discourse on Winning and Losing*.[11] As Dr. Richards states in a 2014 article, "We can't just look at our own personal experiences or use the same mental recipes over and over again; we've got to look at other disciplines and activities and relate or connect them to what we know from our experiences and the strategic world we live in." He believes that if we can do this, "we will be able to surface new repertoires and (hopefully) develop a Fingerspitzengefühl for folding our adversaries back inside themselves, morally–mentally–physically—so that they can neither appreciate nor cope with what's happening—without suffering the same fate ourselves."[12]

The term is associated with Hermann Balck, Heinz Guderian, and Erwin Rommel, and all had an almost magical ability to "feel" the flow of the battle and thereby to influence it. This idea of an intuitive feel for a situation carried over to Boyd's work: "Until you have Fingerspitzengefühl for something so that you can do it quickly, smoothly, and intuitively, you don't have it."[13]

The set of actions for which you do have such potentially effective responses we call your repertoire. Boyd talks about repertoire in his last briefing, "The Essence of Winning and Losing," in which he notes that we need both and according to Chet Richards, "an implicit repertoire of psychophysical skills shaped by environments and changes that have been previously experienced, and the ability to evolve new repertoires to deal with unfamiliar phenomena or unforeseen change."[14]

The OODA loop sketch, by the way, is a schematic for developing and using Fingerspitzengefühl. This perhaps mysterious statement may become more palatable if you read *The Essence of Winning and Losing* and Dr. Richard's brilliant essay on *Conceptual Spiral.*

How do we develop Fingerspitzengefühl? Boyd does not tell us the how-to in his numerous works, but he is great at identifying its strengths and the weakness (when one is not prepared). This is what this book is about, using Boyd's work as a springboard for the outcome we want to achieve in our leaders. This takes out the complicated "how to do it" by providing the tools to achieve the outcome of sound, fast, and decisive decisions. It involves constant practice using innovative education methods, but since the idea behind Fingerspitzengefühl is to deal with "unfamiliar phenomena or unforeseen change," somehow those have to enter into the equation. And perhaps most important of all, we have to do whatever it is we're doing as members of a team or other type of organization. The only advice Boyd gives concerns teams:

Expose individuals, with different skills and abilities, against a variety of situations—whereby each individual can observe and orient himself simultaneously to the others and to the variety of changing situations.

Why ?

In such an environment, a harmony, or focus and direction, in operations is created by the bonds of implicit communications and trust that evolve as a consequence of the similar mental images or impressions each individual creates and

Heinz Guderian at Sedan, France, 14 May 1940. *NARA*

commits to memory by repeatedly sharing the same variety of experiences in the same ways.[15]

The beneficial payoff is a command and control system, whose secret lies in what's unstated or not communicated to one another (in an explicit sense)—in order to exploit lower-level initiative yet realize higher-level intent, thereby diminishing friction and compressing time, hence gaining both quickness and security.[16]

Can groups have Fingerspitzengefühl? Yes, they can, but as cohesive groups that have bonded through difficult events. Boyd used the word *Einheit* (trust or unity) to describe an organization that seemed to be functioning as a unified organism with Fingerspitzengefühl. The quote above suggests that it's best to view Fingerspitzengefühl and Einheit as different aspects of the same underlying phenomenon and develop both at the same time. This is difficult to do, but unless a person can work harmoniously with others in the organization to accomplish the purposes of the organization, Fingerspitzengefühl is just showing off.[17]

Boyd and the "Mission Concept" (Mission Command)

Patterns of Conflict is the title of a PowerPoint presentation given by Boyd on his theories on modern combat and how the key to success was to upset the enemy's "observation-orientation-decision-action time cycle or loop," or OODA loop. *Patterns* developed the idea of a "counter-blitz," a blitzkrieg in reverse, with numerous attacks followed by withdrawals to the rear. The aim was to confuse the enemy by presenting no apparent strategy, reveal the enemy's intentions through the strength of the response, and present a misleading picture of the defender's own actions in order to disrupt the attacker's future plan of action.[18]

Patterns took Boyd twelve hours to present, and was first staged in 1976. Boyd never backed off from giving the entire briefing, as he understood the complexity of decision-making in warfare. When asked to provide executive summaries from politicians and generals, Boyd would reply, "No brief unless the whole brief."[19] *Patterns* grew enormously popular through the 1970s and was presented on many occasions, including a personal presentation to Dick Cheney in 1981. A 1980 presentation to the U.S. Marine Corps led to the development of an entirely new doctrinal system. Boyd's ideas also became the basis for AirLand Battle, the U.S. Army's European war-fighting doctrine from 1982 into the late 1990s. *Patterns* has been widely regarded as one of the most influential works of war-fighting theory of all time and has been compared to the seminal writings of Sun Tzu.[20]

How did strategist John Boyd approach Auftragstaktik in his famous *Patterns of Conflict* briefing?[21] Boyd always began the presentation with a question about how a concept contributed to the decision-making of the particular side using it. He queried, "How do mission and *Schwerpunkt* concepts give shape to this overall scheme?" Before we go further we will briefly define Schwerpunkt, which is important in relation to Auftragstaktik.

The Germans referred to a Schwerpunkt (focal point) and to a *Schwerpunktprinzip* (concentration principle) in the planning of operations. They viewed the Schwerpunkt as a center of gravity or point of maximum effort, where a decisive action could be achieved. Ground, mechanized, and tactical air forces were concentrated at this point of maximum effort whenever possible. By local success at the Schwerpunkt, a small force achieved a breakthrough and gained advantages by fighting in the enemy's rear. Heinz Guderian summarized this doctrine as "*Klotzen, nicht kleckern!*" ("Boot 'em, don't spatter 'em").[22] "The main force and the mass of munitions must be focused on the decisive point. . . . The attack will in this place have its Schwerpunkt."[23]

First Boyd talked about the professional bonding of trust that "mission concept" gave to the German Army. According to General Gunther Blumentritt, such a scheme presupposes a common outlook based upon "a body of professional officers who have received exactly the same training during the *long* years of peace and with the same tactical education, the same way of thinking, identical speech, hence a body of officers to whom all tactical conceptions were fully clear."[24]

This came from tough, but progressive education methodologies that served as the baseline for their leader development with, "Furthermore, à la General Blumentritt, it presupposes an officers training institution which allows the subordinate a *very great* measure of freedom of action and freedom in the *manner* of executing orders and which primarily calls for independent daring, initiative and sense of responsibility."[25]

Boyd goes on to add that "without a common outlook superiors cannot give subordinates freedom of action and maintain coherency of ongoing action. *Implication?* A common outlook possessed by 'a body of officers' represents a unifying theme that can be used to simultaneously encourage subordinate initiative yet realize superior intent."[26]

Boyd provided this summary of the glue that bonded the German army in the execution of high-risk operations, but then asked, "Very nice, but how do the German concepts of mission and Schwerpunkt give shape to this [overall mind–time–space] scheme?" Boyd went on to answer his own question on the next page of the briefing with, "The German concept of mission can be thought of as a contract, hence an agreement, between superior and subordinate. The subordinate agrees to make his actions serve his superior's intent in terms of *what* is to be accomplished, while the superior agrees to give his subordinate wide freedom to exercise his imagination and initiative in terms of *how* intent is to be realized."[27]

Interesting that Boyd uses the term contract between superior and subordinate. In that he means in order to gain the freedom to operate as the subordinate chooses (solve the problem as he sees fit), in return the subordinate will fulfill the superiors' intent (end state or outcome), "As part of this concept, the subordinate is given the right to challenge or question the feasibility of mission if he feels his superior's ideas on what can be achieved are not in accord with the existing situation or if he feels his superior has not given him adequate resources to carry it out. Likewise, the superior has every right to expect his subordinate to carry-out [sic] the mission contract when agreement is reached on what can be achieved consistent with the existing situation and resources provided."[28]

There is nothing like this in any other Western army: a contract of trust (not paper or legal) where a subordinate, in order to gain the ability to solve the problem they are given in the best way they see fit, and in return it gives his superiors the outcome they desire. This of course is easier said than done. It requires a lot of professional preparation and the right force structure, as well as personnel laws and policies that will enable, and not hinder this type of culture.

Boyd does present a possible weakness in this two-way agreement in that, "while this concept of mission gives form and expression to what is expected between an individual superior and subordinate, it does not suggest ways to coordinate or harmonize activities among many superiors and subordinates as a collective group."[29] These come next.

Schwerpunkt and "Mission Concepts" (Mission Command)

Boyd discovered that the Germans used the concept of Schwerpunkt (point of decision) to harmonize the independent actions created through Auftragstaktik, or as he says, "harmonize activities among many superiors and subordinates as a collective group."

Boyd correctly translated the German concept of Schwerpunkt thus: "Schwerpunkt acts as a center or axis or harmonizing agent that is used to help shape commitment and convey or carry-out intent, at all levels from theater to platoon, hence an image around which: Maneuver of all arms and supporting elements are focused to exploit opportunities and maintain tempo of operations, and Initiative of many subordinates is harmonized with superior intent."[30]

In 1933 the Germans drafted the *Truppenführung*, the doctrinal work that formed the foundation for World War II tactics based on lessons learned in World War I and experiments in the 1920s validating those lessons learned. Schwerpunkt tactics emphasized how to break an enemy's defenses. It would begin with a broad advance by light forces to identify a weak spot. Then the Germans would mass overwhelmingly against that weak spot in order to achieve a breakthrough. If the Germans could identify a weak spot before they began their attack, then they would identify a Schwerpunkt in order to achieve a decision. "By breaking through the enemy lines one would create chaos among enemy units and

Another example of Auftragstaktik: Field Marshal Erwin Rommel.

NARA

destroy their ability to fight as coherent units. This was the rule of thumb whether the enemy was large or small."[31]

In English translation Schwerpunkt means "main effort." In Western thought the main effort is where the attack or defense will be weighted with more resources or assets than in other zones (for attack) and sectors (for defense). In my analysis of many operations at all levels, I found that most main effort attacks or defenses had slightly more resources than in ancillary areas. The main effort may have some more air power and slightly more artillery support, but there is not much of a difference. And in some cases, if a senior commander is good, he will even designate his best subordinate commander to be the main effort.[32] But Schwerpunkt is more than that and reflects the philosophy of Auftragstaktik.

Boyd went further to identify this difference saying, "In this sense Schwerpunkt can be thought of as a focusing agent that naturally produces an unequal distribution of effort as a basis to generate superiority in some sectors by thinning out others, as well as a medium to realize superior intent without impeding initiative of many subordinates, hence a medium through which subordinate initiative is implicitly connected to superior intent." This is where the German commander at every level is meant to achieve a decisive decision.[33]

For example, look at Guderian's XIX Panzer Corps at Sedan, France on 14 May 1940. Guderian was the Schwerpunkt of the entire German effort in the 1940 attack on France. Each of Guderian's three panzer divisions was given a zone of attack. However, Guderian's breakthrough unit was the 1st Infantry Regiment under Col. Hermann Balck. Balck thus became the Schwerpunkt of the entire German army on 14 May 1940. He was given all available artillery and the air support from an entire air division of the army group. Balck was to attack in a five-hundred-meter wide zone. This meant that the main thrust of a panzer corps, which was the main thrust of Kleist's Panzer Group (army) and Army Group, came in a five-hundred-meter wide zone. This is the definition of Schwerpunkt tactics and the perfect practical example of how the doctrine describes a Schwerpunkt attack. The Germans wrote in *Truppenführung*, "A Schwerpunkt attack is characterized by: narrow sectors, arrangements for combined arms, including those of neighboring sectors, reinforced by heavy infantry weapons and artillery."[34]

The *Truppenführung* text concludes, "You can never be strong enough at the decisive point. You act contrary to this principle if you try to secure everywhere and waste resources on secondary missions."[35] This is the Western definition of "main effort." It is usually applied as a balancing act, but it is also a sign of a weak character. People who avoid making a decision will try to balance everywhere but will fail to achieve anything. Obviously, one cannot be too strong at the point where one wants to reach a decision. This is more or less the same conclusion that Frederick the Great arrived at when he said: "He, who defends everywhere, defends nowhere."[36]

Boyd's understanding of this was that "Schwerpunkt represents a *unifying concept* that provides a way to rapidly shape focus and direction of effort as well as harmonize support activities with combat operations, thereby permit a true decentralization of tactical command within centralized strategic guidance—without losing cohesion of overall effort."[37]

Just as important, the German commanders who were not the Schwerpunkt understood that it was in their duty to do everything possible to support the Schwerpunkt. In contrast this concept—that it is your duty to support the decision point by whatever means possible—is not expressed anywhere in other Western doctrine. Additionally, one should be prepared to assume the Schwerpunkt if the situation changes. Boyd went on to say that "Schwerpunkt represents a *unifying medium* that provides a directed way to tie initiative of many subordinate actions with superior intent as a basis to diminish friction and compress time in order to generate a favorable mismatch in time/ability to shape and adapt to unfolding circumstances."[38]

Finally, Boyd's summary of "mission concept" was that "the German operational philosophy based upon a common outlook and freedom of action, and realized through their concepts of mission and Schwerpunkt, emphasized *implicit over explicit* communication."[39]

The idea of implicit over explicit led to the core of Boyd's understanding of the power of Auftragstaktik. He stated that *implicit* was rooted in the culture: how a leader had been brought up, rewarded and punished, how he or she had been selected, and so forth. This led to his conclusion, "The secret of the German command and control system lies in what's *unstated or not communicated to one another*—to exploit lower-level initiative yet realize higher-level intent, thereby diminish friction and reduce time, hence gain both quickness and security."[40]

Boyd, who spent decades studying warfare and how people made decisions, narrowed down the German's "result" saying, "The Germans were able to repeatedly operate inside their adversary's observation–orientation–decision–action loops." He went further to employ a quote from one of the many leaders who practiced this approach by adding, "As stated by General Blumentritt, the entire operational and tactical leadership method hinged upon . . . *rapid*, concise assessment of situations . . . *quick* decision and *quick* execution, on the principle: 'each minute ahead of the enemy is an advantage.' "[41]

What Does This All Mean?

Boyd's analysis of the German way of war is brilliant; it clearly stipulates that it takes unique and progressive learning methodologies in the professional development of personnel to make these approaches work. It is not easy! Boyd concludes with a few points that Chet Richards shares with us: "Auftrag = 'contract' or order as in an order to buy a car. Auftragstaktik is a personal device, given the common outlook and the group harmonizing of the Schwerpunkt. It's how you put each of your subordinates into the picture by 'mission orders.' "[42]

Richards elaborates with a few points that apply to Auftragstaktik:

- A "contract" implies freedom to choose (to paraphrase Milton Friedman).
- If there is no choice, then you have a *Befehl* (order), such as "Right face!"
- Communication even after accepting the Auftrag is critical.
- If the subordinate doesn't ask questions, he or she may not be the right person for the job.[43]

If action is flowing smoothly and (nearly) instantaneously from orientation, as it should the vast majority of the time, then the speed that counts is the speed to reorient in response to changing external and internal conditions. That speed is symbolized by three of the most adept practitioners of maneuver warfare: Heinz Guderian, Hermann Balck, and Erwin Rommel. There is no case where slower is better.

Given that your orientation is well matched to reality, you must have actions available to influence the situation, and these actions must flow smoothly and rapidly from orientation. Otherwise you hesitate (perhaps in endless rounds of meetings and conferences) and provide an opportunity for the enemy to figure out what you're up to—to operate inside your OODA loops.

Obviously, this requires the right education, extensive practice, and unit training under constantly changing conditions.

What It Really Means

Note that in some of the components of "implicit guidance and control," the "decision–hypothesis" link is also used when you must exert control explicitly.[44] Against a well-prepared opponent, explicit control should be rare, since it is always much slower than implicit control.

Note also that in the original concept of the OODA loop, speed and accuracy of decisions will tend to trade off. That is, you improve one only by shortchanging the other. This doesn't happen in the OODA loop that Boyd initially conceived.

How do we develop these abilities to make Auftragstaktik a reality? This will be addressed in the second half of this book. The first half lays a foundation of understanding, the "why" behind Auftragstaktik and the associated adaptability required to make it effective. One supports the other, and not the other way around.

2

The German Way of Command

In the German Army we use what we term "mission tactics"; orders are not written out in the minutest detail, a mission is merely given to a commander. How it shall be carried out is his problem. This is done because the commander on the ground is the only one who can correctly judge existing conditions and take proper action if a change occurs in the situation.[1]

—ADOLF VON SCHELL, *Battle Leadership*

As an exchange officer at the U.S. Army Infantry School at Fort Benning, Georgia in the 1930s, Captain Adolf von Schell translates Auftragstaktik as "mission tactics." Although English translations exist, it is difficult to understand the meaning of it unless one strenuously researches into the origins of the concept. The Prussian/German concept is interesting in two ways.[2]

First it explains how the Germans believe in the primacy of speed over enemies. The Germans mean faster not in terms of physical speed, but faster in making decisions. Timely and sound decisions translate into increased speed. Germans would do this with progressive and innovative development approaches. Technology was only seen enhancing the development of their leaders to improve their decision-making. More importantly, it speaks to the kind of leadership an army needed to operate under this concept. This is key to understanding what an army or any organization must do in order to change their culture.

18

U.S. historians have long explained the German victories in the early years of World War II through superior German equipment and numbers. Nothing could be further from the truth. As historian and author Dr. James Corum explains in the introduction of Condell and Zabecki's study, *On the German Art of War, Truppenführung*, "For years after the 1940 campaign the German victory was explained by Germany's employment of masses of tanks, motorized forces and aircraft against an enemy bound to the Maginot Line and a defensive strategy. However, we now know that in terms of numbers of troops and weapons, the Wehrmacht in 1940 held few advantages. Indeed, it was often at a disadvantage against the Allied forces."[3]

Taking into account the Western or Industrial Age tactical principle that an attacking force should have a force ratio of 3:1, this chapter explains the roots of the German success based on the intangibles of leadership, especially how they developed and nurtured the intangibles of leadership. It does this by explaining that it was not the content they taught leaders, but the context environment and the methodology of the trainer. This differs greatly from the methods currently employed by the U.S. Army, which focuses on the content and time, inputs versus outcomes. To effectively practice Auftragstaktik one must practice in war and in peace, every day in everything they do.[4]

On Auftragstaktik

As noted, the common translation of Auftragstaktik as "mission-type orders" or "mission command" is unfortunate. This focuses the attention in the U.S. sense on paragraph 2 of the U.S. operations order. If there is to be a focus on any part of the U.S. operations order, it should be on paragraphs 3a (Concept of the Operation) and 3b (Coordinating Instructions).[5]

Auftragstaktik emphasizes the commander's intent, which gives the subordinate a base from which to make his own decisions, so that they are in harmony with the overall plan. "The German Army used mission statements . . . in the form of the commander's intent. . . . The commander then assigned tasks (Aufträge) to subordinate units to carry out his superior's intent. The subordinate commander decided upon a specific course of action which became his resolution (Entschluss)."[6] Auftragstaktik "explains basic principles of giving orders for operations."[7]

German military training designed to foster this kind of individual initiative was the major outcome of German officer and soldier education. In short, the officer corps was taught how to think, not what to think.[8] Two generals, Hermann Balck and Friedrich von Mellenthin, stated during discussions with Col. John Boyd and Pierre Sprey in 1979 that they "considered the individuality of the German fighting man—his freedom to take initiative and the system which engendered these policies and attributes—to be the key superlative German performance."[9]

The German army culture continued to stress that a higher commander rarely if ever reproached a subordinate if he showed initiative. It was much better to make a good decision now, than to spend considerable time to find the best possible solution or, worse, to wait for more accurate information before taking action. This attitude extended down through the ranks, to the individual soldier. As Dr. Bruce I. Gudmundsson stated, the German army was, ever since the times of Frederick the Great, one of "the most decentralized ones in Europe."[10]

In a situation when contact with the higher commander was lost, the subordinate could be counted on to take appropriate action, rather than to stop and wait until contact was reestablished. This aggressive attitude allowed units to take advantage of local successes. In short, "nothing laid down from above in advance is sacrosanct. A subordinate commander . . . is justified . . . in modifying or even changing the task assigned him," as long as his action supports the higher commander's intent.[11]

The core of the success of Auftragstaktik was the strenuous selection and development of German leaders. There were three personal qualities that the Germans clearly valued in their officers. They were knowledge, independence, and the joy of taking responsibility. Knowledge served at least two purposes. First of all, knowledge was what made the officer know what to do or was the foundation for making a decision.

At the same time, it was also the main source for generating trust among your subordinates. Independence was also related to decision making. Independence was needed because, as an officer, you were the only one present where decisions had to be made. You could not wait for others to tell you what to do and when to do it. The last and the most important personal quality was the joy of taking responsibility. The joy of taking responsibility was what kept you on the battlefield. It was what forced you to stay despite the horrors you were experiencing. It was what made you endure.[12]

The best way to separate the great from everyone else was placing responsibility on their shoulders from the top commander down to each individual soldier. Not only were they responsible for their own units but they were responsible for "service to the people." This leads to the introduction of an interesting German word, *Verantwortungsfreudigkeit*. German doctrine as early as World War I uses this term, but particularly it is highlighted in the 1933 *Truppenführung*. The 1921 manual, *Führung und Gefecht der Verbundenen Waffen* in 1921–23 says, "the most distinguished leaders' quality is the joy of taking responsibility."[13]

Truppenführung (1933) dives into this concept: "All leaders must in all situations without fearing responsibility exert his whole personality. The joy of taking responsibility is the most distinguished leader quality." This reflects the German's emphasis on responsibility. Clausewitz discussed the well-known fact that an officer has to handle the responsibility he has on his shoulders. What is different and new is that the Germans wanted the officer to enjoy responsibility.[14]

Why is it important for an officer to enjoy responsibility? Independence was what equipped an officer to handle uncertainty and still make independent decisions. But when faced with the horrors of the battlefield an officer needs more than just independence to keep him vigorous. When everything is difficult and everyone around him seems to have given up that is when the feeling of responsibility kicks in. It is the feeling that it is up to him to decide the outcome of the engagement when everyone else has given up and he experiences the "emptiness of the battlefield."[15] This is why *Verantwortungsfreudigkeit*,[16] or the joy of taking responsibility, is what makes the officer "endure the situation" on the battlefield, and is why it is the most important quality for a leader.[17]

That is why there are no chapters in the book about single personalities because they do not play a major role in Auftragstaktik.[18] Though there are a few leaders that warrant mention as they had a hand in exemplifying and enabling Auftragstaktik. The Germans were able to teach the concept to a great many officers and NCOs. They found a way to make it a part of their culture. It is Auftragstaktik playing the major role and not the people. The following examples highlight how Auftsragstaktik enabled good leaders to be even greater regardless of their rank. "The Army is inseparably connected with the operations themselves. . . . If the views shaping original deployment are incorrect, the work is completely without value. Even a single error in the original assembly of the armies can hardly ever be made good again during the entire course of the campaign."[19]

In Context and Environment

If one gives a leader his or her mission and flexibility to act within the limits of this mission, that officer/leader will feel responsible for what he or she does. For this to be possible on the battlefield, it must have first been practiced in training. One cannot expect initiative and independent action from junior leaders if this is not a natural part of daily training, or "how they grew up," so to speak.

The best way to implement Auftragstaktik is to examine how others have done it through case studies. Until recently, most historical studies focused on the Prussian and German practice of mission command on the battlefield. Recently, new studies have begun to consider the "peacetime practices" that enabled mission command in the German army. Even the U.S. Army has recently stated in its Field Manual 7-0, *Training*, "If mission command is not practiced in training, leaders will not use it in operations."[20]

Recent research focuses on the link between Auftragstaktik and the German military education system. German institutions had evolved since the reforms of Gerhard von Scharnhorst in 1809. Over the course of a century they evolved together with an emphasis on developing and nurturing leaders of strong character and independent mind. These individuals took and sought responsibility, even taking joy in the challenge of decision-making.[21]

First of all, the German personnel system was decentralized. Leader development was held as the premier mission of commanders in the German army. Officers were strenuously developed and selected through one of the finest professional education programs in the world. Intensive professional education came first in an officer's career, beginning when he was a new cadet and continuing through the last course he would take as a captain at the *Kriegsakademie*. After that, professional education, through individual initiative, was highly encouraged. There was no centralized control of training and education except through the guidance of the General Staff and commanders. If leaders needed updating on the latest tactics, techniques, or technology, it was left to corps and divisions to devise their own courses.[22]

Commanders used staff rides and after-action reviews of free-play force-on-force exercises to further develop their subordinates. Additionally, from the time they were cadets at the military academies throughout their time as junior officers, German officers were given time off and evaluated on their character and conduct during unsupervised time. Conduct off duty was as important as performance on duty. One cannot determine a leader's potential to innovate, solve problems, or make decisions if he is completely controlled in his professional educational environment, be it on or off duty.[23]

Another way to practice Auftragstaktik on the institutional side was to keep written correspondence as concise as possible. This began during the education of officer cadets.

Examinations were used to screen candidates as they advanced from different levels of cadet through lieutenant and then to captain. Examinations centered on tactical problems that put the cadet and junior officers in roles of responsibility two to three levels above their current position. For example, the German cadet or lieutenant would be given a regimental problem to solve, but the solution had to be expressed in the form of written orders as concise as possible, one page being preferred, with no school solutions on which to base their prior knowledge. Their problem-solving ability had been developed through numerous map and staff exercises and an exhaustive study of military history.[24]

Another example is the German approach to training. In 1888, records indicate that German army guidance on training was based on principles and outcomes. A German cavalry squadron was expected to perform certain tasks, expressed in German army training guidance: attack, defend, screen, and conduct reconnaissance. The guidance defined the expected outcome, but units were expected to train to the mission independently with the resources afforded them by the Germany army. Each commander could deviate from the other squadrons as long as he adhered to the principles (or outcomes) of the General Staff and his commanders.[25]

On one occasion, when members of the General Staff later inspected the performance of the seven different squadrons in free-play force-on-force maneuvers, six succeeded and one failed. The German army took actions by relieving the failed officers and promoting successful commanders from the exercise.[26] This example is just one of thousands of how the Germans applied Auftragstaktik to their training institution. British officers after World War I and U.S. Army officers in World War II were amazed by this decentralization of training based sometimes on "little more than a page of yearly guidance." German officers replied again and again that their army valued the independence and innovation of their subordinate commanders over standardization. Standardization in other armies was used so that all units could reach a minimal standard for war.

In *Command Culture*, Jörg Muth describes the impact of Auftragstaktik culture on German military effectiveness:

> The strength of the Wehrmacht officer corps lay in the creativity, leadership capabilities and tactical finesse of officers who commanded anything from platoons to corps. They had been taught to be innovative and inventive, to disregard doctrine when desirable, to surprise the enemy whenever possible, and to live and survive in the chaos of war. They were taught to welcome that chaos and use it against the enemy instead of making sense of it with a "school solution" or a preconceived doctrine. German officers were able to give oral orders an instant after a short tactical deliberation, employing Auftragstaktik, trusting their subordinate commanders to carry out those orders with minimum interference.

They would go forward with their troops into battle to observe the fighting and go into combat themselves if necessary—from lieutenant to major generals. Those abilities were the power of the German officer corps that enabled them to hold out for so long, inflict catastrophic casualties on their enemies, and made them the terror of Europe.[27]

As mentioned later, there is the need to reform the U.S. Army personnel system, and there are multiple efforts beyond the scope of this book that promise effective reform if put to practice. What can take place today to enable Auftragstaktik is a revolution through the application of Outcomes-Based Training and Education (OBT&E). This methodology supports the Army Learning Model (ALM) 2015 while preparing soldiers to perform under Auftragstaktik. In the spirit of Auftragstaktik leaders and soldiers are already taking the concept of ALM 2015 and implementing new learning methods that, after sixteen years of war, will better prepare our soldiers and leaders for the future.

Assessing Leaders: It Is All about Strength of Character

Through all of an officer's education and training, the individual's decision was honoured, and if wrong, corrected without condemnation. To do otherwise would have stifled initiative . . . officers who completed the military schools found it unnecessary to receive detailed specifics from higher headquarters in orders and directives. . . . Their thinking was not limited to specified doctrine or techniques but had more to do with a professional devotion to fulfilling the commander's intentions.[28]

Making decisions sounds easy but being able to make decisions in battle is very challenging. One should therefore ask which qualities are needed for a leader to make sound decisions.[29]

What choice did Prussia have to defend itself? Could it rely on a larger landmass to buy time while defending? No, it could not. Did it possess a large amount of resources without having to import them? No, it did not. By the time of Napoleon, Prussia was a small country with little population. They could not afford long wars, especially situated in the middle of Europe surrounded by many hostile nations.[30]

Enter Frederick II (later known as Frederick the Great) the first king who was drilled in the line with regular soldiers in the 1740s. He started his first war at age twenty-nine with little knowledge of battle. Frederick had the well-drilled Prussian army at his disposal. Meticulously crafted by his father, Frederick Wilhelm I, Frederick's army was a standing, professional force capable of significantly greater rates of fire than its adversaries.[31] As Prussia had been at peace for some time, the effectiveness and potency of the Prussian army was largely unknown in Europe. As a standing force, his army was able to quickly muster and strike into Silesia. Overwhelming the majority of the Austrian border forces, Frederick's men secured most of region before the Austrians could assemble an army to oppose him.[32]

In his first battle, at Mollwitz on 10 April 1741, both wings of the Prussian army were defeated. The king went away to gather reinforcements because he was the best rider in the army. His second in command, the grizzled old Field Marshal von Schwerin ordered the center to attack while the enemy expected the entire Prussian army to flee the battle. Working to restore order, Schwerin was enabled by the Prussians' excellent training. Several units pivoted in an orderly fashion to meet the threat. Unleashing devastating volleys, they killed the Austrian cavalry commander and successfully turned back the attack. In an attempt to maintain pressure, the Austrian commander, Neipperg, ordered a similar cavalry attack on the Prussian left but was defeated by intense fire. Prussia won despite sustaining heavy casualties.[33]

From this battle, Frederick learned two significant lessons: never leave the battlefield again, and draw from the experience of his battlewise regimental commanders (who had recommended the course that ultimately won the battle). From this battle onward, Frederick insisted that his regimental commanders act on their own initiative and act aggressively. This concept was unheard of in early modern times when a regimental commander was only responsible to form a line, maintain order in battle, and follow orders. It was the beginning of a culture that encouraged its officers, and eventually even its privates, to demonstrate initiative and independence when the situation called for it.[34]

Frederick the Great and staff at the Battle of Leuthen, 5 December 1757.

Hugo Ungewitter, NARA

Frederick also became a harsh taskmaster, but not in the way that myths have portrayed him. Yes, the Prussian army had the highest number of officer court-martials (up to general rank), but never was an officer court-martialed because of a mistake made due to aggressiveness.[35] This is a key aspect that later reformers would remember about Frederick, while he encouraged aggressiveness and initiative he also tolerated mistakes, made while taking decisive action. In desperate moments during battle, the king would also move forward into the first battle line and thus set the example for all officers. This was also unheard of in early modern times.[36]

But for all of Fredrick's greatness, he left no capable successor. As he was both king and battle leader of the army—especially the officer corps—the officer corps slowly withered away.[37] The rot of the officer corps came apart in the Battle of Jena and Auerstaedt (central Germany), October 1806. The battle stretched over more than twenty miles with three different points of gravity. Prussian soldiers showed themselves to be far superior to the French, but Prussian command and control was horribly top-down and centralized; thus, the double-battle ended in a humiliating defeat (officers may be extremely brave but will not make decisions without higher permission—they cannot adapt to changing battle).[38]

Prussian army reformers led by Gerhard von Scharnhorst studied Frederick the Great's numerous writings on leadership and initiative and reemphasized the independence of the commander on the spot during Prussian army reform.[39] The reform movement began in 1801 with Scharnhorst forming an intellectual group to write papers and foment debate regardless of rank. The first reforms followed the disaster of Jena–Auerstadt with the Act of 1809 emphasizing leader development, restructure of corps and divisions, and first application of general staff specialist to advice commander (follow-on reforms focused on the training, treatment, and punishment of soldiers).[40]

Helmuth von Moltke was a crucial figure in late-nineteenth-century European warfare. Following the French Revolution and the Napoleonic Wars (1792–1815), technology—such as the telegraph, railroads, and breechloading firearms—grew rapidly, complicating military operations. In particular, offensives became increasingly difficult, as the Crimean War (1854–56) and the American Civil War (1861–65) clearly demonstrated. These new technologies coincided with the dramatic rise of mass armies.[41]

More than any other individual, Moltke balanced the new technology and mass armies with the unchanging characteristics of war. He guided Prussia to victories over Denmark (1864), Austria (1866), and France (1870–71). Prussia became the leader of a new, unified German Empire. Moltke's art of war was not based on a strict set of rules; rather, it followed general outlines that allowed for flexibility. Most important, however, it was practiced by highly developed professionals.[42]

Field Marshal Melmuth von Moltke, the "Father of Auftragstaktik."

NARA

Moltke was a follower of Carl von Clausewitz, one of the most influential military writers of the modern age. Clausewitz argued that war was too unpredictable to be explained by specific theories. In his foundational study, *On War*, he stated, "Everything in war is very simple, but the simplest thing is diffi-cult." He also cautioned, "No other human activity is so continuously or universally bound up with chance," and declared in conclusion, "War is thus an act of force to compel our enemy to do our will."[43]

Moltke also followed Clausewitz' belief that probabilities would determine each encounter while an army adapted to each circum-stance as it arose. Moltke served as chief of the Prussian General Staff from 1857 to 1888. He almost immediately expanded the General Staff's influence, developing it into a permanent, peacetime war plan-ning organization.

Helmuth von Moltke was a student of Frederick's writings; as well as a pupil of Carl von Clausewitz. Moltke realized that in the age of mass armies and rapid transportation by railroad—independence in com-mand was more important than ever. Moltke was the first to formulate the concept of Auftragstaktik as critic of maneuvers in 1858 when not yet chief of staff. He was appalled by the sluggishness of the chain of command and the lack of initiative shown and states that "as a rule an order should contain only what the subordinate for the achievement of his goals cannot determine on his own." Moltke began to feel that everything else was to be left to the commander on the spot.[44]

After becoming chief of staff of the General Staff, Moltke and his pupils relentlessly championed Auftragstaktik as a new command sys-tem. It remained heavily embattled within the German army, while professional debate was encouraged among all ranks regarding how to implement and develop leaders. Finally, it was formally introduced in the *Manual of 1888* as the empowerment of subordinates, while not burdening them with too many details. It stated "give subordinates enough guidance in terms of your [a superior's] vision of success to get them going without telling subordinates how to do it."[45]

Additionally, the results of the debate were seen in the wars of 1864, '66, and '70 with the independence of subordinates winning many battles as they adjusted out-of-date orders on their own accord. This cultural independence of subordinates, encouraged as low as private, was unheard of in other armies of the period. Ironically, the 120-plus American officers who visited Europe and Prussia during the nineteenth century completely missed out on the discussion of Auftragstaktik. They attribute the professional German military culture to efficiency and prevailing business models (bureaucracy was the fad of the day).[46]

The Germans also had a cultural foundation upon which Auftragstaktik existed. German public education was considered among the finest in the world. The officer aspirant had several hurdles to overcome. He had to possess an *Abitur* degree (general qualification for university entrance). Ironically, while discipline was already established in a highly authoritarian society, the army began a cadet's professional journey through one of the most advanced and liberal educations in the world. As Dr. Jörg Muth observed, "Civil War hero and military reformer General Emory Upton, USMA 1861, noted after his tour through Europe that the entire mathematics curriculum of the *Hauptkadettenanstalt* [military academy] would be taught at the United States Military Academy in one year. This observation shows remarkably well the narrow focus of a former West Pointer and the misunderstandings about an officer education."[47]

The selection of potential officers began with stepping into a regiment as *Fahnenjunker* age sixteen to nineteen. The individual could also enter a cadet preparatory school (*Voranstalt*) age ten to fifteen, before entering the main cadet institution (*Hauptkadettenanstalt*) between the ages of fifteen to seventeen. The POI of the Voranstalt and Hauptkadettenschule was the curriculum of a civilian school with added military drills and a large portion of athletics including bayonet fighting. In contrast to the U.S. Military Academy and other American military schools at the time, and with the introduction of Auftragstaktik (1860s), hazing was banned from all schools.[48]

Of the total officer population, 50 percent of officers came from *Kadettenschulen* (cadet schools) and 50 percent from the ranks during expansion. The Prussian NCOs corps maintained high standards as well as focused on combat leadership so transitioning them to officers during mobilization made the process of professionalism easier. The focus here will be on the Program of Instruction (POI) for the Kadettenschulen. They were all considered Voranstalten. Aspiring officers were admitted as early as ten years but normally fourteen years (to the *Hauptkadettenanstalt* [HKA] in Berlin) until as late as nineteen years old. Three years later, and after a difficult entrance exam, as well as a recommendation for their regimental commander, the new ensigns (officers) would be sent to the *Kriegsschule* (war school) for eight months to one-and-a-half years (last formal school overseen by general staff at the army level). Army schools focused on combat leadership, weapon handling, and the training of subordinates for combat—the art of decision-making.[49]

The curriculum was taught by the "best of the best." The top officers were selected as cadre for duty at formal schools (American officers were "fascinated" by German officers' teaching abilities in the nineteenth and early twentieth centuries). Leadership and faculty took active debate in evolving curriculum based on latest learning methods (no centralized driven curriculum apart from outcomes). Even free time or time off was part of leader evaluation and was handed out quite liberally compared to the U.S. Military Academy of the same period (another way to look at character and self-discipline). Additionally, the element of surprise was common in German leader development (routines and schedules were discouraged).[50]

The graduating and grading system was complicated. Cadets were evaluated equally for character and scholarly abilities. One could outperform others with higher academic standing due to their own leadership abilities. The curriculum consisted of little lecture—the focus was on using tools, such as map exercises, war games, tactical decision games, as well as a liberal education (a lot of reading and discussions). "Technical" fields, such as engineering, signal, and medicine, were the only ones focused on math- and science-intensive fields.

The Germans found that hazing was detrimental to developing self-confident, innovative, honest, and quick-thinking leaders, and had eliminated it by the end of the nineteenth century. The measures against hazing included having upperclassmen directly responsible for the protection of younger cadets. There was no "Beast Barracks" at German schools. There were officers present at all times, and they were role models in treating the young cadets humanely and professionally. The newcomers got upperclassmen helpers to introduce them to the system. One upperclassman (room elder) was responsible for one room of young cadets. The upperclassman was judged by his performance, motivating every room elder to protect his flock.[51]

Leadership performance determined the cadet's advancement and promotion rather than scholarly ability alone. In exceptional cases cadets who had failed many courses but showed themselves to be exceptional leaders were still advanced through the school. All cadets, no matter their seniority, were divided into five moral classes. Their promotion was based on standing in moral classes not seniority (they were not managed by year groups but by performance and potential). In showing exceptional performance, younger cadets could be promoted over the heads of older cadets.[52]

Several problem-style or essay-centric examinations also determined advancement. With each successful completion of a given phase or level, the uniform of the cadet changed slightly. In the Hauptkadettenanstalt, after successfully finishing all ensign examinations, cadets could stay on and get their Abitur degree (general entry to a university). Of those, a few were selected for an advanced class, which was similar to a cadet version of today's U.S. Army's School of Advanced Military Science (SAMS).

Of this class only a handful had the chance to be commissioned as lieutenants (for most of the nineteenth century and early twentieth century, German officer ratio to the enlisted force remained at 2.5 percent versus the United States with 9–12 percent during World War II, and today over 15 percent). All the other cadets were moved to their assigned regiments *without* being commissioned. After several months at the regiment, some more at a Kriegsschule and after that a council of the regiment's officers would decide if the officer candidate would become a lieutenant.[53]

Formal schooling ended at the first lieutenant and captain level (if chosen to attend the Kriegsakademie). Formal schooling for all officers was the cadet schools and the war school (five to eighteen months). There were two formal army professional courses. They were the Kriegsschule (war schools) and the Kriegsakademie. The Kriegsschule was five to eighteen months long based on ability of individuals to progress based on results of free-play force-on-force war games (exams). The focus was platoon and company tactics (students were still ensigns).

Teaching tools included tactical decision games and war games, with all sessions with discussions on student solutions to problems.

Other classes included military history and weapons training. Ensigns were also put together in classes regarding their branches, individual knowledge, and learning speed. In all courses, the Germans sought clarity and brevity in their orders. As with the cadet schools, free time and social events continued to be used as tools to assess character off duty.

All first lieutenants (*Oberleutnant*) with five to eight years of service had to take defense district examination (*Wehrkreis-Prüfung*) to determine attendance at the Kriegsakademie for the General Staff. They took the examination when their regimental commander deemed them ready. Preparation for the examination took over a year. The examination took five to seven days and included applied tactics (command a reinforced regiment in two cases), a map problem, a history essay, a constitutional law essay, and a "What do you think?" question. Is the new armored car of the cavalry also suitable for the artillery? What kind of modifications would you recommend?

Additionally, German officers needed to demonstrate the ability to translate in two languages. U.S. Army officers were impressed by the English proficiency of the German officers they met in the interwar years, as well as ones they captured in the World Wars. There was also an athletic test consisting of running several miles cross-country as well as on a track and a tactical foot road march with equipment. Finally, after all this between 15 percent and 30 percent of officers were allowed to enter the Kriegsakademie. The breaking determination was the character assessment by the regimental commander; this counted as much as examinations results.[54]

The Kriegsakademie was three years, with class sizes ranging from twelve to fifteen officers. It was not a General Staff school (which focused on process and procedures), but a military university to advance the level of military knowledge within the army. The strength of the Kriegsakademie curriculum was the teachers. There was one main teacher (*Hörsaalleiter*) per class and he was only slightly more senior than students, usually teaching military history and tactics. He had to earn respect of students by performance. There were other instructors for different topics. But it was the Hörsaalleiter who would write a character assessment for each student.

Only one stint was allowed for the Hörsaalleiter. The Germans felt that he had to be rotated back to his unit because of fear to become *truppenfremd* (alienated to troops). The teacher's position was not a career dead end but highly respected (this applied not only to the Kriegsakademie, but all military course and cadet schools). He was selected after teacher journey and trial lecture where officers from the high command assessed his teaching. Once selected, he was completely free in his teaching and not bound or restricted to doctrine or an approved curriculum or lesson plan.

Also, included in the curriculum is that students would rotate to the different branches for six months: infantry officers would serve in artillery units and so on. There was no emphasis on a "school solution" during all exercises, students were also free to criticize teachers' solutions and vice versa. Free-play, force-on-force war games were freewheeling and not scripted. They often lasted several days, and the situation changed depending on which solution was adapted at the end of the day. Often the students' solutions solved the war game problem. There was an element of surprise during every war game. The teachers would also implement *Führerausfall*—leader fatality. Preset positions for all members of war games were instantly rotated.[55]

The final determination to enter the German General Staff was the written character assessment for each student after three years. From this only 15 percent to 30 percent were selected for general staff classes after finishing Kriegsakademie. Further weeding out also occurred during those classes. Only a fraction made it to the Great General Staff. Not making the General Staff in the German military culture, though, was not considered failure, with officers seen as receiving additional education to add their abilities to the army.[56]

The focus on leader development under Auftragstaktik continued in the peacetime practices of the operational army. There was no TRADOC (Training and Doctrine Command), no centralized control, except General Staff guidance, which was minimal (one-page directives outlining outcomes reference to training, and what war plans specified). Other than mobilization plans, which were strictly enforced to meet deployment times and railroad movement tables, actions during mobilization were one area in which the culture did not allow Auftragstaktik—maximum efficiency was sought. Promotions in peacetime were decentralized to the regiment and division up to lieutenant colonel, while colonels and general officers' promotions were centralized. The overhead of field grade and general officer was very low. Overall officer ratio to enlisted was 2.5 percent and later in World War II it climbed as high as 3 percent.[57]

Commanders were responsible for the development of their subordinates and the training of their units. Independence of commanders was valued over everything else. Wide latitude within the framework of commanders' intent was given in training of units based on outcomes. Commanders and their units were evaluated on the results of yearly free-play force-on-force exercises and in division, corps, and army level war games. Divisions were responsible for integrating the latest lessons learned from General Staff officers sent to observe the most recent conflicts. Except for the two formal courses mentioned above, it was left to divisions to form their own training-courses based on battlefield lessons learned. Additionally, debates through professional journals and papers were highly encouraged.[58]

The so-called peacetime culture easily translated to wartime conditions. This culture encouraged independence, initiative, decisiveness, and innovation over conformity, loyalty to process, regulations, and chain of command. This was demonstrated in the wars of Unification, when officers and NCOs were encouraged not to obey out-of-date orders if they felt the situation demanded it. Later, in World War I, NCOs and squad leaders, were given the authority during the attack to change avenues of follow-on units if it avoided enemy strengths. Also in World War I the battalion commander in contact could decide where reinforcements would counterattack even if the reinforcing commander outranked him.[59]

German officers of all ranks felt an obligation to lead by example that was at the heart of unit effectiveness. Policies and practices sustained unit cohesion (until late 1944). Divisions were pulled off line, where they took in new replacements built around a cadre of veterans from the same regions and integrated lessons learned in division-ran schools, and then returned to combat. Time and time again divisions could be destroyed in a previous battle, but the unit manning system of returning the unit back with a core of veterans, would allow it to return later more effective than it had been.

What Does It All Mean?

The more formal process for developing orders used in peacetime (both in education as well as in training operations) is much too slow. The thorough education of the officers referred to earlier also ensured that they all thought along the same general lines. This went a long way in reducing the length of orders, since details did not have to be mentioned.

"Orders in combat at the division level were normally given verbally, either by telephone or, if possible, in person. Later, when the pace had slowed down somewhat, a written copy of these orders would be prepared for the unit diary. Balck even went so far as to forbid the use of written orders in his division, including his largest and most important operations orders, except to complete the unit's diary."[60]

Officers also get to know each other better, the longer they work together, especially through tough training exercises, and most importantly, in combat. Generalmajor von Mellenthin said, "Commanders and subordinates start to understand each other during war. The better they know each other, the shorter and less detailed the orders can be."[61] Von Mellenthin stated that in Russia he and Balck usually allowed themselves only about five minutes in which to decide how to deploy their division for the next battle.[62] On the eastern front, a division often received its orders for the next day around 2200 hrs. By midnight, the order had been analyzed, translated into regimental (*Kampgruppen*) objectives, and dispatched.

The professional manner in which commanders planned and executed missions parallel the small size of large unit staffs. For example, division staffs were small compared to today's standards. There were no deputy commanders or chiefs of staff. All these positions, as well as that of operations officer, were combined in the Ia, who was normally a captain or major of the General Staff.[63] The other General Staff officer was the Ic, responsible for intelligence. A division staff, assisting the commander in running an organization from anywhere from 10,000 to 18,000, as well as thousands of various types of vehicles and horses (depending on the type of division, the front, and year), including drivers, clerks, radio-telephone operators, and the like, on average came to fifty soldiers.

One of the finest tacticians of World War II, with commands from regiment through army group, General Hermann Balck had seen as about as much combat as anyone in any army, but said, "the less [officers] there were, the less aggravation."[64] General der Panzertruppe Otto von Knobelsdorff's staff, when he commanded the 48th Panzer Corps in late 1942, consisted of a total of twelve officers. "Germans of the Wehrmacht vintage see this as essential to the proper exercise of [Auftragstaktik] . . . an operational level headquarters should have only ten or a dozen officers, and a minimum of supporting personnel—this meaning a minimum, not the kind of circus that traipses around in the wake of American and British formation commanders."[65]

The commander and his key staff worked as a team; a small headquarters helped to foster the team spirit. The decision-makers were normally the commander, Ia, and Ic. The decision cycle was quick, without much detail or staff analysis, although the underlying staff work and planning was both competent and detailed.

A system of reliefs among staff officers was not used. Instead, the staff officers were stretched to the breaking point.[66] This practice helped hold down the size of the staff and ensured continuity. General Gaedcke describes his experience as a divisional Ia during World War II:

My division commander and I would sit together in a half-track vehicle with the map on our laps, [and] exchange opinions . . . then we'd scribble down our instructions, give them to the driver next to us, and he'd pass the orders along to a couple of radio operators in the back of our vehicle.

[In the postwar period,] we've built the division staff into a little city with operations centers, communications centers, the whatnot—with everything now in formal writing and transmitted by teletype machines.

The daily command briefing—with 10 to 15 experts ranging from weather to religion—simply didn't exist in World War II. The Ia (or chief of staff) would go with is papers to the commander, who was perhaps at his cot or his morning coffee; the verbal report would be delivered quickly. There was not huge theater required.

There are lots of disadvantages to [today's] huge staffs. You get far too many vehicles which are too hard to move and that attract the attention of enemy aircraft. The whole apparatus becomes sluggish and slow. All of that needs to have the fat thoroughly trimmed away one of these days.[67]

General Gaedcke's comments are based on his vast experience in both World War II and after where he served as Ia (operations) and chief of staff during World War II and later served as a corps commander in the *Bundeswehr* (post–World War II German army). While this author was serving in Afghanistan, it was easy to see nine-hundred- to a thousand-man division- and corps-size staffs. The ratio of generals to enlisted personnel was one to six hundred (resembling the Confederate army in April 1865). Operations orders and fragmentary orders (or "frags"— abbreviated orders that adjust or change the original orders) were issued for all events from the most complex to the simplest.

Despite the previous talk of operations orders and staffs, no German professional course from cadet through captain (the last professional course was the Kriegsakademie) prepared the German officer for staff work. They prepared them to command and make decisions under pressure. The commander could not lead his forces from the rear. As often as possible, he would move forward to the regimental or even battalion lines. According to General der Panzertruppe Hasso-Eccard von Manteuffel, "The place of all commanders of armour up to the division commander is on the battlefield and within this wherever they have the best view of the terrain and good communications with the hard core of the tanks. I always located where I could see and hear what was going on 'in front,' that is, near the enemy, and around myself—namely the focal point [Schwerpunkt]. Nothing and nobody can replace a personal impression."[68]

Generalfeldmarschall Erich von Manstein described how he and his chief of staff operated:

The Chief of Staff had to stay behind [at] the command post to deal with the work and telephone calls. I spent the days, and often part of the nights, out on the road. I usually left early in the morning, after receiving the dawn situation report and issuing any orders that were necessary, to visit divisions and forward troops. At noon I would return to the command post for a while and then go out to visit another division, for as often as not it is just around eventide that success beckons or a fresh impetus is needed. . . . Such flexible leadership on my part was, of course, possible only because I was able to take a wireless vehicle along with me on these trips.[69]

As chief of staff to General der Panzertruppe Balck (Army Group G), Generalmajor von Mellenthin made it a point to visit the front every two or three days, while Balck would man the desk at the command post. The chief of staff would in this way maintain up-to-date personal experience of conditions at the front, which was imperative since he often made tactical decisions.

The commander would often locate himself at the anticipated crux (Schwerpunkt). Here his personal presence not only provided a boost to morale but allowed the most talented and experienced man to be in the place to make the most critical decision at the decisive point quickly. He could sense the situation for himself rather than get it secondhand.[70]

To achieve this type of effectiveness, the Germans had a very "comprehensive approach to training where the whole officer was shaped as a human being."[71] Knowledge and independence were fostered through demanding theoretical studies and realistic training that built self-confidence. The joy of taking responsibility was a more difficult matter; it could not be achieved through ordinary training. This quality was a result of *Erziehung* (refinement education and childhood training, no precise English translation).

Erziehung of the officer's character was shaped over a long period of time. "Responsibility implied not just for taking care of one's own men, but the pride and honor of one's uniform, men, unit, profession and Fatherland."[72] If one failed as an officer he had not only let his unit down, he had also brought shame on his country. It was this kind of responsibility an officer was supposed to enjoy taking or be entrusted with. Only then would he be able to endure the situation on the battlefield.

It is therefore wrong to claim that the Germans had a broad spectrum of revolutionary training methods. Instead, they created an environment characterized by high standards and a "relentless pursuit of professional-ism, out of which grew self-assurance and self-confidence." Not only in ordinary education and training of their leaders, "but professionalism in everything which interfered with the officers' lives and professions and which ultimately shaped the officers' personal qualities." It was in this environment and within this framework that every German officer was "brought up" (Erziehen/Erziehung) to always take responsibility and to enjoy it. Therefore, it is fair to say that in interwar German officer devel-opment the framework of, and the environment in which the education and training took place, was even more important than the content.[73]

3

Barriers to Mission Command

Interestingly, the literally hundreds of American observers who were regularly sent to the old continent during the course of the 19th century to study the constantly warring European armies completely missed out on the decade long discussion about the revolutionary command philosophy of Auftragstaktik. Instead they focused on saddle straps, belt buckles and drill manuals. This is one reason why the most democratic command concept never found a home in the greatest democracy. The U.S. officers simply missed the origins because of their own narrow-minded military education.

—DR. JÖRG MUTH, *Command Culture*

Before a culture of Auftragstaktik can succeed, the Army must possess the moral courage to identify countless Industrial Age barriers. These barriers must be torn down. If they are not, the current focus on mission command will only remain rhetoric and countless buzzwords on PowerPoint slides and doctrinal slogans. The real damage will be done to the next generation of leaders when they hear one thing, yet see the same old actions that run counter to efficacy.

A little history will help us understand "the why" behind today's Army's Industrial Age approach to leader development. In 1899, President McKinley picked Elihu Root as secretary of war to bring "modern business practices" to the "backward" War Department. Root was a highly intelligent lawyer who specialized in corporate affairs. He acted as counsel to banks, railroads and some of the great financiers of that era. Root's approach to reforming the American military was to insert the ideas of management science then in vogue into the Army's ossified decision-making process. He wanted the Army to run like a large corporation (sound familiar?).[1]

To this end, Root took "progressive ideas" in personnel management—ideas such as social Darwinism—and applied them to the Army's personnel management. This approach should not be surprising. Root was a product of the big corporations that dominated the Progressive Era and would soon dominate the U.S. government.[2] Root was also a disciple of the management theories propounded by Frederick Taylor. He believed that Taylor's theories could be used to make the military more efficient.[3]

Fredrick Taylor is one of the intellectual fathers of the modern industrial production system. Perhaps his greatest contribution to production efficiency was to break down complex production tasks into a sequence of simple, standardized steps. This permitted him to design a standardized mass production line around a management system that classified work into standard tasks and workers into standard specialties. This combination established work standards, and the people who were trained to these standards became interchangeable cogs in the machine. This greatly simplified personnel management in a vast industrial enterprise.[4]

To be sure, "Taylorism" transformed industrial production, but it also had a dark side: Taylorism treated people as unthinking cogs in a machine. By necessity, these people had to accept a social system based on a coercive pattern of dominance and subservience. Every action and every decision made in the organization was spelled out in the name of efficiency. In theory, the entire regimen flowed from the brain of one individual at the top of the hierarchy.[5]

A complimentary management dogma also emerged during the Progressive Era. This was the theory of "Ethical Egoism,"[6] which asserted that all people are motivated solely by self-interest. By extension, all people would respond predictably to a variety of positive incentives (money, pleasure, advancement, distinction, power, luxury goods and amenities) or negative incentives (which took the primary form of a fear of losing the positive benefits, but also of outright punishment and pain). Easier accessions, faster promotions, no obligation to attend professional courses, and quicker pay raises are fully consistent with this theory of human behavior.[7]

Taken together, the idea that people are interchangeable cogs in a machine and the idea that self-interest is the only significant motivator of behavior help to explain why the Army thinks that increasing its "production" of lieutenants, cutting out necessary training for young leaders and reducing the promotion time to major will solve its statistical readiness issues with deploying units, meet near-term requirements, and solve potential retention problems. The ideas of Taylor and Root dominated management science and War Department circles a century ago, but their ghosts are haunting the Army's Human Resources Command and the deputy chief of staff for personnel (DCSPER) staff. Moreover, the ghosts of Taylor and Root will continue to haunt the Army's personnel managers as long as Congress shows no interest in rooting out the causes of our personnel crisis.[8]

The Assembly Line of the Minuteman

Before World War I, the Army employed the European depot manning system. As regiments received replacements, noncommissioned officers would integrate (socialize) them at the lowest level. Attempts were made in the Spanish-American War and the Philippines insurrection to rotate units. In 1899, each of the regiments in Cuba designated one of its three battalions as a depot battalion. The depot battalion would rebuild and then rotate overseas with one of the other two battalions. Many officers liked this program because of the cohesion that it built. On the other hand, some soldiers did not like the unit rotation system because they were forced to stay overseas for two of their three years of service. As long as the Army stayed at a stable strength, and remained a constabulary, this program worked. Despite the merits of unit rotation and raising regiments from distinct geographical regions, the Army decided in 1912 to move to an individual replacement system to meet the need for mobilization.[9]

The new individual replacement system (IRS) was based on Taylorism because it viewed the individual as an identical component part that could be created on an assembly line. In World War I, the Army adopted a classification system that responded to the needs and wishes of the individual. Through interviewing and testing, the system (and all others since) determined a recruit's prior trade, and tried to place him in a parallel military job. Although considered efficient, this approach actually hurt combat units by steering potentially superior soldiers away from the fighting jobs. This concept led the Army to stop experimenting with a unit-based system for replacing casualties and adopt the individual system it has used since.[10]

In the IRS, soldiers are trained in a set of skills needed to perform their military occupational specialty (MOS). It was hard for the Army to cope with any other system because the only time it ever required massive replacements was during war. In peacetime, the Army was so small and its strength fluctuated so much that it could not maintain a permanent regimental system. This inability to understand the benefits of a well-educated and trained officer corps was due to long cultural resistance to a professional army.[11]

Because of its rapid growth in the Spanish-American War, and the demand for overseas deployments thereafter, the Army also set up a schedule to rotate individuals to and from the United States. The preparation of units to go overseas using the depot system with a small manpower base and force structure conflicted with the mandatory rotation times of individuals. Units would shed soldiers who could not serve the entire time overseas and replace them with new soldiers who could, causing terrible turbulence in the rotating unit. By 1912, the Army was forced to adopt the IRS based on sudden dramatic surges in strength from a small peacetime army to large wartime force.[12]

World War I again caused a swelling of army manpower. A tenfold increase in the Army again caused conflicts between force structure and doctrine and with unit rotations and replacement system. One proposal called for establishing "replacement divisions" so that two divisions could be maintained in France, with one held in reserve, trained and ready to rotate into the line when another division suffered too many combat losses.[13]

This proposal flew in the face of Taylorism. A unit-based replacement system also conflicted with the Army's decision to maintain a few large divisions (the strength of a U.S. division was 28,000 men compared to roughly half that for an Allied or German division).[14]

The decision to maintain large divisions was based on a number of assumptions. There was a lack of experienced commanders available as the Army moved from a small peacetime force that could barely field one division to a global force of millions. The Army, particularly Gen. John J. Pershing, advocated a doctrine of "open warfare." This doctrine relied on the skill of the individual rifleman in much the same way as congressional leaders saw the minuteman arising from the public masses with his rifle to repel invaders. The World War I U.S. division with its thousands of well-trained and disciplined riflemen was expected to overwhelm the German defenses.[15]

Finally, to compensate for the lack of a professional officer corps, Pershing and his staff were forced to employ a centralized command system controlling fewer divisions. In the end, although the Army was able to deploy forty-two divisions, reality surfaced as a larger number of casualties was incurred as officers learned how to employ artillery, armor, and infantry; slowly discarding open warfare; and adapting combined arms. The French and the British were coming into their own in 1918 with combined arms and attempted to train the U.S. officers in its execution, but were largely ignored by the overconfident but poorly trained U.S. officers. A large number of casualties were incurred in the fighting over the summer and fall of 1918.[16]

The campaigns in the Saint-Mihel salient and the Meuse-Argonne forced the Army to keep its few divisions on line and maintain them to strength by stripping newly arrived units of men for replacements. Additionally, wounded and returned soldiers were sent to different divisions with no regard for unit loyalty. Such an approach to war was a comfortable fit with the scientific management theories of Frederick Taylor. The U.S. Army was really only involved in the war through six months, which allowed it to fight a war of attrition without needing the strength of cohesion or the professionalism of an officer corps. The officers were managers of death, feeding an endless supply of manpower and equipment into a never-ending grinding machine of death, finally wearing out a German army that had been at war against the world for four years. Brig. Gen. William "Billy" Mitchell, a military aviation pioneer, observed, "The art of war had departed.

Attrition, or the gradual killing off of the enemy, was all the ground armies were capable of."[17]

A cold industrial approach to war was gradually being adopted by the Army officer corps (a tradition upheld in the latter part of the Civil War). Efficient methods were achieved for mobilizing mass armies as industry geared up to provide the needed weaponry. Effectiveness was translated into mustering as many men, weapons, and machines as possible to achieve an enemy's physical destruction. There was little incentive left in peacetime to create and maintain an effective standing army. A regimental system could provide cohesion and unit replacement, but a doctrine requiring intellect and experience from officers was too hard to measure by a U.S. society dedicated to short-term efficiency.

The long-term negative impacts of Root's reforms on effectiveness due to the American tradition of compromise would have an adverse impact on the Army. Uptonians had stressed that the training and education of officers coupled with tours of troop and staff duty took years to develop professionals. But the armed progressives coming to power after Root's era believed "six months would probably suffice . . . in the progressive mold, they emphasized the individuality of each person." This lack of military professionalism would be highlighted in World War I as the Army scrambled to find effective commanders and staff officers.[18]

The selection of officers, particularly division commanders, was based more on "parade ground" appearance and youth than ability. Calm demeanor and sound judgment as well as strength of character were not criteria for command selection. Additionally, ambition was seen as a necessary drive to accomplish short-term goals and missions, not as a liability.[19]

The U.S. Army, however, seemed to have no alternatives because it had not acquired officers based on demanding selection procedures at the beginning of their careers. There were no tests linked to evaluations used to eliminate poor performers. The Army quietly dismissed merit promotions early in an officer's career and reverted back to a seniority system. The Army that arrived in France in World War I had to take draconian measures based on how well the commander in

France, General Pershing, felt his officers would perform in command or staff positions. The de facto centralized personnel system for selecting officers also moved into the way the Army built and sustained its combat units with individual soldiers. In 1919, many valuable lessons learned during the war about the personnel system were forgotten. Unfortunately, this trend of forgetting mistakes and emphasizing successes has continued to dominate the Army.[20]

The French Way of War

The principles of management science and the influence of the French were in use during the U.S. Army's interwar period from 1919 to 1939, and if one looks close enough, remain so today. The way of training leaders under the guise of the mobilization-based leader paradigm evolved out of the Industrial Age way of war and centered on the rote memorization of process, or what is today called the "military decision-making process" (MDMP).

MDMP evolved from a scientific way of organizing thoughts in the preparation and execution of missions. It goes so far as to tell commanders and their staffs that certain decisions should be made through events and time on a matrix. Additionally, MDMP evolved to represent how the U.S. Army prepares civilians to become officers. The Army's education system has centered on memorization of the process, or the "checklist approach," to war fighting.

U.S. Army Maj. Eben Swift created the MDMP in 1897. At the time of the emergence of the philosophy of "scientific management," based on the theories of Frederick Taylor, Swift's methods were seen as the basis for a professional military education. The source of his process has a twist of irony to it, however. Swift's approach was based on his examination of a French interpretation of a German book on tactical decision games by a Prussian officer named Verdy Du Vernois.[21]

In Du Vernois' system, most calculations and die rolling were eliminated in favor of an umpire who would determine results based on the situation and his own combat experience. War games had become a mainstay of German military training. Du Vernois proposed to eliminate the written rules and govern opponents by tactical rules that would become obvious during the course of the game.[22]

On the other hand, the French military organized Du Vernois' book of tactical decision games by structuring the games and their presentation. Swift went even further, organizing the answers to the game into what we now call the five-paragraph operations order. It is important to note that, at the time, more U.S. officers spoke French than German. This made the adherence to French principles of war easier.

Swift then institutionalized his game at the Army's Command and General Staff College (CGSC) at Fort Leavenworth. Over time, the Swift method evolved into our task, condition, and standard approach to task training, and the U.S. Army's crawl–walk–run approach to education and training systems. The Leavenworth methodology for teaching problem-solving skills has remained constant since the 1890s, when Swift introduced an educational technique known as the applicatory method, under which lecture, recitation, and memorization gave way to hands-on exercises in analytical problem-solving, such as map exercises, war games, and staff rides—all designed to teach students what to think not how to think. The irony is Germans used them to teach critical thinking, while just the opposite as the U.S. misinterpretation of the French misunderstanding of the German methods of teaching.[23] The United States used these methods to confirm the "school solution."

By the late 1930s, such exercises accounted for more than 70 percent of total curriculum hours. The applicatory method survives in the form of curriculums, practical exercises; terrain walks; staff rides; and the capstone exercise, Prairie Warrior, which relies heavily on computer simulation. While these methods may sound progressive, they were diminished with an adherence to process and checklists, and school solutions that students could not argue against.[24]

Today's crawl–walk–run—or lecture–demonstration–practical application—system used in leader development curriculums is overwhelming. This contrasting American approach was born out of necessity in World War I. The U.S. Army, arriving on the field of battle unprepared for large-scale war, followed the French military approach to education based on the philosophy of René Descartes.[25]

Descartes was a famous mathematician who broke down engineering problems in sequence, making it easier to teach formulas to engineering students. This approach was translated into French military training, where the French found it easy to break down military problem-solving into processes (checklists) to educate their officers and their awaiting masses of citizen soldiers upon mobilization.[26]

The Cartesian approach allowed the French (and later the United States) to easily teach a common, fundamental doctrinal language to many who were new to the military. It significantly reduced the time it took to master basic military skills. The downfall of this approach is that it simplifies war (complex problems) into processes where the enemy is only a template, not a free-thinking adversary with a very important voice in determining how the plan might be executed.

The Cartesian approach also slows down a decision cycle by turning the planners' focus inward on process instead of outward on the enemy. The problem with this approach is that it does not fit in with the problem at hand. It is the same thing with operations research, which is a powerful tool for solving certain well-defined problems. The problem that we have within the Armed Forces is that we try to apply it to all sorts of inappropriate problems. The French, relying on a massed citizen army in the late nineteenth and early twentieth centuries, had to find a way to instruct many citizen officers quickly in military doctrine.[27]

Additionally, because of the casualties of World War I and the advance of modern weaponry and its destructiveness, the French needed a way to teach its officers how to control these resources to concentrate firepower so they could compensate for their lack of unit skills on the battlefields. They used an orderly and systematic approach to planning that was similar to the MDMP.

When the United States arrived in Europe in 1917 with its new Army, led largely by citizens who had been transformed into officers almost overnight, it needed to learn the fundamentals of the profession of arms quickly. All U.S staff officers and commanders attended French schools in planning and controlling forces in combat. The United States and France were the victors in World War I and saw that victory as a validation of their training process.

When the French developed methodical battle in the interwar years, the United States copied it with all its accompanying process-focused education. The U.S. Army carried this over to its education and training, as well as its doctrine. The analytical approach to leader development supported the nation's mobilization doctrine. For the Army it worked well for World War I and World War II.[28]

The U.S. Army's attrition doctrine in World War II was based on intense supporting firepower. This doctrine is called "fire-and-movement tactics." It relies on one unit firing while another one moves, supported by massed indirect fires (a carryover of the French doctrine of methodical battle). These fire-and-movement tactics are linear—Napoleonic on an operational level. The doctrine's focus is tying in flanks with adjacent units, adhering to detailed map graphics, with nearly every aspect of the operation centrally controlled. The end result of this type of detailed, analytically driven doctrine forced Army officers, who were educated to rely on inherent rote procedures, to focus inward instead of outward on what the enemy was doing.[29]

This French-based doctrine was institutionalized when George C. Marshall became commandant of the Infantry School at Fort Benning, Georgia, in 1929. Though Marshall countered the doctrine's demand for strict obedience by modifying the curriculum to align more with the progressive approaches employed by the Germans. Marshall's three-year stint was but the lone bright spot in leader development during the interwar period. As soon as Marshall left Benning, it reverted back to its linear and French way of leader development. Both the Army's infantry school and the Command and General Staff College at Fort Leavenworth, Kansas, drilled its officer students in tactics devised by the French in the latter part of World War I and during the interwar years. Marshall was the sole exception, who tried to get away from this top-down, rote dogma being taught everywhere in the U.S. Army.

Although there was a great doctrinal debate in the interwar years among officers, the French way of war was deemed acceptable. It was more easily identifiable and explained than the German approach. American doctrine called for a systematic approach—from strategy, at the highest level, to tactics, at the lowest level—so coherent and so simple that even an army of half-trained amateurs could soon learn to fight effectively.

To properly gauge the French influence on Army doctrine, one must go beyond what is promulgated in doctrinal publications. That the 1930 manual for large-unit commanders was never raised to the full status of permanent doctrine is less important than the fact of its popularity. Put another way, what a general stamped "official" is far less important than what resonated in the minds of captains, majors, and colonels of that period.

One reason that the *Manual for Commanders of Large Units* was so popular is that it was familiar. It fit well into the military mentality of an officer corps that had absorbed the French approach to war from a number of directions. These include West Point (which emphasized a Cartesian approach to education); the writings of Antoine-Henri baron de Jomini; the extensive study of the French language; the use of French translations as a means to study German methods; the influences of the centralized corporate culture of the Progressive Era; and, what was perhaps most powerful of all, the experience of World War I.[30]

"This does not mean that most American officers were slavish imitators or even enthusiastic admirers of the French army. Indeed, most American officers who served during the interwar period would deny that they practiced anything but a uniquely 'American way of war.'"[31] This was particularly true where infantry tactics and the 'spirit of the offensive' were concerned."Yet, at a time when maneuvers involving forces larger than a regiment were rare, the U.S. Army needed a means of making sense of the tactics of divisions and corps. The French approach in general, and the *Manual for Commanders of Large Units* in particular, promised to fill that need. The dependence on the trained amateur also institutionalized the doctrine of centralized command and control and authoritarian leadership that began in World War I.[32]

George Marshall was the lone bright spot in interwar educational practices. Marshall pushed many approaches similar to German officer education methods of the same period (more so than the rest of the U.S. Army schools). He would take students to different locations and then change the mission on them, forcing them to adapt to the new situation. He also allowed students to challenge the school solution (unlike Leavenworth) with their own courses of action. Marshall's practices in education were advanced for the day, but were also an aberration to the norm in all other Army courses and schools. Also significant was that Marshall took tactics study away from long formal operations orders more reliant on short or verbal orders. Again, it was similar to what the Germans were practicing in all levels of their schooling.[33]

Graduates of other schools, such as the CGSC at Fort Leavenworth, did not hold their institutions in high regard. U.S. Army professional journals carried articles whose writers criticized the teaching methods for failing, familiar to any post-secondary education instructor. One writer complained that the instructors were "insufferably boring" and that he counted a third of the officer students who were "frankly and openly asleep" before the writer "himself succumbed." A more serious criticism appeared in a 1937 *Infantry Journal* issue. The writer pointed out that the practical problems might last "two or three hours" but in combat the decision-maker might have only minutes to reach and communicate a solution.[34]

Students and journal writers criticized the school solution as a basis for grading the important pay problems. The school solution was the solution to a map exercise, or a tactical problem, considered best by the instructors, and was applied to the student solutions. The school solution grading method inhibited students from presenting innovative solutions to complex problems, and those students complained about the inflexibility of Leavenworth's grading system. The Leavenworth faculty took the complaints about having one right solution, the school solution, seriously. They devised a system of student appeals that recognized that the school solution might not be the only possible solution. The system of appeals and acceptance of innovative solutions resulted in a sharp decline in student dissatisfaction.[35]

What Does It All Mean?

Centrally controlled, attritional doctrine made up for the lack of thoroughly trained and cohesive combat units and educated officers. The doctrine also fit into the culture begun by Elihu Root. The Army's (and society's) culture liked the idea of imposing an artificial order on things like war, which were seen as inherently disorderly. Army officers were comfortable with this type of doctrine because they were trained to think analytically. Exceptions were few, as in the case of the famed 4th Armored Division commander who knew better and taught his officers how to integrate different combat arms and to think holistically.[36]

Finally, the Regular Army officer corps adapted to its new responsibilities of leading a large number of amateur officers being continually fed into non-cohesive new units and practicing a doctrine that embraced applying massive amounts of firepower. They had perforce to employ an authoritarian style of leadership. Some senior leaders, such as First Army commander Lt. Gen. Courtney H. Hodges, treated their subordinates with indifference almost amounting to contempt.[37]

An example of this negative command climate occurred when Hodges, despite the contrary advice of subordinates, decided to attack into the restricted and heavily forested terrain of the Hurtgen Forest in September 1944. Many division, regimental, and battalion commanders lost their positions between October 1944 and February 1945. It was expected that orders would be carried out at all cost. Failure often resulted in the relief of subordinate commanders. Officers would often threaten their subordinates that if they did not carry out an order it would adversely affect their careers. This kind of distant, authoritarian, and hostile attitude toward subordinates persisted throughout World War II.[38]

The actions of officers at all levels could not be ignored despite the glory derived from victory in World War II. Studies and courts of inquiry conducted shortly after the war discovered that poor leadership was directly tied to poor accession standards and a climate that bred competition. This negative environment was created at the top by Marshall. For all his intellect, brilliance, and moral strength, Marshall "expected subordinates to be right all the time; the subordinate might be right many times and then err; he was then 'finished.'" Worse, it remains the dominant army leadership style.[39]

Maj. Gen. James Gavin, commander of the 82nd Airborne Division in World War II, perhaps best sums up the cost of these practices: "Summarily relieving senior officers, seems to me makes others pusillanimous and indeed discourages other potential combat leaders from seeking high command. Summarily relieving those who do not appear to measure up in the first shock of battle is not only a luxury we cannot afford—it is very damaging to the Army as a whole."[40]

4

Institutionalizing the Process: TRADOC

The emergence of the progressive view of military professionalism at the turn of the twentieth century left a lasting impression that military genius was superfluous, if not hazardous. It was "the end of the era of the so-called 'military genius' whose individualism and unpredictability became an anathema." Skeptical of military genius, the army required its officers to be perfected machines of technical skill and tactical ability, not brilliant individuals. War essentially became an industrial process directed by a trained corporate elite. In 1907, students at Fort Leavenworth were advised, "In any office in the military service, search should be made nowadays, not for a brilliant soldier, not for a genius, but for one that knows thoroughly the duties of the office."

—MAJ. DANIEL P. SNOW, "United States Army Officer Personnel Reforms and the Decline of Rank Flexibility, 1890s–1920s"

Commanding generals convene transition teams to explore critical questions about training and doctrine.[1] Training and Doctrine Command (TRADOC) oversees training and soldier development. The results are visions for the way forward into the future. Post–Desert Storm, senior Army leaders recognized the need for change and were not blind to the symptoms of inertia throughout the Army. They took action by creating special study boards, initiative groups, and handpicked protégés to guide decisions on transformation. However, as with other vision statements, ground observations of execution in the field reflect an effort that is still tied to rigid, time-consuming processes; questionable assumptions; insufficient resources (primarily the "right" people); unresponsive or relevant to the needs of the operational Army; and overly concerned with TRADOC internal protocols and priorities.[2]

To their great credit, senior Army leaders are fully aware of this perception. One of the most interesting pieces of evidence is the open dissemination of a TRADOC white paper titled "Adapt or Die: The Imperative for a Culture of Innovation in the United States Army." This study was published as an article in *Army* magazine, a journal read throughout the Army by all ranks. Finally, TRADOC made an audiotape, "Adapt or Die," expressing the need to change the culture. While the publication of the article is a start, there is no discussion of why it was published. In other words, there is no mention of the aspects of Army institutional behavior that indicate the Army does not have a culture of innovation. Also, the article "Adapt or Die" discusses the Army in aggregate and not specifics. What is not said, but becomes clear to the reader, is that while the operational Army has "transformed" in many ways since 2001, institutional Army organizational barriers to self-change are only now starting to be brought down.[3]

There has long been a disconnect between the intentions of the Army's senior leaders and the execution to achieve those intentions by the organization itself. Reading the intent statements of TRADOC commanders, and indeed of any TRADOC subordinate organization, it is hard to find argument with their intent. However, intentions are only slowly evolving into practice in the eyes of the operational Army. Compounding the problem is rather fierce and defensive insistence by TRADOC that they are already doing the right things, the right way—even by people who were once critical of TRADOC when assigned in the operational Army.[4]

The central problem is a cumulative effect of culture, combined with organizational design, combined with changing Army assumptions about how to fight and how to train the Army to fight that inhibit TRADOC transformation and mission effectiveness. The Army generally defines culture as a collection of shared values, beliefs, and behaviors. When he was Army chief of staff (2003–7), Gen. Peter Schoomaker articulated the need to change the behaviors of the Army to reflect new operational realities. He also emphasized adapting an institutional Army that provides soldiers, leaders, organizations, equipment, and training to the operating force. The Army must change its cultural frames of reference and move beyond "task/conditions/standards."[5]

First and foremost, TRADOC is a large organization. Although everyone in the Army passes through TRADOC-sponsored activities periodically, and some spend time immersed in one or two specific activities, very, very few officers or NCOs have deep knowledge of the entire entity. Simply to establish some context to the discussion, consider the following:

> The TRADOC mission is to recruit, train, and educate the Army's Soldiers; develop Army leaders; support training in units; develop doctrine; establish standards; and build the future Army. TRADOC has 11 core functions, 3 key enablers, 3 specified proponents and 16 branch proponents. TRADOC has 37 general officers. There are five deputy commanding generals and five field operating agencies. The TRADOC HQs staffs are functionally unique and do not follow the G-staff model. There are six primary coordinating staff departments, with approximately 31 subordinate directorates. The DCSOPS&T alone has 12 sub-directorates. One specified proponent, The Combined Arms Center, itself has 27 functions, 11 subordinate commands, eight subordinate centers, seven schools, and eight special activities.
>
> If one were to follow the TRADOC model to create a new training topic, concept, or program, this model requires compliance with 22 DA Pamphlets (Pams) and Other Procedural Guidance; seven capstone Field Manuals; 19 HQ TRADOC Regulations and Direct Guidance; and 37 TRADOC Pams and Other Procedural Guidance (averaging 140 pages each). That does not include any of the topics specific FMs, TMs, and other proponent-generated procedural requirements, nor does it include the approximately 32 training related Federal/DoD/Joint Guidance documents. It does include the responsibility to ensure accomplishment of all required communications and coordination, both within the proponent parent organization, with external and

higher organizations, and across TRADOC. At a minimum, that would be the three specified proponents and their subordinate activities (particularly CAC), the six TRADOC HQs coordinating staff departments, and many of the 31 directorates all before recommending approval of new policy or guidance, generating a tasking, or beginning to implement a new command initiative.[6]

A discussion of how the Army got to this point is in order, because there are many in the Army who have an almost religious allegiance to the unchallenged doctrine of training to task/conditions/standards, yet they cannot explain *why* it is the Army way. The impediments to change are easier to counter when the culture is defined as something that can change, and has changed before, without destroying the organization.[7]

Remember, also, that the Army's training responsibility is much more than mechanical, repetitive tasks. Training tactical proficiency also requires education to develop tactical judgment. Current Army behaviors are also not something that must be defended based on tradition. The warrior ethos is not in the same cultural category as task/conditions/standards. In other words, culture defined by organizational behavior is not the same as culture defined by organizational values.[8]

The Army's 1973 reorganization of Continental Army Command into two separate commands, TRADOC and Forces Command, roughly coincided with three related events. First, the experience of the Vietnam War and its effect on Army "culture," which was captured in 1970 in *Study on Military Professionalism* and the *Board for Dynamic Training*. Second is the Army's transformation from a conscript to a volunteer (but not yet to a professional) Army. And third, the assumptions that the Army must be able to fight outnumbered and win a major conventional war in central Europe.[9]

The impact of each of these events was strongly influenced by observations from the 1973 Yom Kippur War that became extrapolated to potential war against the Warsaw Pact. Today, critics who declare that the Army ignored the lessons of Vietnam often discount the importance of these three events. There is, however, a very important part of Army culture that did not discount lessons of the past, but does struggle with how to adapt them to new wartime realities, specific war-fighting requirements, and service budget program requirements.[10]

Gen. William DePuy, as the first TRADOC commander (1973–76), had a vision for changing the new volunteer Army into one capable of fighting outnumbered and winning the first battle, while buying time for mobilization of reserve forces necessary for fighting a long and global war. National security strategy, as well as the political realities of the time, cast the Soviet-led Warsaw Pact as both the most dangerous and the most likely threat for the U.S. Army. This Army transformation led by TRADOC in the 1973–90 period can be characterized by the following doctrine as the unifying engine of change.[11]

General DePuy's personal leadership philosophy became the institutional culture for how to train. DePuy was very much a product of his personal experiences as an operations and commanding officer of a battalion in 90th Infantry Division during Normandy and the drive across France in World War II, and then as commanding general of the 1st Infantry Division during the Vietnam War. In each experience, DePuy was immersed in a second-generation warfare (2GW) culture or linear top-down firepower-heavy culture. Most importantly, he had experienced draftee soldiers and inexperienced leaders, which fit 2GW culture.[12]

The Army's assumptions about the nature of a conventional war in central Europe were based upon a need for forward-deployed draftees, then, later, volunteers to hold long enough for guardsmen and reservists to be mobilized and deployed. General DePuy's personal experiences with draftees and volunteers reinforced his beliefs about how such forces would have to be prepared to fight that war and win. He believed that there was insufficient time and capacity to develop civilians into professional soldiers. Therefore, the institution would have to be top-down and in centralized hierarchies able to "tell them what to do, tell them how to do it, and check that they did it right."[13]

This is an important element because, over time, these assumptions about forward-deployed forces fighting outnumbered, while reserves in the United States went through mobilization that transformed guardsmen and reservists into combat-ready reinforcements established a culture in which leaders expected to be told what to do, how to do it, and what the standard was by TRADOC. This top-down approach was not intended to negate leader initiative, because General DePuy also believed that leaders must exhibit initiative in order to prevail in combat. Unfortunately, the scope of the Warsaw Pact threat model and its Industrial Age tradition evolved the U.S. Army to function as a machine, not a thinking organization.[14]

"Initiative" is hard to define quantitatively, and it does not meet the quantifiable standards or measures that satisfy the peacetime military operations research systems analyst (ORSA) that dominates DOD and DA. ORSAs are aimed at achieiving predictability and uniformity, and that is what leaders—both military and civilian—look toward to help answer their questions. They then use it as a guide to determine whether they are "doing the right thing" to move up in the system.[15]

DePuy was not wrong, but his ideas were specific to the strategic conditions of his time and to an Army grounded in 2GW, or linear/industrial warfare. Strategic conditions have changed, the operational Army has evolved (as have the people the Army draws from U.S. society), and threats have certainly changed. However, Army leaders are just now beginning to reevaluate DePuy's basic assumptions and the influences of Frederick Taylor's theories on industrial management on how the Army trains.[16]

To evolve the Army culture—personnel management system's hold on recruiting and retention, as well as its training doctrine—2GW cultural behaviors were further influenced by three additional significant events: the end of the Warsaw Pact as a threat model, Army assumptions regarding war in the Information Age, and the Cold War drawdown effect on Army leader behavior[17]

After the end of the Cold War and Desert Storm, new Army study groups were convened, new doctrinal manuals written, and new operational concepts explored. Army leaders recognized that the single-enemy focus of 2GW would not be relevant to the Army in a fourth-generation warfare (4GW) world. Army transformation to a more deployable, adaptive, and agile force began. Information dominance across the tactical and operational levels, enabled by technology, formed the basic assumption about how the Army would fight. The models for designing, testing, and evaluating new concepts remained tied to 2GW types of mathematical and linear threat models used by DePuy to justify force development funding in the 1970s. This model needed definitive assumptions about how the Army would fight that could be rationalized mathematically on the linear battlefield.[18]

Even though the nature of conflicts in which the Army would engage was changing, the Army's assumptions about threat models used to create change did not. After thirty years and victory in Desert Storm, it could not question them without calling into question the basis upon which the size, composition, and required capabilities of the force were justified in terms of budgetary requirements. The evolving face of war into fourth-generation warfare (non-state groups using terrorism to achieve strategic ends) through new world situations in which non-state groups were becoming more powerful, as discussed earlier in the book, combined with technological advances on which the Army was spending development funds, led many to conclude that the Army would be able to "do more with less."[19]

This was and is a troubling paradox for a large institution, and its inability to reconcile the desire to be a doctrinally based Army, in a world in which the desired doctrinal measurements cannot be defined quantitatively, persists today. The Army had firmly attached itself to a force development model in which doctrine was not "how we will fight" the nation's wars, but "how we will justify acquiring and managing resources" on a macro level. Doctrine no longer was the engine of change, because the extensive bureaucratic systems that were built in the post–World War II 2GW world now held doctrine captive to process. Doctrine became overly dogmatic, which defeated the entire concept of doctrine![20]

Not only did assumptions about how the Army must be developed remain unchanged, but many assumptions from the 1970s about how the Army should train also remained unchallenged. No one would now argue against the accepted methods used to train soldiers for World War I did not apply to the new battlefield realities of World War II a mere twenty-three years later. But oddly enough, there are many in the Army today who passionately argue that methods developed to train for winning a first battle in central Europe in the 1970s and 1980s are still unquestionably valid for the current war-fighting environment.[21]

In fact, the success of Desert Storm exacerbated the problem by apparently validating DePuy's task/conditions/standards philosophy, although it was no longer recognized as his philosophy, but rather was firmly embedded in the Army culture. Leaders raised under that philosophy chose not to question it—even in the light of Somalia, Bosnia, Kosovo, and 4GW around the globe. Tactical problems are viewed as either the failure of subordinates to understand doctrine, failure to develop detailed standard operating procedures for applying the doctrine, or political failures resulting in the improper (non-doctrinal) use of the Army, certainly not indicative of a need to critically examine Army assumptions and doctrine.[22]

Mission essential task list development (how commanders determine training priorities based on their analysis of the missions they may have to conduct) has evolved from a tool for commanders to focus efforts to their mission, to a very broad listing of approved task words related to larger and centralized higher headquarters' use of certification as the primary method for assessing readiness.[23]

While the direct connection between how to train doctrine and how to fight doctrine was unhinged by the emergence of fourth-generation warfare or 4GW, Army leaders' attempts to retain 2GW training doctrine remain strong. To challenge the rationale of the methods used to train was to challenge the doctrine itself, which was a professional behavior increasingly less desired by an Army that celebrated the leaders and successes of Desert Storm.[24]

A concurrent event, unrelated to war fighting, helped entrench organizational conservatism upon the Army: the dramatic drawdown of the 1990s, in which the Army shrank by half. The effect of the drawdown was to instill a strong professional conservatism and groupthink. In the 1980s, public Army internal debates about how to fight and how to train that had accompanied evolving Army doctrine were often supported indirectly by robust resources.[25]

Even with DePuy's powerful philosophical influence, there was still the flexibility to experiment, improvise, and exercise command initiative. This was especially true in U.S. Army Europe and in first-deploying forces, where units were closest to enemy realities, and also where operational commanders had much more practical influence on their subordinates' thinking than did TRADOC policies. Army internal debates certainly included TRADOC but, interestingly, the adaptive concepts for light infantry divisions and the High-Tech Light Division (HTLD) in the 1980s were directed by the chief of staff of the Army's (CSA) prerogative, and was not a TRADOC initiative.[26]

The abundant resource environment in the 1980s allowed robust debate about, and innovation within, Army doctrine. The soldiers and officers who participated in small-scale combat, as well as those who conducted mission-focused training in the Combat Training Centers (CTC) at Fort Irwin, California, Fort Polk, Louisiana, and in Germany developed into professional, not just volunteer, soldiers.[27]

The drawdown and resource crises of the 1990s slowed and almost stopped innovation. Resources, and thus training, became increasingly centralized. Junior leaders could not be allowed to squander limited resources learning their craft; they needed to be taught "what right looks like" by their seniors, because there was too much risk in allowing junior officers and NCOs to develop professionally the same way their seniors did. Innovative training methods such as those employed by Special Forces were considered inappropriate for conventional forces. Junior leaders emulated the behaviors of their seniors, centralizing and directing the task/conditions/standards activities–driven subordinate activities, and held doctrinal correctness as an essential measure of leader competence.[28]

Training as a leader competency was also replaced by training resource management as a leader requirement quite unrelated to the actual execution of training. Careful stewardship of resources, and the satisfactory completion of resourced events, culturally took precedence over the actual effectiveness of training. Training itself changed from experiential training (proficiency gained through experiencing realistic training, incidentally a key part of DePuy's training philosophy) to event-driven training, following strategies determined by TRADOC.[29]

These strategies determined the approved methods and allocated resources and external "trainers" for unit commanders. The CTCs changed from an environment in which leaders trained their units to fight, to a place where outsiders told leaders to follow approved doctrinal methods. The fundamental training methods remained unchallenged by critical analysis and became the hallmark of leader risk mitigation. Leaders who survived the drawdown ended up following doctrinal methods precisely and evaluating others by how well they followed the same methods.[30]

In 2000, the gap between intentions and reality became public as Army officers and NCOs began voting with their feet. The volunteer professional Army was losing staff sergeants, captains, lieutenant colonels, and colonels faster than even a smaller Army could handle and still fulfill its requirements. Command climate surveys showed wide and deep dissatisfaction with senior leaders, with Army schools, with training methods, and with overly restrictive command climates. "Highlighting the disconnect, it is interesting to note that while General Eric Shinseki, Army chief of staff from 1999 to 2003, commissioned a series of Army Training and Leader Development Panels to try to understand why the gulf existed, the TRADOC commander continued to insist (in testimony to the House Armed Services Committee [HASC]) that training and leader development were the strengths of TRADOC and that there were no issues requiring fundamental change."[31]

By 2003 General Schoomaker (in coordination with the Army CSA) engaged in changing the Army, not only to help win an ongoing war but to prepare for future security needs, still found him hamstrung by a generation of subordinate leaders in the institutional Army who survived and thrived by not changing any systems without first being told the approved answer. Army leaders—officers and NCOs—became victims of goal displacement. Faced with uncertainty and ambiguity, they transformed what their cultural experience told them they could do (and could not do), into what they believed they should do. It only became worse when the broader organizational and senior leader culture did the same, misusing methods such as quarterly training briefings to measure events as if they were measures of effective training.[32]

Until recently, the Army was using training methods for wartime readiness as if it were still the 2GW volunteer Army of General DePuy's day, expecting to be told what to do, how to do it, and what the standard is. It was assumed that personnel knew nothing until trained and certified by an outsider. Indeed, in the operational Army there is reliance on TRADOC doctrinal products (and the hierarchy of multitudes of quality assurance inspectors) as a substitute for commanders' vision, concepts of operation, and innovative training strategies.[33]

On the unexpected eve of 9/11 and the following campaigns in Afghanistan and Iraq, the Army found itself with new operational requirements and many new technologies, but a professional officer and NCO corps that did not really know how to train it to fight and wage 4GW. "It could execute published tasks, under defined conditions, to simulated standards, but the culture imposed upon the Army caused it to struggle with how to fight and how to train to fight when conditions or requirements did not conform to officially approved assumptions." The Army had, through its own cultural behaviors in the 1990s, taught itself what to think, not how to think.[34]

Col. Casey Haskins, commander of the Army's 198th Infantry Brigade, responsible for the training of new Army infantry soldiers at Fort Benning, Georgia, describes the result in an observation he made in his own unit in August 2007:

> The training program lacked focus and often seemed to drill sergeants and company leaders like a non-stop series of events without connecting themes or clear priorities. A company commander trying to manage all the training could easily feel like the ball in a pinball machine, bouncing from one event to the next. The printed documentation governing 14 weeks of training was a stack of papers over three feet high, virtually unreadable.
>
> Much of the training had an assembly line, check-the-block feel to it. Soldiers firing on a machinegun range would move forward, pull the trigger, and then are moved off the line. They did not leave the training feeling confident they knew what to do.[35]

Colonel Haskins attributed this observation of training to three factors that evolved from DePuy's influence; these factors led to greater centralization and a top-down Army culture. First, outsiders—usually trainers from 2nd Battalion, 29th Infantry (2-29)—delivered much of the training. This left the company chain of command and especially the drill sergeants with little sense of ownership and little vested interest in seeing that the training was effective. The second factor was the low expectations embedded in the TSPs (training support packages), the documents governing what was to be trained and how. Not only did the TSPs often assume that soldiers were capable only of achieving minimal standards, but they sometimes dodged the issue altogether, requiring only "familiarization" with a topic—a vague term usually defined down on the ground to require mere presence and rarely requiring anything rigorous. The third systemic factor discouraging excellence was that training was governed by inputs rather than outcomes or results. Number of hours spent, number of rounds fired, number of classes attended all counted; true proficiency at the task being trained seldom did. This system made it easy to calculate resources and provide support but, unsurprisingly, did not maximize the training effect. Attendance at land navigation training was a prerequisite for graduation; the ability to read a map and navigate from one point to another was not.[36]

As a result, recent leader and soldier training does not encourage thinking and decision-making. In fact, it often discourages it. Although the best instructors—and especially those recently returned from combat—take great efforts to explain to their soldiers why things were done a certain way, the program itself stressed only the mechanical application of tasks. Worse, the atmosphere established during some courses emphasized "total control." In some units, particularly basic training units extended beyond the point of usefulness, that atmosphere sometimes remained nearly until graduation. Drill sergeants yelled, while instructors at leader courses assumed the "know all and be all" stance that prevented anyone from questioning their authority. Cadets, candidates, and junior officers, as well as soldiers, asked few questions, and infractions were answered by mass punishment, while education techniques are rote and boring.[37]

The process for training mobilized guardsmen and reservists was even more obsolete and narrow. Guardsmen and reservists, many of whom had active component experience, were treated as if they had never trained their units, and training at the mobilization centers has continued to be lockstep in compliance with that of the First Army, FORSCOM, HQDA, and CENTCOM training requirements for theater. Many guardsmen and reservists have stated, "I'll deploy again, but I never want to go through another mobilization center run by First Army."[38]

Young leaders and soldiers are not forced to work things out for themselves or to learn to be individually responsible. Not understanding why tasks are performed a certain way, they often fail to adapt properly to changed circumstances. Fortunately, thousands of leaders at the officer, NCO, and retired levels in the Army have recognized the downfalls of today's training and education doctrine and are moving from the bottom up to fix it, better preparing tomorrow's Army for the changing face of war.[39]

5

The Result: What Happens Today?

The institutional army began to observe expanding negative effects as the reforms became more extensive and deep-rooted, especially in the post–Industrial Era of the late-twentieth century. Army internal reports (1970, 1985, 1995) indicated an organization-wide "professional climate" reflecting the worst aspects of a managerial way of war and a promotion system that rewarded ticket punching functionaries and corporate managers over professional competence and bold, creative individuals. A century after the Root reforms, warnings in Army internal memos highlighted the Army's "disproportionate loss of high-potential, high-performance junior leaders." A 2011 survey of active duty general officers rated personnel management as one of the Army's weakest functions.[1]

—MAJ. DANIEL P. SNOW, "United States Army Officer Personnel Reforms and the Decline of Rank Flexibility, 1890s–1920s"

Since the 1980s, the U.S. Army has incorporated the lessons of military history in its education system to increase an understanding of doctrine and pride in the Army's past. Additionally, the Army has instituted a "training revolution" focusing on self-paced individual training, realistic training for units, and candid and rank-blind after-action reviews for soldiers and leaders. In addition to improving these institutions, there was an emphasis on leadership doctrine built upon trusting, respecting, and empowering subordinates.

Together with new material, the reforms moved the Army for the first time toward institutionalizing a total cultural change, something that had surfaced only briefly during the nineteenth century.[2]

One must address other developments including education and training to explain synchronization. The thinkers and writers who created the AirLand Battle doctrine defined synchronization as several operational and tactical echelons occurring at different levels at the same time. Commanders would employ different weapons systems with their own inherent strengths and weaknesses to attack opposing enemy systems in order to disrupt the enemy's sequential actions. This would be easy to translate if the officer corps had been educated to think holistically. However, thanks to the influence of events from the Civil War through Vietnam, the officer corps translates synchronization into centralized control through systematic thinking.[3]

How synchronization is taught and understood in the Army's officer education and training system appears similar to the French World War II doctrine of methodical battle described in the previous chapter. Illustrations of synchronization feature enemy forces arrayed in perfect templates while commanders and staffs manage sequential actions on an orderly decision matrix. Methods of teaching involve "synchronizing the battle." These are taught in an orderly sequence as well. In professional courses, or in officer professional development classes on war fighting, officers learn how to synchronize checklists.[4]

A number of younger officers who have attended Army schools, especially the Command and General Staff College, express frustration over the difference between what is desired or understood and reality. According to one observer: "'Out of the box' thinking is given lip service for appearance sake, but in the end, dismissed . . . rather than encourage free thought, CGSC's (mid-level staff college for field grade or majors) curriculum focuses on the circumscribed use of templated processes, pre-determined phases, matrixes, laundry lists, and pages of commander's guidance."[5]

Scenarios at the schools have changed little since the development of "active defense" (or since World War II for that matter, according to Gen. Omar Bradley).[6] The Army's approach to education, or the instruction of a "systematic approach to problem solving," is being transferred to scenarios in the Army's use of simulation or its "training revolution of the future." A broad array of simulators, including the simulation network (SIMNET) and the emerging close combat tactical trainer (CCTT), employ the terrain databases of the combat training centers.[7]

Mission accomplishment in the simulator can be evaluated by using the same checklists observer controllers (OC), the Army's doctrinal experts, used at the CTCs. Mission accomplishment or the outcome (the result achieved) is not as important as how the commander, his staff, or the unit go about it (inputs over outcome). The question asked by OCs and observing senior officers is, "Was the process employed?" Following the "process" or the "matrix" makes it easier for commanders and staff with little experience. It is thought that if new commanders and staffs train and rehearse on the same terrain, then they are all able to succeed. The thought ingrained in most officers is: "If you follow the process you will succeed." As a result, the tendency is for commanders and staffs to focus more on the numerous charts and matrixes posted on the walls of their tactical operations center (TOC) than on the opposing forces (OPFOR) actions.[8]

The tool that officers employ to ensure that all available battlefield operating systems (BOS) are in the fight is the "synchronization matrix." This is a complex chart depicting the various arms and battlefield operating systems on the left side of the matrix while phases of the operation or times are posted across the top. This enables the commander and staff to check off critical events as time progresses. The Army theorizes that this will help officers who have little experience with joint operations to properly integrate them. At division and corps level, commanders and staffs employ the "decision support template (DST)," which is a more complex synchronization matrix.[9]

Again, younger officers complain that these tools are overemphasized: "Tools such as the deliberate decision-making process and the synchronization matrix do provide excellent fundamental bases for analysis. However, once trained in their basic applications, students are not free to experiment or further develop their own cognitive abilities using these tools as frameworks."[10]

Ironically, this process was developed after officers such as Emory Upton in 1876 and Arthur L. Wagner in 1885–86 examined the way the Germans taught their students to view combined arms in combat, or to think "outwardly." Wagner and Lt. Eben Swift developed and standardized the "estimate of the situation" in 1888. This process, combined with the American experience in World War I when the French and British taught the Army, resulted in a systematic approach to solving tactical and operational problems. This evolved into the rote and methodical approach to fighting on the battlefield that would come to be recognized as part of the "American way of war."[11]

The difference between the Prussian/German and U.S. military education systems is that the Germans did not use any process or checklists in teaching decision-making. They threw the students into tactical problems later introducing field regulations as only a guideline. Their teaching tool to help students at the fundamental level view the separate arms in combined arms as solutions to tactical problems was through tactical decision games and war games. Doctrine was not even introduced until later in an officer's development, so it did not confine his problem-solving ability. Students, starting at the cadet level, were graded on how they went about solving and communicating solutions to the problem as concisely and quickly as possible.[12]

In contrast, the U.S. Army saw it as a solution to get its officer corps ready for war. The process and matrix would be employed at all levels to ensure the corps of trained amateurs mobilized for war checked all the blocks. Officers were taught how to use a matrix. They then transferred this process to the field, where they exemplified the slogan "train as you fight" in their units. For over a century major U.S. Army schools, particularly the Command and General Staff College, focused more on the process and the school solution than how students solved the problem. The outcome did not count, what mattered was that the student understood and applied the process correctly.[13]

Army education has come a long way since the 1960s, not, unfortunately, at a level that teaches officers to think holistically or simply how to make decisions and possess the character to stand by those decisions in the face of instructors and peers. The education system stresses repetition instead of thought. Still, there have been advances in education. Along with the doctrinal revolution of the 1970s and 1980s and the continual evolution of education, there was also a dramatic training upheaval during this same period. General DePuy's active defense concept encouraged better and more detailed training at both the individual and unit levels. A component system was developed by TRADOC, which traced training from the basic or individual level through higher levels of unit training.[14]

For example, manuals described how tank crewmen trained. These were linked to tank gunnery, how tank platoons and company/teams maneuvered, how tank battalions/task forces operated, and so on. Thus the types of tasks at each level were effectively aligned with those at a higher unit's level. The Army training and evaluation program (ARTEP) was developed to enable commanders to evaluate their unit's training.[15]

Although this program helped to train units better the Army turned it into a checklist measuring tool or test of commanders and their units' combat abilities against inputs instead of outcomes. If units completed the assigned training missions on time and adhered to prescribed checklists for an array of missions, then the commander and unit would be successful. Evaluations for units thus became a drill involving "checking the block on the ARTEP Training and Evaluation outline."[16] Manuals focused on the management of the systematic conduct of training have emerged from this system.

Another brilliant officer, Gen. Paul F. Gorman, contributed to the development of the tactical engagement simulation (TES). The advent of laser technology and sensors led to the development of the multiple integrated laser engagement system (MILES), or what civilians call "laser tag." Soldiers and vehicles using MILES are able to engage one another with laser fires for real-time assessments of casualties. It has made training vastly more realistic and, in terms of tempo, almost as intense as combat. At the same time, Gorman's efforts led to the creation of the National Training Center a Fort Irwin, California. There new brigades with two battalion task force elements, a cavalry squadron, supporting artillery engineers, and aviation, as well as direct support assets conduct both force-on-force training against the OPFOR, and live-fire training against automated target arrays. Today they do an array of training from counterinsurgency (COIN) operations to high intensity warfare. Such training tools and the amount of training space

(Fort Irwin is larger than the state of Rhode Island) would provide incredible training and readiness opportunities for the Army if it were used to its full potential (the Army now has evolved to Simmunition in the place of MILES II).[17]

Prior to the 9/11 attack, the friendly or blue force (BLUFOR) units were given wider zones of operation than the OPFOR so they can flank the opposing forces. However, even this advantage is of little help because most commanders fail to exploit the opportunity to maneuver. Those who do so generally fail because they lack experience making rapid decisions and their education has been focused on how to synchronize the battle. According to a RAND study, in 1996 Lt. Col. Douglas Macgregor had the most successful rotation against the OPFOR. He did this by not following doctrine. His award for achieving this, as well as leading heroically in the first Gulf War was not to receive a brigade command.[18]

When training at the National Training Center (NTC), commanders continued to emphasize checklists and follow procedures in order to synchronize operations. Detailed planning and then following the plan within the framework of the ARTEP (or, more recently, the mission training plan, or MTP) checklist is deemed more important than mission accomplishment. Successful rotations are based on "did we follow doctrine and execute the process?" and "no one got hurt."[19]

Since the 9/11 event the training at NTC has improved dramatically, simulating a COIN environment with villages and role players. The Army has transformed the base dramatically in the last thirteen years, adding fifteen towns and villages all linked through simulation and video to enhance learning through the AAR system. They have employed 350 soldiers operating as role players in these villages and make-believe country. The OPFOR (the 11th Armored Cavalry Regiment as of this writing) plays both insurgents and conventional enemy troops. Fort Irwin is the only place where the U.S. military can train using all of the systems it will later use in theater either in Iraq or Afghanistan. Its airspace is unrestricted and its truly remote location ensures an uncluttered electromagnetic spectrum, meaning that troops can practice both collection and jamming, while they maneuver.[20]

Still, when commanders are sent against a well-trained OPFOR in conventional force-on-force scenarios, they can explain away their defeat because "it is impossible to win against the OPFOR. They do this all the time on their home turf." Commanders have a defeatist attitude, and most battles wind up being head-on bloody battles of attrition. Brigade commanders are given orders from a planning cell in the NTC operations group that may read: "Destroy the enemy in zone" and include "no bypass criteria." With these restrictions, scenarios at the NTC are structured to stress the system—from soldiers through brigade commanders—ensuring that all battlefield operating systems (BOS) are used in the "close" or battalion-level fight. Units have little ability or opportunity to use judgment to exploit enemy weaknesses and attack his vulnerabilities.[21]

Under these conditions, it is almost impossible to distinguish who the best thinkers on the battlefield are. Even worse, the NTC is evidence of the Army's mentality with regard to tactical proficiency. The conventional wisdom is that any tactical situation can be solved with a "two up, one back" tactical solution, or by just following the formula, going back to French tactical doctrine at the end of World War I. With few exceptions, rotations at the NTC prove that the personnel system promotes and selects managers rather than battlefield commanders. One experienced OPFOR commander told Congress: "Combined-arms battalion and brigade commanders are not required to prove and demonstrate a mastery of battle command skills and tactical competence before being placed in command. It is not, and has not been, a prerequisite for command selection. It shows at the NTC, year after year."[22]

Although the NTC has improved the Army's readiness, it also highlighted the costs and weaknesses of the IRS. Under such conditions, Army combat units "cannot achieve their full combat potential, given existing conditions within our army today." The constant turmoil among units rapidly lessens the unit's "band of excellence" due to large officer and enlisted personnel turnover rates. Of course this loss is written off or ignored as business as usual. At upward of $10 million, the rotation of a brigade to the NTC is not a cheap venture. Even with the unit normally rotating overseas to Afghanistan after an NTC rotation capitalizing on the experience gained, no sooner does a brigade return from an intense rotation than the personnel managers take over, to send hundreds of officers and soldiers to other assignments. Commanders within the chain of command also move personnel to other "career-enhancing" positions within their organizations. While about 70 percent of the unit that rotates to NTC stays the same for its deployment overseas, still 30 percent, almost one third of the unit will still change over.[23]

Rhetoric Does Not Match Reality

While the emphasis is on the importance of "institutional culture" in embracing the concept of mission command, the Army culture is shaped by a personnel system that runs on out-of-date assumptions. The regulations, policies, and laws that guide the personnel system impact behavior throughout the Army. Personnel bureaucrats fight the wars of today with practices from the past.[24]

Little has changed since Vietnam. While the names of key players are different, the substance of their policies is not. As Jörg Muth wrote in reference to the 3rd Infantry Division's 5 April 2003 "Thunder Run" into Baghdad:

> The episode shows a command culture that has only gradually evolved from the days of World War II. While the technical knowledge of today's U.S. Army officers is far superior to that of their predecessors, their leadership capabilities are not. There are exceptions as some of the aggressive officers of the 3rd Infantry Division have demonstrated. Before the second Thunder Run, [Col. David] Perkins outlined for his officers which decisions were his to make and which ones they could make. That is as close as the U.S. Army has ever come to Auftragstaktik, but Perkins has proven to be an exceptional officer. This most effective and democratic of all command philosophies has, 120 years after its invention, been studied but not yet understood nor yet found a home in the armed forces of the most democratic of all nations.[25]

As a retired command sergeant major who spent his entire career in special operations stated, "Soldiers succeed in spite of the system, not because of it."[26]

For example, standards in officer accessions (how we prepare individuals to become officers) leader development, promotions, and attendance to military and civilian education opportunities were recently lowered to meet the need for "bodies" or "spare parts." Despite lessons that ought to have been learned from the mistakes made in the personnel arena during World War II, Korea, and Vietnam, these mistakes were repeated during the past ten years due to being corralled by legacies of the past. In 2010, the Defense Science Board report on the personnel system concluded that the Defense Officer Personnel Management Act (DOPMA) [with "up or out" as its centerpiece] and other policies and regulations "have the effect today of inhibiting the Department's flexibility and adaptability."[27]

The 2011 Secretary of the Army Human Dimension Task Force found that the Army's solution was to balance input with output by pumping up the input, in this case by beginning to demand more from accession sources, raising the percentage of soldiers who just made major, considering cutting down pin-on time to major, and in one of the worst decisions, sending lieutenants to a combat zone without going to Ranger School in order to fill "lieutenant slots" in battalions deploying to an insurgency war. In short, despite past evidence of its weaknesses, the conveyor-belt method of mass production of soldiers and officers ensures only that the quantity of service members remains high; their quality, on the other hand, is compromised by the inadequacies present in these current methods of educating them.[28]

This leads the Army to do two things that undermine its ability to practice mission command. Today, and in the future, asking lieutenants to make decisions with strategic implications, while decreasing their development opportunities and the time available to learn the soldierly arts at the small unit level, is a recipe for disaster. However, we continue to move them along this conveyor belt with frequent, and short, tours of duty in complex assignments.[29]

For nearly two decades, the Army's solution has been to increase the size of the bilge pump rather than to plug the hole that is sinking the ship. Why is this happening in the twenty-first century? As introduced in the previous chapter, the Army still views the management of its people through the tired old eyes of Secretary of War Elihu Root and turn-of-the-century industrial theorist Frederick Taylor. This was further impacted by the institutionalization of management science by Secretary of Defense Robert McNamara in the 1960s.[30]

In recent years, the Army has retained officers by promoting them, trying to solve a structural problem by bribing people to stay, hoping that the positive incentive of faster promotions could buy their loyalty, patriotism, and the moral strength to go into harm's way. Yet this kind of appeal to self-interest is precisely the kind of policy that has failed repeatedly in the past and will actually increase the exodus of our "best and brightest" young people, thus jeopardizing the Army's future. It is based on the dehumanizing assumption that our officers (and non-commissioned officers) are mindless, undifferentiated, replaceable cogs in a machine. This implies that any body of a certain rank will do—so much for highly developed professionals.[31]

But Congress and the press are blinded by the sterile promises of another technocentric analogy—the Air-Sea Battle (revolution in military affairs on steroids)—which is based on the idea that war is a mechanistic process and that machines are the true source of military prowess as U.S. opponents stand in the open all day and let us kill them. It was with this belief that the Army went to war with Iraq. As soon as the troops were out of Iraq and drawn-down in Afghanistan, the Air-Sea Battle and the specter of Root and Taylor began to haunt the Pentagon once again.[32]

There are dangers of reasoning by analogy. Used properly, analogies are powerful reasoning devices because they unleash the genius of imagination and creativity (Einstein's thought experiments being cases in point). But analogies are also very dangerous, because they simplify complex problems and capture our imaginations. Used improperly, they shackle the mind and take it over the edge of the cliff. Believing that the Army is like a business or that good business practices will solve military problems are examples of flawed and dangerous analogies.[33]

Effective business practices are often very different from effective military practices such as mission command. This is particularly true in the area of personnel policies, where the idea of soldierly virtue embodies the ethos of self-sacrifice and where, as Napoleon said, the moral is to the material as three to one. Numerous studies over the years have pointed out these issues with the American way of war.

In 2011, Eitan Shimar stated in *Transforming Command: The Pursuit of Mission Command in the U.S., British, and Israeli Armies*, "The American approach [to war] was influenced by Frederick Taylor's principles of scientific management. They sought to control war through efficient planning and execution processes. Thus, the regulations emphasized loyalty as opposed to independent action."[34]

Army Chief of Staff Gen. Mark Milley and Chairman of the Joint Chiefs of Staff Gen. Joseph Dunford have endorsed a belief in mission command and leader development as their top priorities. To succeed, they must also boldly take on the personnel bureaucrats to undertake the necessary reforms in regulations and work with Congress to change laws such as DOPMA 1980. To make mission command a powerful combat multiplier, they must exorcise the ghosts of Root and Taylor from Human Resources Command and the staffs of DCSPER and U.S. Army Training and Doctrine Command.[35]

6

What is OBT&E (ASLT&E)?

We've gone to outcomes-based training. . . . What we've learned in
this fight is that Soldiers really need to be able to figure things out.

—GEN. MARTIN E. DEMPSEY, Commanding general, TRADOC, October 2009

The challenge the Army faces today is not one of overthink-
ing situations; rather, it is the failure to think clearly in situations that require sound judgment at junior levels, and
leadership's hesitation to believe that juniors can or will think clearly.
Soldiers who are trained or conditioned to "look" at the situation—
that is, to assess, exercise judgment, and make decisions—are more
decisive, deliberate, and correct in their actions. This is particularly
important in the complex environment of full-spectrum operations.
The most important capability needed for these organizations is
thoughtful leaders and personnel who seek after the "why" of a situation, task, or directive, to understand and make better use of the
purpose behind it.[1]

In light of this, thinking young men and women who have been
taught the purpose behind military operations understand that anarchy
leads to failure, while unity of purpose leads to success. An organization of thinking individuals, working in unity of purpose with a strong
understanding of intent, is more readily able to adapt to the unexpected realities of today's mission sets. Therefore, individuals and some
courses in the Army were adopting a new approach to training and
education called Outcomes-Based Training & Education (OBT&E)

and developing two teaching methods—the Combat Applications Training Course (CATC) and the Adaptive Course Model (ACM)—under the OBT&E doctrinal umbrella.[2]

OBT&E evolved out of the efforts of the 198th Infantry Brigade at Fort Benning, Georgia from 2006 to 2008; it is now being embraced by parts of the Army (the latest incarnation is the Adaptive Soldier Leader Training and Education, or ASLT&E). Simply put, OBT&E looks for results. It puts a greater burden of professionalism (including accountability for prior knowledge and training) on the shoulders of the student, with guidance from the instructor. OBT&E is best described as "developmental training," that is, development of the individual within the training of military tasks.[3]

The constant change in personnel forced compliance to a veritable mountain of rules. These rules in turn diminish the soldier's ability to be adaptive; they destroy innovation. Additionally, as people see that compliance is rewarded—just another part of the incentive program—they perhaps fail to see that it also confirms and narrows their ability to solve complex problems. Thus, more rules lead to a lack of critical thinking and trust that in turn undermine the principles of mission command. Until recently, these causes were not well understood, so there was little the Army could do to influence soldier development in a meaningful way. Based on my own contemporary research and experience, this issue began around 1970. Today, the Army needs to embrace the fact that the actions we take during the earliest stages of a soldier's career manifest themselves much later.[4]

To counter an array of opponents, we must employ a full range of new military training and education courses. To meet this end, current educational and training ways and means must be assessed, evaluated, and changed. Weak spots and points of failure in education and training must be identified in the interest of retooling the system in ways that facilitate the development of leaders who are intuitive and adaptive.

Acknowledging the need for change, the Army has begun an evolution in the way it develops leaders and soldiers—from recruitment and selection to training, education, and promotion. The recently published training doctrine field manual, FM 7-0, *Training for Full-Spectrum Operations*, states:

> Traditional training and education may not meet all the needs of an expeditionary Army; as appropriate, training and education must adapt to the needs of a new operational environment. The training and education requirements are different for a full spectrum-capable force. Development of new approaches may be necessary to ensure Soldiers and Army Civilians are confident in their ability to conduct full spectrum operations anywhere along the spectrum of conflict with minimal additional training.[5]

In the past, the "competency theory" of learning dominated course curriculums, and there remain signs of it today in leader development. Competency theory is a product of the Industrial Age outlook that once governed the way military forces prepared for war. During the time when we relied on a massed citizen army of draftees, this "assembly line" mentality made sense, but its disadvantage was its emphasis on output over the individual product.

Competency-based education evolved from the *Principles of Scientific Management* developed by management and efficiency theorist Frederick Taylor in the 1890s. By the end of World War II, most public schools had adapted it as a foundation for their curriculum. It was designed to fit time constraints with objectives used and defined as reaching a given proficiency selected by an organization (such as "federal standards") in order to achieve efficiency and define an agreed upon minimum level of effectiveness. Industrial Age organizations seek routine and habit achieved through standardized procedures. Complex tasks are broken into simple steps that are assigned to organizational positions to ensure that employees are both interchangeable and easily replaced. Bureaucratic hierarchies tend to value quantifiable assessment of specific aspects of complex managerial tasks. "Leaving no child behind" is an example of competency education, as well as the phrase "teaching to the test"; it is teaching *what* to think rather than *how* to think.[6]

Today, some leader-centric programs within the Army still reflect the old assembly-line approach. But order and control are perpetuated by TRADOC through programs of instruction (POI). These

POIs are based on the Frederik Taylorism competency theory, circa 1905. TRADOC has adopted the term Adaptive Soldier Leader Training and Education (ASLT&E) to advocate for the development of a mission command mindset, but the influence of the Industrial Age has proven hard to shake.[7]

Leader development for the full spectrum of twenty-first-century military operations must be based on quality, not quantity, at every grade level. The rule should be, "Soldiers deserve and require trained leaders." Schools must constantly put students in difficult, unexpected situations and require them to decide and act under time pressure. Schooling must take students out of their comfort zones. Stress—mental, moral, and as well as physical—must be constant. War games, tactical decision games, map exercises, and free-play field exercises must constitute the bulk of the curriculum. Drill and ceremony and adherence to task, condition, and standards (TCS)—task proficiency—in the name of process are not important.[8]

There are many tasks for which TCS is still relevant. But under CATC and ACM, the emphasis is on growing the decision-maker by explaining the reason for the task and teaching in the context of a problem-solving exercise. Higher command levels overseeing officers and noncommissioned officers schools must look for flexible courses guided by outcomes rather than inputs while allowing instructors to develop their lesson plans using innovative teaching techniques and tools for a dynamic environment.

Those leaders who successfully pass through military schools must continue to be developed by their commanders; learning cannot stop at the schoolhouse door. The question that arises repeatedly is, "How does one teach in an OBT&E environment?" There are two techniques that answer this question: CATC is better for lower-level/individual soldier-centric tasks, and ACM is focused more on leader tasks; both approaches focus on growing decision-making. OBT&E is the guiding philosophy from which CATC and ACM were developed as education methods.

In both CATC and ACM, Army standards remain the baseline for training, although they are no longer the primary or exclusive goal of training. Within this idea is the realization that a generalized standard designed for the success of the Army at large may differ from what is required for the success of the individual or small unit in unique situations. In this manner, the task to be trained is looked upon as an opportunity to develop soldiers, primarily by creating a foundation of understanding that allows them not only to perform the task to standard but also to take ownership of the task and to exercise problem-solving skills.

Combat Applications Training Course (CATC)

The Army's Asymmetric Warfare Group (AWG), as well as other courses and units, are teaching the employment of CATC. It offers a method to instruct and develop mastery of any given subject. Its premise is that soldiers should understand the how and why of training. At the center of CATC is the use of problem-solving to teach a task. In the OBT&E doctrine, CATC uses rifle marksmanship as the training vehicle to demonstrate how to teach under OBT&E. AWG selected basic rifle marksmanship (BRM) as a vehicle to demonstrate OBT&E because BRM is an Army-wide course of instruction. CATC has been utilized by several basic training battalions throughout the Army; it has also been employed by infantry training brigades at Fort Jackson, South Carolina; Fort Benning, Georgia; Fort Sill, Oklahoma; and Fort Leonard Wood, Missouri (though it has since been discontinued at these sites). It was also employed at the drill sergeant school at Fort Jackson.[9]

When problem-solving exercises were taught using CATC techniques, teaching a particular military skill generally resulted in mastery of that skill for the majority of students. The teacher guides the student to discovery of a desired solution or outcome through established principles or demonstrated facts, and with student-generated evaluation throughout the learning cycle. Mastery of the skill results in confidence, accountability, and initiative; it also offers an introduction to the skill of discursive reasoning and the norm of problem-solving.[10]

AWG instructors believe this is applicable to all manner of military training; its efficacy has been readily demonstrated in history and in such current military initiatives as land navigation, squad tactics, room-clearing, and convoy operations. The term "mastery" defines reasonable ownership of a skill in terms of knowledge, expertise, and application. CATC abides by the following OBT&E principles:

- Training to grow problem-solving teaches soldiers to "teach themselves" the skills necessary to the success of their mission.
- Training to increase intangibles develops the intangible attributes of confidence, accountability, and initiative.
- Training to increase understanding and awareness teaches through contextual understanding of the task and its mission application.
- Training to increase deliberate thought conditions soldiers to always exercise a deliberate thought process while under stress.
- Training to improve combat performance conditions soldiers to overcome the psychological and physiological effects of combat.[11]

The CATC program uses rifle marksmanship as a foundation to improve the professionalism, confidence, and character of the soldier. One example involves a task for clearing a jammed rifle called SPORTS (*Slap, Pull, Observe, Release, Tap*, and *Shoot*). The traditional approach to basic soldier skill training only utilizes the TCS approach. In this case, the problem for the soldier is to correctly perform a mechanical function in five seconds or less in a sterile environment. This not only offers no opportunity to employ the problem-solving skills required in combat, it also places the responsibility for the outcome on the instructor, not on the student.

In contrast, the OBT&E approach presents the problem in a combat scenario. When the weapon jams, the soldier not only uses the SPORTS process to clear the jam (if that makes sense under the circumstances) but also considers and executes other essential tasks, such as taking cover and notifying comrades of the problem—in roughly the same amount of time. From leaders at all levels, the response to CATC's approach has been positive. For example, SFC Steve Case reported, "While at the Drill Sergeant School (where I received CATC training), we made a great attempt immediately to implement the training from CATC. Introducing the training methodology was easy, in that it is merely a shift in leadership style and does not take much outside approval to make it happen. We also wanted to integrate the basic rifle marksmanship training itself; we thought it would be a great addition to the curriculum at the Drill Sergeant School."[12]

It is a natural process for individuals in leadership roles to solve problems without regard to the potential impact on those below them. But problem-solving in a vacuum is a short-term solution that may do harm to the long-term development of an organization. If an individual in a position of influence or authority identifies a problem of concern within an organization, a solution is generally presented in a top-down manner. In effect, this takes the responsibility out of the hands of the individual performing the task, making him or her dependent first on the instructor and later on the chain of command for trivial tasks.[13]

It can be argued that there is nothing systematically wrong with this approach. It is to the point, it appears efficient, and it is quantifiable. The Army, and society, will solve organizational problems using the mechanical approach or find a process wherein the solution is thrust upon the group with a means of enforcement. The focus of this type of problem-solving is the problem itself, and it often relies on principles of manipulation associated with models like Maslow's hierarchy of need. One soldier reflects on the contrast between the Army's Industrial Age approach and CATC's OBT&E method: "The course exceeded my expectations. I expected to get the basic rifle marksmanship class that I gave while a drill sergeant. I was wrong. I was introduced to a new method of providing information to today's young leaders, as well as honing my BRM skills. The BRM portion was presented in a well thought out manner, time was well spent, the instructors were the subject matter experts, and the range was well set up."[14]

CATC developers have discovered another approach to problem-solving, but it is counter to current cultural ideas and is not inherent in the Army or U.S. society. It is extremely powerful in building a sense of accountability, responsibility, and confidence in the soldier in addition to solving the problem. The focus of this type of problem-solving is equally divided between growing the intangible attributes of juniors and the problem itself, and it relies on the principle that individualized, purposeful action is superior to mandated action.

In this approach, CATC instructors have discovered that when an organizational problem is encountered, a solution is still defined (to a degree), but it is not directly presented. The leadership works with the soldier to help him see and analyze the problem from an operational perspective. The instructor demonstrates to the soldier that the resources required to solve the problem are within the soldier's means. In this manner, the soldier plays an active, creative, role in discovery of the solution.

Two things are accomplished with this approach: The solution is found through the positive experience of discovery, and the soldier takes ownership of the solution and experiences the process of problem-solving from an operational perspective. Revisiting the simple example of a rifle stoppage: "An obstacle in your mission to engage the enemy is a stoppage in your rifle. How can you overcome this obstacle? First, determine what causes a stoppage and then how to correct it."[15]

Leadership talks the matter out using its defined or partially defined solution as a guide—for example, the logical process of SPORTS plus thoughtful problem-solving versus a mechanical function that must be performed correctly in five seconds. The intent is for the soldier to discover the cause and solution by his own deliberation. This builds in the soldier a sense of accountability for his actions, responsibility for taking action, and confidence in deciding on the correct action. The goal in this approach is for the soldier to understand the problem and the solution. The standard of correctly performing the task in five seconds will be a natural by-product and, to a degree, secondary to the growth of the soldier.

Asking questions in a positive manner involves the soldier in the process of discovery. Using the word "we" means the leader is joining with the soldier in finding mission success for the soldier: "This is your mission (or task), but I am committed to helping you find success."[16]

Contrast the two methods of dealing with organizational problems—the competency theory and OBT&E—and discover that the first method is not concerned with developing the problem-solving ability of the soldier. It focuses the efforts of leadership on solving an increasing number of problems for the soldier. A by-product of this method is a growing sense of frustration in the leadership over a perceived lack of initiative and responsibility in soldiers. The second method, concerned with encouraging the problem-solving ability of the individual, sees problems as opportunities. It focuses efforts of leadership on providing the environment and resources for the individual to succeed. The first method defines what the soldier *must* do for success while the second method empowers the soldier to discover what he *can* do. "It is better to be called a mentor than an instructor."[17]

In the BRM example, an instructor states the problem (a jammed weapon) and then states the solution (execution of SPORTS within the mandated five seconds). For the soldier, the problem has shifted from the need to clear a rifle stoppage in combat to the need to perform a task correctly in five seconds. This places a requirement on the student not related to the task of war fighting and contrary to the initiative expected of American soldiers. A mentor helps the individual understand the problem as it relates to the task of war fighting and then guides him to discover the solution. A mentor does not have to know the solution; he has only to ask the right question and be willing to help find the solution.

Field Manual 3-22, *Rifle Marksmanship*, contains the word "must" more than four hundred times, with more than a hundred references to "Soldier[s] must." The Army has solved the problem for the individual and retained ownership of the solution. In doing so, it also removes operational accountability, responsibility, and confidence from the individual. Leaders and advisers may find it rewarding to solve problems—as we all do—if the Army is not teaching soldiers how to solve their own problems, then the Army is the problem.[18]

Adaptive Course Model (ACM)

Parallel to the CATC program of instruction is the Adaptive Course Model (ACM)—the second innovation used to apply the principles of OBT&E; ACM evolved from an effort at Georgetown University between 1999 and 2005 to develop ROTC cadets to be better decision-makers and leaders of character. While CATC and ACM use different vehicles—ALM uses situational exercises in a tactical environment—to develop professionalism, decision-making skills, and, ultimately, strength of character, the methodology used by the instructor is similar.[19]

According to Maj. Chris Kennedy, CATC and ACM are "two sides of the same coin."[20] CSM Patrick Laidlaw describes ALM as:

> Training as it has always been done but now more focused for the team to share and not just the leader. ACM reinforces the events that all Soldiers and future leaders learn in a long period of time what they can now do in short periods receiving instant feedback and input. This should be a course that gets into every aspect of decision-making from reception station to mission rehearsals for future combat operations at the lowest level. ACM is a great asset for early leader development at all of our training bases.[21]

Dr. Gary Klein tells us that the dominant type of decision-making for leaders in a time-critical environment is based on recognition, which requires a large amount of experience. Research also tells us that making a large number of decisions in a stressed environment solidifies competence in decision-making.[22]

Dr. Robert Bjork, dean of the School of Psychology at UCLA, tells the Army that there is room for improvement in its training methods. In his presentation "How We Learn Versus How We Think We Learn: Implications for the Organization of Army Training," Bjork emphasizes:

> As instructors, we can often be misled in this determination because what is readily available to us is the performance of our students during instruction, which can be a poor indicator of how much durable learning is actually occurring. If, for example, all we consider is the rapidity and apparent ease of learning during training and instruction, we can easily be led into preferring poorer conditions of learning to better conditions of learning. Additionally, as learners, it seems that we do not develop—through the everyday trials of living and learning—an accurate mental model, so to speak, of those operations that result in learning and those that do not.[23]

Leaders must understand that deciding when and how to close with an enemy may be the least important decision they make on an asymmetric battlefield. Instead, actions that build and nurture positive relationships (with a community, local leaders, and children) may be among the defining factors for success, along with the primary tools for containing an insurgency, building a nation or stopping genocide. True tactical prowess often entails co-opting the local population's will while shattering the cohesion of asymmetric adversaries. The Army—and for that matter the other services (with a few exceptions)—has focused on the competency model, which produces leaders who are good at *what* to think, but as Bjork stresses, "When instruction occurs under conditions that are constant and predictable, learning appears to get what we might call contextualized. It looks very good in that context, but doesn't support retention later when tested in other contexts and the learning acquired in the original context does not transfer well to different contexts. In contrast, varying conditions of practice, even just the place where you study, for example, can enhance recall on a later test."[24]

Bjork's work, as it relates to evolving the current task-centric and process-centric approach to Army education, can be summed up in the following: "Conditions of instruction that make performance improve rapidly often fail to support long-term retention and transfer, whereas conditions of instruction that appear to create difficulties for the learner, slowing the rate of apparent learning, often optimize long-term retention and transfer."[25]

Army courses moving to OBT&E as doctrine can use ACM as a basis for their Program of Instruction. It exposes students to classical education in conjunction with existing leadership programs on campuses where they are taught to find the answers, as opposed to a competency-based curriculum that gives students the answers. If students are exposed to an environment in which they want to find the answers for themselves, the lessons are emotionally marked in time, building intuition—a necessary trait of adaptive leaders. This approach in ACM immerses the students in their education and training.

According to Lt. Col. Chad Foster, former course director for Military Science 300 in the Department of Military Instruction at West

Point, "The implementation of key elements of ACM has been the best thing to happen to our Military Science program during my time here as an instructor. After seeing this new methodology of teaching applied to our courses in tactical problem-solving and small unit tactics this semester, I am even more convinced of its value. In just a few weeks, I felt that I was able to get my cadets to a level beyond that which I was able to achieve over several months during previous semesters."[26]

ACM is a leader development approach incorporating recent advances in the field of experiential learning. It is an answer to the call for a new leader education model to reshape a fundamental Army learning process for a dynamic operating environment. ACM provides an answer to the 2006 TRADOC Area of Interest 2 requirement to "Change the Professional Military Education (PME) model to adapt to the contemporary operational environment (COE) and the Army Forces Generation (ARFORGEN) model, and leverage Army Distributed Learning (ADL), which supports Army TRADOC Campaign Plan."[27]

Some companies of the former Basic Officer Leader Course (BOLC) II program at Fort Sill and Fort Benning used ACM from July 2006 until the BOLC II program ended in October 2009.[28] Since February 2008, the demand for information on ACM has intensified, as have requests for its instructor certification workshop "Deciding Under Pressure and Fast." Since January 2008, ACM and the workshop have been presented to the Joint Conference on Military Ethics in San Diego, and at Fort Huachuca, Fort Benning, Fort Gordon, Fort Monroe, Fort Knox, and at the USMA.

According to Lieutenant Colonel Foster, "The ACM workshop was instrumental in getting our new instructors to 'buy in' to the new teaching methodology [ALM] that we are utilizing in our new MS 300 course. It built on a lot of things that I had been saying to them previously, but it went farther in communicating the spirit and intent of ACM than anything else that we did as part of our new instructor integration and training."[29]

ACM became institutionalized on 24 April 2008 when Lt. Gen. Benjamin C. Freakley, commander, U.S. Army Accessions Command, signed a policy letter, "Basic Officer Leader Course (BOLC) Policy and Guidance," mandating ACM certification for BOLC instructors. Of course it was largely ignored by other courses that fell under the Accessions Command until September 2008 when Chief of Staff of the Army Gen. George Casey sent out a copy of chapter 3 from this author's book, *Manning the Legions of the United States and Creating Tomorrow's Centurions*, to all the two-star commands in the Army with recommendation to consider employing OBT&E and ACM to improve training.[30]

The Asymmetric Warfare Group has also used ACM in its OBT&E activities; it hosted its first Adaptability Conference 3–4 June 2008, with day one focusing on an ALM workshop while day two focused on OBT&E. AWG continues to host these workshops; they have offered them a few years ago at Fort Benning and at Fort Sill in December 2008.[31]

Many other institutions within the Army, including leader-centric courses such as the Noncommissioned Officer Academy (NCOA) at Fort Benning, are starting to use ACM in their POI and lesson plans. As CSM Zoltan James, commandant of the Fort Benning NCOA, describes,

> ACM has outlined and changed the way we teach at Fort Benning's NCO Academy by giving us the ability to develop NCOs to think for themselves instead of current training outlines that provided them with a Task, Condition and Standard. We have changed our training culture adding the utilization of tactical decision games with no additional resources or increased Program of Instruction time. This new training tool allows our Noncommissioned Officer Education System (NCOES) students to share their combat experiences with their peers and provides a training vehicle to develop and practice adaptability. Most important, they gain knowledge and understanding of how to deal effectively with a continually changing environment.[32]

ACM and OBT&E support Army Chief of Staff Peter Schoomaker's vision of adapting Army culture to teach adaptive leadership. The issue before TRADOC is instituting a methodology that moves beyond this vision to a method that teaches leaders *how* to think versus *what* to think. Command Sergeant Major James continues, "Creating adaptability in our leaders attending NCOA is a huge challenge for the current methods available of training by the standard training support packets (TSP) provided for NCOES classroom instructions by the institutional Army."[33]

The institutional Army must understand the ACM principles, which include providing contextual interference during learning (for example, *interleaving* rather than *blocking* practice); most tasks are learned through doing and are subordinate to leader development scenarios taught as part of the conditions of learning.

- "Experiencing the thing before they try to give it a name."[34]
- Conducting scenarios three levels higher to understand their (units') role in the bigger picture through use of tactical decision games (TDGs).
- Executing free-play, force-on-force exercises, with missions used as vehicles to develop leadership adaptability.
- Distributing or spacing study or practice sessions (providing the opportunity and access to find answers).
- Reducing feedback to the learner, forcing the student to find the answer rather than providing it.
- Using observations and evaluations by conducting scenarios (rather than presentations) as learning events.

Instructors' feedback and that of students involved with ACM reflect the positive impact this cultural change will have on the Army's future leaders. According to Capt. Thomas Pike, course director for Military Intelligence BOLC III, "Adaptive Leader Methodology" has had a paradigm-shifting impact on the Military Intelligence Basic Officer Leader Course (MIBOLC). ACM has not only improved the way in which material is presented to the students, it has also changed the way in which instructors understand their material, dynamically changing MI BOLC's training environment. ALM is what is needed to train junior intelligence officers for the 21st century."[35]

This change has required no additional resources or a lengthening of the total period of instruction. ALM takes advantage of current combat veterans' insights and experiences, their continued initiative, and their desire to grow future leaders. ALM does this because it continues to build on the Army core principles and values. The warrior ethos underpins everything in ACM, while ACM adapts Army leaders to the current and future operating environment.

ACM is a cultural change rather than the specific implementation of exercises; as Captain Pike continues, "It is a completely different mindset for the instructor."[36] ALM develops adaptability by employing the rapid decision-making (RDM) process, using the experiential learning model in scenario-based learning. According to Capt. Casey Giese, BOLC II company commander, "ALM is a system that promotes self-actualized learning via weakly structured situational problems."[37]

Additionally, ACM parallels the latest findings in leader and cognitive development. The ACM POI employs techniques that are "desirable difficulties" as pointed out by Dr. Bjork in his keynote presentation at the TRADOC-hosted "Science of Learning" workshop in August 2006. Capt. Alec Barker states, "ALM espouses institutionalized inductive reasoning in order to prepare leaders for the complex wars of the future."[38]

According to former BOLC II company commander (and formerly commander of 1st Squadron, 11th Armored Cavalry Regiment) Lt. Col. Paul Wilcox, in a course using ACM,

> Students are quickly thrown into problem-solving exercises that would be viewed in the past as too complicated for them without first learning the basics [from a classroom lecture]. They then review the results of their actions in an after-action review (AAR) in which the instructors facilitate the students in finding their answers. The instructors avoid telling the students how to do it—there are no book solutions—but guide the students toward workable solutions they already discovered in experimenting during the course of the scenario.[39]

Before introducing theory or doctrine, instructors use tactical decision games (TDGs) or symposium-based case studies as tools to facilitate learning.[40] Then, whenever possible, they follow up with force-on-force, free-play exercises. A USMA cadet contrasts the old with the new:

> [I] wanted to express to you how thankful I am for the change in the program. Last year as you know was death by PowerPoint, where the quizzes were a bunch of form numbers. Myself and many of my classmates deemed that of little use considering how most of those forms can be found on Google and that most of us have forgotten what we memorized and dumped for that course. I was very happy to find out that the yearlings [second-year cadet, sophomore] did not have to suffer through what I did, and instead, are developing their tactical thinking and applying them to scenarios we may see in the future. Many of my classmates and myself agree that this course makes one realize why they came to West Point, to lead Soldiers and be real good at it. I just read the homework assignment for MS 300 and it was full of good information that I can use for the future. This class prepares me a lot better for [Operation Iraqi Freedom] and [Operation Enduring Freedom] than last year's class. Thank you for that, and I hope this development continues.[41]

Students are allowed to run as much of the course as possible. For example, for rifle qualification required to meet Army regulations, students not only learn how to shoot, they also learn by running the range. These approaches do not absolve the cadre of the responsibilities of teaching and ensuring the safety of the students. According to BOLC II instructor SFC Robert Elzy, "The approach called for in the ACM POI is more difficult because the instructors must stand back and let the students learn through doing, but also know when to step in to keep students on course without wasting too much time as some student leaders will flounder in trying to lead and solve the problem."[42]

Lieutenant Colonel Foster added,

> ACM works, but it takes the right kind of instructor. Gone are the days when you could just plug any officer or NCO into a teaching position. Teaching in a course that applies ACM requires a

high level of passion and competence. It is tough for those who want to implement this methodology, but nothing worth having is ever easy. After seeing it first hand, I will apply the principles of ACM in everything that I as a leader, trainer and mentor do during the rest of my Army career. I will also seek out subordinate leaders who understand this philosophy and can put it into practice.[43]

ACM holds to the idea that every moment offers an opportunity to develop adaptability. Every action taken by a student in the classroom or in field training is important to the process of inculcating a preference for new solutions. If students err while acting in good faith, they do not suffer anything more than corrective coaching. Constructive critiques of solutions are the norm, but more important are the results of actions, and the reasons for those actions. The role of coaching and 360-degree assessment is to develop students so their future actions will make a positive contribution to their unit's success, no matter what the mission. This idea is based on the premise that one learns more from a well-meaning mistake reviewed critically and constructively than from applying an established and memorized process.

ACM teachers are concerned with why the students do what they do—an action learning approach. The emphasis of the course is on ensuring that the students gain and maintain a willingness to act. During numerous AARs and mentoring sessions—occurring during and after numerous scenarios with different conditions—the teacher analyzes why the students acted as they did and the effect the action had on the overall operation. As Capt. Andrew Watson, an instructor at the Infantry Basic Officer Leader Course III (formally Infantry Officer Basic Course), said,

> I was skeptical at first of ACM's utility for a number of reasons. We had to really bite our lips during the painful execution of very poor React to Contact Drills during the live-fire exercises [LFXs]. However, we noticed during the AAR we were no longer confronted with the statement, "But that's the way the sergeant told me to do it." I was now able to ask leading questions during the AAR, i.e., "Why did you assault back toward your support-by-fire position?" I found myself rather than in a position of convincing

the lieutenants of a way to do it, and even confrontational at times in the AAR, the lieutenants now fully accepted and took owner-ship that they were not ready. I was now coaching, teaching, and mentoring on team, squad, and platoon leadership. The lieuten-ants then went back and conducted several hours of rehearsals and then executed a second iteration of the LFX. They performed the best set of squad LFXs we've ever conducted.[44]

The ACM curriculum and leader evaluation system use two criteria to judge students' decisions and ultimately their strength of character: the timeliness of their decisions and their justification for actions taken. The first criterion will impress on students the need to act in a timely manner, while the second requires students to reflect on their actions and gain insights into their own thought processes. Since students must justify their decisions in their own minds before implementing them, imprudent decisions and reckless actions will be less likely. During the course, student decisions in terms of a "school solution" are relatively unimportant. The emphasis is on the effect of the students' actions, not on the method they may have chosen. This encourages a learning envi-ronment in which there will be few formulas or processes to achieve optimum solutions—an environment that will solicit creative solutions.

The learning evaluation system in ACM is based on the philoso-phy that feedback should be given in a way that encourages a will-ingness to act and then reflect on actions in a manner that maximizes learning. Unconstructive critiques destroy the student leader's will-ingness to act. This can lead to withholding of adverse information or false reporting. The course will avoid formulaic solutions and pro-vide room for over a generation of leaders, teaching new dogs new tricks. As Command Sergeant Major James remarked, "With ACM we have a better trained and developed NCO Corps that become critical thinkers and can adapt to a changing operating environment to sup-port senior leaders' mission requirements."[45]

Egos Are Not Invented Here
Maj. Gen. John M. Custer III confessed: "I am the Commander of the Intelligence Center of Excellence and have very little say in how my Captains' Career Course is run."[46]

Moving beyond traditional instructor-led "blocks of instruction" requires a "cultural learning evolution" affecting significant changes to established TRADOC institutional processes. TRADOC's Army Learning Coordination Council has taken on the task of synchronizing learning across the Army to ensure implementation of *ALM 2015*. They have identified key institutional challenges that involve reforming current training resourcing and policy to accommodate One Army School System initiatives and Regional Learning Center fielding. Improving instructor quality and utility to ensure selection, assignment, development, and sustainment of the best personnel as faculty cadre is also important. This further enhances network access and infrastructure to ensure soldier accessibility and point-of-need delivery of learning content. Finally, there is a retooling of the current training development model to develop, maintain, and assess learning outcomes across TRADOC.[47]

OBT&E requires a different method of allocating resources to training and more flexibility in using them; resources are aligned to tasks being trained rather than to skills attained. The OBT&E model can be instructor intensive. It requires a much different level of instructor quality than current practices. It necessitates reexamining instructor selection, promotion, and development, including empowering instructors as leaders. The key to quality training and education relies on a cadre of experienced faculty who are leadership mentors, coaches, and teachers.

One of the advantages of the Army having been at war for nearly two decades is the increased level of tactical and operational experience its instructors now possess. OBT&E requires additional instructor training not currently provided by the Army Basic Instructor Course. In OBT&E, the instructor is required to change the conditions of the operational environment based on the ability of each student to produce the desired level of skill proficiency versus one standardized instruction approach. This instructor skill set requires additional training not currently offered—except at Fort Benning for the 316th Cavalry Brigade (Armor Center), as of the summer of 2014.

Delivery of training and education dependent on actual learning outcomes requires that some consideration be given to multiple learning models, including OBT&E. A primary benefit of *ALM 2015* is that we do not have to choose a "one-size-fits-all" approach to how the Army trains and educates. It further emphasizes that the Continuous Adaptive Learning Model must continually assess outcomes in meeting the needs of the force and be responsive to operational changes and evolving trends in learning technologies and methods. As Army Chief of Staff Gen. Raymond T. Odierno has stated, "Adapt leader development to meet our future security challenges in an increasingly uncertain and complex strategic environment."[48] The Army is expected to fight and win on difficult and rapidly changing complex battlefields. Aligning the institutional Army to the culture desired through mission command will vastly increase Army capabilities. But some hard decisions must be made in terms of how to support and institutionalize the mission command concept.[49]

While reforms to the personnel system may take years to implement and must overcome deep bureaucratic resistance, OBT&E is already providing an alternate route to prepare leaders to operate under mission command. It aligns more closely with the way individuals actually learn and communicate. While results are preliminary and anecdotal, evidence is clear that OBT&E results in superior mastery of fundamental skills, increased retention, and higher levels of confidence while promoting improved judgment, initiative, and accountability. Further, as an approach that encourages broader development of capabilities, its implementation will better position soldiers and units for the uncertain missions and ambiguous realities consistent with full-spectrum operations.[50]

OBT&E represents an integrated approach to planning, managing, and delivering training, education, and self-development. It teaches soldiers and leaders how to think rather than what to think by developing a deep sense of understanding and increased will to adapt tasks under realistic, complex conditions. It connects the classroom to the operational environment, tapping combat experience and integrating it with mission command. OBT&E is consistent with FM/ADP 6-22, *Army Leadership*; FM/ADP 7-0, *Training*; and the ALDS, and it is linked to the development of essential characteristics, attributes, and competencies of the profession of arms.

OBT&E has diverse application across the force. However, achieving an outcomes-based learning approach consistent with the *ALM 2015* framework and the ALDS imperatives will require a "cultural learning evolution" that includes major institutional challenges for TRADOC (i.e., resourcing and policy, instructor quality and utility, network access and infrastructure, and training development). Implementing OBT&E also requires an organizational climate with a consistency of collaboration and flexibility in doctrine, policy, and allocation of resources to ensure accountability for results. Finally, OBT&E necessitates reexamining instructor selection and development that includes empowering instructors as leaders.[51]

Evolution Must Continue

In their article, "Adapt or Die," Brig. Gen. David A. Fastabend and Robert H. Simpson make the case for teaching critical thinking, saying, "Most Army schools open with the standard bromide: 'We are not going to teach you what to think . . . we are going to teach you how to think.' They rarely do. Critical thinking is both art and science. There are techniques to critical thinking, such as careful application of logic, or alternative application of deduction and induction. These techniques can be taught and learned."[52]

Superior (innovative) military education and training is critically important to the institutionalization of adaptability, which will assist with recruiting and retaining good personnel. Not only does the Army need to produce adaptive leaders, it must ensure that the institutions tasked with developing them become adaptive as well—evolving as the operating environment changes.

The Army's cultivation of adaptability requires a vast effort—both from the top-down and the bottom-up. It is so central to the future of the Army that it applies to squad leaders as well as the joint force commander. Moving the Army toward a learning organization structure will bring its collective creativity to bear in solving problems at the tactical, operational, and strategic levels of war. The culture will become one that rewards leaders and soldiers who act, and penalizes those who do not.

The Army's future leaders will also have the responsibility to self-police their ranks, particularly early on if they become teachers within a CATC, ACM, or an operational unit. This makes evaluating—"racking and stacking"—graduates easier. It will also help determine early on who will have the character and traits to become an adaptive leader. The criteria should include observations of the student leaders in several scenarios. Before selecting or promoting subordinates, a commander and teacher should always ask, "Would I want this person to serve in my unit?" Throughout a course, an instructor or teacher will instill in students the importance of accurate reporting and taking action when the situation demands it. The Army's culture of the future will not tolerate inaction.

The teacher's role in employing OBT&E principles cannot be overstated. The instructor is central to the learning process, be it training or education. One could argue that OBT&E is dependent on specific instructor skills, whereas the skills of course managers and training developers are enablers to OBT&E. It's the instructor who interfaces with the student and is accountable for facilitating the student's attainment of the desired outcome while maintaining a safe learning environment that does not stifle initiative. Under OBT&E, safety is opportunity for the individual to preserve life, equipment, and resources in training, mission, and combat.

Safety allows training and mission to go further, resulting in more realistic training (learning in more complex scenarios) and greater success in mission or combat. Safety is more than risk management—it can be instilled in the individual as an awareness of situation, instead as an additional annex in an operations order (OPORD) or as a mandatory event done to get training approved called risk management matrix.

Adaptability will become a product of the future Army; it will depend on what appears to be a relatively simple change in teaching technique to deal with the increasing complexities of war. The understanding and mastering of adaptability will come through rigorous education and tough training early on—quality, not quantity—to produce adaptive leaders. Leaders' ability to adapt will guide their decisions while also helping them to recognize and compensate for differences in the temperament and ability of other Army officers, NCOs, and civilians through unit training and professional development.

Adaptability will provide a stable support structure to infuse and sustain Army leaders' initiative in future operating environments. Most important, as Lieutenant Colonel Foster concludes, "ACM creates leaders and soldiers who can truly 'think on their feet' because they are forced to do so in every aspect of the course. I don't think there is any other method or theory that could be better for developing leaders, especially those in the military."[53]

7

Who Teaches (Facilitates)?

We cannot expect to be able to issue long-winded orders, either
written or oral. Whatever order we are able to issue must be short
and must be clear. If we hope to do this in war we must practice
it in peace.

—ADOLF VON SCHELL, *Battle Leadership*

T
rust is the glue that bonds everyone together and makes
Auftragstaktik work, while the leaders and teachers strengthen
that glue. As we discovered earlier, the Germans spared nothing
when it came to selecting their best officers and NCOs for teaching
positions. They believed this assignment was second only to leading
and commanding in combat.

Not everyone has the temperament, personality, experience, professional knowledge, and foresight to perform as an effective teacher
(referred to in the Army as "instructors"—an Industrial Age term).
After determining who can do the best job, the Army must accept
what it will be giving up when assigning the "right" person at the
right time and place. "Any good officer can perform as a teacher"
is an inaccurate assumption, but it was the basis in the decisions for
selecting for instructors in the past. Conversely, good teachers are
good leaders.

Each MOS branch is required to fill quotas for officers and NCOs
who are assigned as teachers. The subject the officer or NCO would
teach, their experience, or their personal merit have not been a part of

the selection process in the past. The argument that any good officer or NCO should be able to do this job is correct *in theory*. The instructor selection process in the past has also contradictory to FM 3-24, paragraph 6–87 calls for in the field for advisor positions as well, "The importance of the job means that the most capable individuals should fill these positions."[1]

The role of teachers and their methods are different in a culture of Auftragstaktik than in the Army's traditional teaching model. Learning through many scenarios relies on a teacher's ability to introduce increasingly difficult unit tasks in the development of adaptive leaders. The program should constantly expose students to individual and collective tasks that they have never seen. Teachers should not get "wrapped around the task"; rather, they should introduce and show students how the task fits into solving the larger problem. A better term would be to say students become "familiar" with most tasks instead of spending an incredible amount of time becoming "trained" (qualified) in any particular one.[2]

The burden of imparting adaptability on students is the teachers'. Individuals who qualify for these key roles in an ACM are called "teachers of adaptability" (TA). They are constantly updating and preparing new challenges for their students through a rigorous study of the latest lessons as they apply to the profession of arms. Teaching cognitive skills involves exposure to new ideas, encouragement to experiment with theories concerning what works and does not work, and the ability to learn, evaluate, and assess. An ACM sets the conditions where evaluation occurs with the student through various mission scenarios, each with different conditions.

There is an art to teaching. In the Army, it requires an understanding of war, proficiency in the technical aspects of the profession of arms, imagination, and patience. There is no room for big egos in a classroom. With these ingredients, the teacher of adaptability will find many ways to utilize tasks to employ the teach–facilitate–mentor approach. The goal of a true teacher is to prepare the student to be a better problem solver than the teacher.[3]

The key to the ACM is that individuals must know how to *teach*, *facilitate*, *mentor*, and *evaluate* adaptability. How the Army certifies the leaders it chooses to teach these courses is critical to the success of the ACM. This goes far beyond today's demand that instructors must master certain tasks or win certification as instructors by passing an online course consisting of multiple-choice questions.

Certainly teachers must understand individual tasks, but their knowledge cannot comprise only the ability to reinforce memorization of how to perform a certain task. Teachers of adaptability must understand the threads of knowledge that allow a combat leader to choose the appropriate number and type of tasks, how to combine these individual tasks as part of more complex tasks in order to solve the challenges that they will encounter in a kinetic or insurgent environment. More difficult, instructors must understand theories, and how to experiment to solve unknown or unfamiliar problems that might arise in the classroom or on the battlefield.[4]

With these general insights into the nature of an ACM teacher, the next step is defining the selection and certification of teachers of adaptability. Currently, the Army Instructor Training Course (AITC), which certifies many of the Army's instructors—with the exception of the one at the Fires Center of Excellence at Fort Sill, Oklahoma— is dominated by a linear format that includes "how-to" briefings on putting together lesson plans, schedules, and calendars—all of which are focused on task proficiency. Selection of individuals to be Army instructors is usually based on the need to fill a slot, which in today's personnel system is not considered a "career enhancer." The ACM will be limited if the personnel system fails to provide the necessary resources for leader-centric courses, including the best and brightest individuals for instructors.[5]

Certification for an ACM begins with the selection, is followed by the education, and finally the certification of those individuals who initially demonstrate the potential to teach adaptability. First of all, the Army as a learning organization needs to rank the importance of teaching at an ACM as second only to command or leading soldiers. The feeling among Army leaders should be, "If [I am] not in command, then teaching at an ACM is the next best option." Becoming and being a teacher of adaptability does not come from a career need, but from a burning desire to teach and develop future leaders.[6]

The organization should then select potential TAs based on rec-ommendations from a soldier's chain of command and mentors. The evaluation reports of soldiers should also mention the traits and attri-butes mentioned in the beginning paragraphs of this section. In addi-tion to the wishes of the individuals and recommendations of others, there could also be a competitive entry examination or an interview process wherein current TAs can further screen for the right teachers. Just because the candidate is selected to attend ACM certification does not automatically qualify them to teach in an ACM.

Those chosen to attend the ACM must be prepared to *erase their memory.* That is, they must unlearn how they themselves were trained in their careers. This will be a challenge to establish: preparing these newcomers to teach adaptability must occur within a positive and encouraging environment. Those training the teacher teach adaptabil-ity should impress upon them that the new methodology will come as a great shock, but that success will bring significant rewards—such as knowing that in turn their students will become well prepared for the most challenging endeavor, leading the other battle.[7]

TA candidates attending the ACM certification course will encoun-ter a course similar to the one that they will teach if they are certified as a TA. Learning for adaptation begins in the preparation prior to arrival to the course: students should be given minimal instruction but expected to have administrative requirements completed prior to their arrival. Websites should provide them with necessary materi-als, but the student should be forced to do the work and complete the tasks on their own. Then, upon arrival on the first day, candi-dates should be put in positions where they have to teach to their peers. Intermittently between their stints as teachers, students will be taught by teachers of adaptability, or "Jedi knights"—those who pos-sess the most profound commitment and astute mind—on how to teach, infuse enthusiasm, and relate the importance and development of implicit communication.[8]

As candidates proceed through certification, they should be intro-duced to the ACM principles by experiencing them firsthand, and then encouraged to discuss their value during an AAR. TA candi-dates should be constantly thrown into leading and teaching classes, as well as observing other students conducting training. They should participate in AARs where current TAs introduce facilitation techniques such as active listening, the art of asking questions, teaching to the objective, and how to brief instructions. Teachers of adaptability may highlight these techniques by demonstrating how to perform them correctly or incorrectly while the students critique the teacher's demonstration.

After the exposure to teaching adaptability in the classroom, students should be introduced to the scenarios and how to develop their own scenarios, as well as to the tools used to deliver scenarios through the experience of using case study methods, tactical decision games, or free play force-on-force exercises. All scenarios should conclude with a group AAR exercise, evaluating the candidate that facilitated the scenario. The observing cadre should counsel the candidate on their performance through a questioning process. The TA should not provide answers during the counseling session, but merely provoke thought.

The students come to understand the nature of the feedback loop after going through several scenarios, AARs, and counseling sessions. While the AAR can revolve around the performance of students in the scenario, students begin to grasp that the focus of feedback is not on whether decisions made during scenarios were good or bad. The key to feedback is that students come to understand the process, that is, why and how the decision was made.

Furthermore, students demonstrate in front of a TA that they can also facilitate an AAR and teach this process to their fellow students. An ACM certification course should conclude with current TAs evaluating each student in his or her conduct of a scenario using a TDG. Each student should be given a scenario that they have not seen before, with little time to prepare. Then the student should demonstrate their ability to teach, facilitate, mentor, and evaluate adaptability while conducting the scenario. The class will be composed of other TA candidates with one of the current TAs serving as an evaluated student (the student who will present their solution to the problem in the scenario). The scenario concludes with an AAR, followed by a discussion facilitated by a TA candidate, wherein the

TA acting as the student will be questioned about his performance by the TA candidate.

Some candidates will pass this evaluation and move on to be certified as TAs, others will not. Those candidates who do not attain the status of TA return to their units with valuable skills they can apply to their current leadership roles; at a later date they may apply them when they take another shot at the ACM certification course. Even if the ACM is accepted as the new professional educational model for instilling adaptability in future Army leaders, it will fail if it is not resourced to attract not only talent, but those who want to teach. On the other hand, it is also unrealistic, with today's demands for good leaders and quality soldiers, to expect an ACM to get all the talent from the field. With this in mind there are a couple of ways the Army can ensure the ACM has quality teachers.

First, not every cadre member that occupies the traditional role of tactical officer (TAC) course that uses the ACM needs to be certified. The Army can focus limited resources on preparing and certifying selected individuals who then take their abilities and skills, and occupy positions where they not only teach, but also oversee other cadre members who are not qualified.

Second, the Army can compensate for shortfalls by the establishment of visiting teaching fellowships. These fellowships could be offered to civilians, as well as retirees that have already won awards and demonstrated their ability to teach. They would still have to be certified to teach at the ACM, but this would ensure the continuous flow of new ideas into and out of those leader-centric courses. If the ACM is to grow and produce the adaptive leaders the Army needs to win in future complex environments, it must animate its cadre and prevent stagnation.[9]

Teaching in an ACM

Teaching in an ACM is mastering the art of facilitating. Facilitating or coaching requires understanding and using different techniques: asking questions, using sarcasm, and stepping in at the appropriate time and place with encouragement to continually push and guide students to rethink what they are doing without being demeaning.

Teaching in the ACM avoids (unless it is absolutely necessary) giving the student answers.[10]

When the TA is acting as a coach it's possible to see another example of the art of facilitation. At appropriate times during a briefing, a TA can interject reality into a student's proposed solutions. The instructor may comment with phrases like "that's not possible," or "in reality this is what 'x' can do for you in that type of terrain." Or the instructor can ask probing, Socratic questions such as, "Does your course of action coincide with the spirit of the commander's intent?"; or, "What caused you to change the mission you were given?" These repeated sessions aim at building character, adaptability, and intuition over time, through constant 360-degree assessments, feedback, mentoring, and coaching.

"Professionals have coaches. Amateurs do not."[11] In other words, those students aspiring to be professional officers should be coached in a way that teaches them how to think. Coaching does not involve giving them the answers. Coaching is the art of guiding the student toward the answer and encourage them to find it on their own; in that way, it becomes embedded. This is *education* rather than *training*. Teachers of adaptability are professionals, and coaches are indeed needed and appropriate. Beyond merely talking about it, effective coaching must be made a cultural cornerstone and practical reality of a course that teaches adaptability.

As Col. Jon Moilanen observed in a recent *Military Review* article, "Leaders mentoring leaders in a clearly defined manner, and complementary coaching of soldiers and teams, reinforces learning and motivation to adapt. Direct and recurring advice and counsel among leaders reinforces adaptive behaviors. Coaching has been demonstrated to contribute quantifiably to organizational productivity (up 53 percent), retention (up 39 percent), and job satisfaction (up 61 percent) according to 100 executives from Fortune 1000 companies."[12]

The major benefit of this type of education is that students can experience situations that are either hard to enact in actual training or too expensive to enact in the field or as a computer simulation (war games). Student leaders can go over literally hundreds of scenarios without ever leaving the classroom. At the same time, all types of training, from physical exercises to field exercises, can be facilitated with scenarios. Scenarios establish a solid foundation to understand decision-making prior to moving into the field and where repeated trials can be much more costly. Obviously, scenarios are not a substitute for free-play, force-on-force exercises, but they do make the time and expense in the latter more valuable.[13]

The course environment of an ACM must be one that treats, relies on, and trusts its teachers as professionals. It is imperative in teaching adaptive learning to treat students—whether cadets, lieutenants or sergeants—with respect, while strongly challenging the students to think for themselves. TAs know that they are teaching correctly if they are initially unpopular with their students, especially with younger students when society has taught them what to think in providing road maps in everything they do with safety nets that prevent them from failing.

The ACM teaching approach forces students to work hard to find answers. Then, they work even harder to self-assess their performance in scenarios. Good TAs constantly test their students, and respond to their questions with even more questions. Such a philosophy will quickly define the teaching environment. This approach will end trivial and insignificant aspects of current Army education, such as signing in and out, drill and ceremony, or marching students to an event in formation, while both training and educating. These methods also apply stresses and challenges to students without using the "rabid dog" approach (i.e., yelling).[14]

In the latter context, task training and leader development become one. Any training task should be seen as a vehicle to teach adaptability. Striking a balance between training conducted through task performance and education of adaptability is important. The accomplishment of the task alone is not as important as the environment that is used to create it, while the teacher facilitates learning. Given the Army's long-standing emphasis on skill mastery through competency based education, the need for this innovation is hard to instill.[15]

The students in a class might be using the same tasks and mission, but the teacher has to have the ability to change conditions. The teacher should continually revisit the progress of each student daily to evolve his or her lesson plans. This leads to constant AARs, and the mentoring and counseling of individuals.

The TAs use several methods to impart knowledge, and this includes the use of changing conditions of the situation while the students execute the scenario, the use of time, and asking questions. In changing the conditions of the scenario, the TA creates conflict between what students are ordered to do, and what is really occurring. Instructors can also issue vague operation orders. This forces students to make assumptions or educated guesses. Teachers continue to plug small bits of information into the problem to encourage the students to ask questions and create solutions that will help the students work toward a given outcome for the class and course.

Time is another factor teachers use to induce stress and enable adaptability. Teachers should time scenarios. When time is up, the student presents his or her solution. Peers then evaluate the student's decision-making ability, rather than how he or she accomplished the specific tasks and mission. If the student did not accomplish the mission goals, the peer group and the student leader should discuss where they fell short. Limiting time also goes hand-in-hand with another stress-inducing approach: teaching students how to ask questions.

Telling students "there are no dumb questions" is counterproductive to teaching them how to think for themselves. Allowing them to ask dumb questions only reinforces bad habits such as not listening attentively when orders or guidance is given. In the real world, there is not much time for extensive follow-up questions over the tactical radio. Everything falls back to teaching the student how to deal with the stress of combat in the shortest amount of time.[16]

Teachers must encourage students to seek more knowledge when they ask pertinent questions. The teacher will do this through the student brief-back of the proposed solution. Students should offer a solution to the TDG to their peers, who in turn should evaluate that student's decision. In this case, the instructor is there to guide and facilitate the discussion and to force the student to seek more answers (with the condition that they should not provide the answers). Students should seek more knowledge, either in the syllabus or verbally from the instructor on their own time.

With vast preparation required, the learning organization strives to keep TAs in one of three states when "on duty": first, they will be teaching or facilitating, either in the classroom or in a training environment; second, they will be preparing for their next lesson or scenario; and finally, they will be evaluating student adaptability, which should always be accompanied by the provision of mentorship and feedback. The POI of the adaptive leader course puts more responsibility on the shoulders of both teacher and student to manage their time.

Teaching and coaching relies on the art of facilitating. Teachers and coaches facilitate by knowing the right time and place to say something to urge the student forward. They say just enough to let the student think and figure out the solution.

Scenario and Case Study Education

A new leader paradigm will permit building richer and deeper understanding of the self and alternative approaches to problem-solving.[17] The Army's current and future operating environments demand emphasis on adaptability and "learning to learn," not the mere ability to memorize information.[18]

In the ACM, teaching does not rely on the podium lecture or the use of PowerPoint presentations; the POI is experiential and scenario-based.

Scenarios constantly expose students to individual and collective tasks that they may have never seen before. Students are not "wrapped around the task," but instead encouraged to see how the task fits into solving the larger problem. Under OBT&E tasks are taught in the context of problems. Students become familiar with the task while participating in a scenario. Students should always be in a situation conducive to the development of personal initiative and adaptability. Everyone takes an active role in the course. This may consist of learning how to evaluate students during scenarios, the observation of movie clips where adaptability was or was not demonstrated, briefing solutions to the class or their group, or assuming a role during one of many exercises. This serves two objectives: first, it demonstrates experiential learning and second, it keeps students actively engaged.

The teacher must thoroughly understand the multiple aspects of adaptability in order to pass this on to students. Some aspects that are associated with adaptability include: cognitive ability, problem-solving skills, and especially metacognitive skills. Taken together, they constitute the ability to critically assess your own thoughts, always questioning, "Have I thought about this or that?" as well as looking from the outside in and saying, "What consequences does my decision have?"

Think of scenarios as guideline- and principle-based lesson plans that serve as templates to teach students the aspects of adaptability. In the POI, responsibility for the improvement of training plans centers around the teacher's scenario development. It is not left to combat developers or academic committees.

Teachers develop their scenarios for their students, while coming together during planning sessions to coordinate the next phase of leader development and to determine scenarios and the timing for events that will involve larger units and more resources. Scenarios are used to expose students to many different experiences in order to build and nurture intuition.

The purpose of the scenario-based education concept is to provide opportunities for each student to gain experience. Through multiple types of participation, either as a leader or team member, students receive breadth of experience and skills in decision-making to meet a specific set of circumstances. It is important to note that the teacher must also prepare to teach lessons from errors the students made in the execution of their plan.

Scenario-based education used with the proper tools provides students with supplemental information so that they can rely on experience when a new situation presents itself. Even so, these scenarios and the prescribed teaching approaches in this monograph are not substitutes for actual real-world experience. Scenario-based concepts benefit student leaders by improving their pattern recognition skills, allowing them to exercise the decision-making process, improving and practicing their communication skills, increasing their leadership potential, and building character.

Scenarios to build these skills take many forms, which is why the instructor's selection of a specific tool to deliver the scenario-based education is critically important. There are three other factors that must work together to produce learning synergy and successful scenario-based education: the way in which an instructor facilitates, the ability of students to understand what is being taught (material should be presented in a context the students can relate to—another skill of good teachers), and the instructor's capacity for mentorship (either individually or in a group through an after-action review).

Scenario packets integrate the required skills of adaptive leaders, to be practiced and evaluated in the course of a seminar discussion or exercise. While in some respects scenarios are built to be accomplished by a team, they should ideally be integrated seamlessly into the conduct of regular classroom instruction. In addition, principle-based lesson plans should include a history lesson that compels students to consider multiple perspectives. Some other components of scenario packets in an ACM include: a tactical planning exercise that compels students to visualize plans to accomplish an objective, a leadership lesson that may compel students to challenge their own biases, and time for students to identify new skills and discuss them.

Every scenario offers opportunities to practice leadership and decision-making, as well as to develop one's level of adaptability, letting the learning objectives (rather than resources) drive the event. Time is set aside for instructors to prepare opportunities for students to seek answers, or to prepare for the next mission, as well as to observe students when no specific activities are being pursued.

Teachers should continue to adjust scenarios through "lessons learned" and student feedback from previous classes. The goal is to create better and more efficient ways to nurture students into becoming adaptive leaders. All parts of the "learning organization" should contribute action and feedback—command and control—through overall cooperation. The development of adaptive leaders is fundamentally an activity of reciprocal influence involving give-and-take among all parts, from top to bottom and from side to side.

Each TA can develop scenario packets based on his or her own experiences and key events in the course. These are points in which instructors assess the progress of their students and provide them feedback in order to make improvements. It does no good to give a very complex scenario if the student does not have the abilities or understanding of adaptability to attempt to solve the problem presented in a scenario, so in turn it assists the teacher with the evolution of the curriculum based on the evolution of the student.

The TA can change the scenario cases based on what the students achieve as well as the level of proficiency of a student unit. While students should "experience the thing before they try to give it a name," the teachers also want to give students problems that they can manage. This means that there should be some reasonable chance for them to solve a scenario, but only with a degree of stress. By exposing the students to overly complex problems, teachers may discourage them early on from taking risks and thinking boldly about their solutions.

On the other hand, whenever possible, the teacher should use scenarios that place selected students three levels of command above their own. This assists teachers in observing what the student would do when presented with a complex problem involving a chain of command. Teachers should not be concerned with the student's ability to repeat information already given to him—what he knows—but rather, the focus should be on the student's willingness to use different types of information to solve the problem.

The teacher places the student in a command level to be able to understand the place of their unit in the context of larger unit operations. It is not seeking to make them "experts" in higher-level operations, but to familiarize them with what goes on above their own level and giving their interpretation back to their peers. This raises the bar, challenging selected students whose abilities require more difficult problem-solving.

Following each scenario, the TA must sit down with the leader and his or her team, both together and separately, and go over what they have learned. With the individual, it should be similar to counseling. With a team, this can resemble the existing Army after-action review process. Also, due to the Army's adherence to a "zero-defects" mentality, students will often use caution when admitting to their mistakes or allowing others to criticize them. The AAR can turn into a session of "who shot who" if not properly facilitated by the teacher.

Some people recommend a "pre-mortem" to the AAR. The pre-mortem should occur before the scenario is finished or before any presentation of solutions by students. In the pre-mortem exercise, the teacher tells his students to imagine that the situation has ended in failure. The teacher then facilitates the students through all the things that could have gone wrong with the scenario.[19]

Principles of Teaching in an ACM

Effective teaching in the ACM as part of the doctrine of OBT&E incorporates as many of the following guidelines as possible when conducting a session with students using the tools to be discussed here and in following chapters:

- Infuse enthusiasm
- Craft tactical proficiency and interactive perspective into the TDE
- Demonstrate mental agility and adaptability
- Stimulate and maintain player interest
- Integrate mentorship into the TDE
- Manage players and scenario

Enthusiasm is the ability to realistically paint the scenario and place the participant into the play. Enthusiasm is contagious and absolutely necessary to effectively build the scenario.

Proficiency and respect are fostered when the teacher knows the skills and abilities of the participants; the scenario through the appropriate delivery tool can be used to challenge cadets without overwhelming them. It is absolutely crucial that the instructor not over design the TDE and pick the right delivery tool beyond the scope of their capabilities. An instructor should conduct a self-analysis of their own skills and abilities, and keep the TDE to where it generates positive results, not professional embarrassment.

Mental agility and adaptability are paramount. The teacher should demonstrate the ability to react to unanticipated solutions and responses. Incorporating critical and creative thinking requires the instructor to adapt to the response and redirect the play as required. Becoming mentally mired in the TDE as the facilitator could limit the decision-making and experiential learning potential. Encourage frank discussion on COAs, but watch too many sidebars.

Stimulating player interest starts with design and development, but finesse in execution is even more important. Do not beat concepts or observations into the ground. Keep the play and discussion rolling at a light and brisk pace. Leave room for mental maneuver. Ideally, the instructor will be a senior approaching the TDE from the position of a mentor. Positive communication and approach increases the effectiveness of the TDE.

- The seminar can target areas such as teaching or illustrate warfighting or tactical concepts
- Teach warfighting or operational techniques
- Relate the importance and development of implicit communication

Student or cadet critiques are essential to recap the play of the TDE and create lessons learned. The game facilitator will have to make notes during the game to analyze and capture the thought processes used to make decisions during the TDE. Critiques can identify adaptability objectives that can be implemented in future TDE, curricula, and field applications.

In the POI of the adaptive leaders course, the instructor has direct input on the schedules or may do the actual planning, so the results from TDEs can be used to create similar situations for future TDEs as well as what tool will be decided upon to deliver them.

TAs conduct discussions during or after every TDE enhances the lessons learned since it requires the players or observers to think critically. Discussion is the oral application of decision-making, since it requires the players to assess the information and then provide feedback to the TDE facilitator and other players. Critiques, discussions, and after-action reviews are all similar, but can be directive, interactive, and informational, respectively, depending on the personality and approach of the facilitator and the training objectives that support the design of the TDE and the appropriate delivery tool.

"Manage the TDE" is when the instructor attempts to set a tone of candor when the group participating in the TDE is made up of varying experience levels.

Facilitation

When the teacher is determining the method of delivering the TDE, the number of students, cadets, or personnel to be enabled and the adaptability objectives are the determinants. The instructor is most likely going to use a TDE to deliver a scenario. The three basic methods to play a TDE are:

1. Solitaire (students will do on their own, but lack frank discussion by others on COA)
2. Seminar
3. Force-on-force (dynamic, multi-resource)

The *solitaire method* requires the player to solve the problem in a fashion similar to solving a crossword puzzle or brainteaser. The paper TDG is the ideal application for the solitaire game in that the individual reads the problem, produces a solution, compares a response with the one provided, and then reflects on the rationale that is used to determine the solution.

The *seminar* approach involves a designated facilitator and a group of players. The facilitator presents the information and guides the solution produced by the players. Ideally, the number of students, cadets, or personnel should be limited to twelve or fewer.

Force-on-force is a dynamic, multi-resource method; it is a more advanced approach that evolves along a timeline. Players may represent opposing or adjoining forces and must respond to changing situations. When playing from opposing perspectives, the teams simultaneously solve the TDE from opposing viewpoints. The instructor also assumes the role of an observer-controller facilitating and comparing the two solutions and generating a new scenario based on how the two scenarios match up.

The instructor uses judgment to assess outcomes or casualties of the solutions. In this case, the facilitator must control the evolution of the TDE with the purpose of generating new tactical challenges. The new challenges must be "on the spot" or intuitive decisions versus the collaborative thinking and planning used for the initial scenario. After four or five engagements, the opposing side will have completed an engagement.

Limiting force-on-force play can be useful. In this approach the instructor limits the size of the teams to four to six students, cadets, or personnel. Larger- or smaller-sized teams limit the amount of inter-activity, increase the amount of time to play the TDE, and expand the decision-making capacity of the players. In this approach, it is harder to direct and control the objectivity of the game.

Facilitator Responsibilities

The instructor facilitating the TDE should be able to incorporate the following concepts to create the desired benefits from the TDE based on how it was delivered:

- Prepare for the exercise
- Present the scenario
- Choose students to present solutions
- Enforce the "time limit" rule
- Enforce the "decisions as instructions" rule
- Question the thought process
- Lessons learned

In *preparing for the exercise* the teacher must have a thorough knowl-edge of the TDE, and be prepared to address a variety of possible deci-sions made by the players. The experience and expertise of the cadre has to be at such levels that it makes them excellent TDE facilitators, but it also requires them to think tactically.

Thinking tactically is not necessarily thinking in terms of combat, but more of a conceptual perspective of war fighting. Creating an atmosphere that forces the game play to use the OODA process intui-tively can be challenging with novice players. Designing TDEs that unroll quickly for more advanced players requires the controller to combine war fighting, tactics, techniques, and occupational specifics to speed up the decision-making process.

How the instructor *presents the scenario* to the group is important. This can be done with an explanation supplemented with an orientation of a map or sand table, as applicable. The controller should also be prepared to answer any questions that the students may have about the situation. Answering questions does not mean that the controller should eliminate all uncertainty.

Choosing students, cadets, or personnel to present solutions is generally better than asking for volunteers. The player should not feel as though they can escape the challenge by simply not volunteering. Creating a TDE environment that makes the players feel as if they have as much chance as anyone else is important since it adds to the stress of the TDE. The controller should not tolerate players that actively try to avoid presenting a solution.

Enforcing the "time limit" rule forces the students to act quickly. Time compression creates stress, which is normally part of the decision-making process especially under operational conditions.

Enforcing the "decisions as instructions" rule requires the players to issue their decisions as combat orders utilizing the appropriate format. The player should be prepared to discuss the decision made later in the game. The facilitator should ensure that the TDE forum is focused on "Decide now, discuss later."

In *questioning the thought process*, the TDE facilitator inquires about the rationale used to make the decision. Useful questions include:

- What was your reasoning for that action?
- What was your overall estimate of the situation?
- What would you have done if . . . ?
- What were your assumptions?
- What was the biggest concern about your plan?

Summarizing lessons learned at the conclusion is essential for creating greater decision-making ability.

Brief Instructions

The facilitator should provide the players with a briefing and clear instructions for the TDE. The briefing and instructions should convey the following essential information:

1. *Overview of the situation* includes elements or anticipated changes in the situation that could significantly influence the actions of the unit.
2. *Mission and commander's intent* describes the task, explains why it needs to be done, and outlines the intended end result of the action.
3. *Coordinating instructions* that state what each unit is to do and when.
4. *Communication methods* are used between individuals and between adjoining forces.

Facilitation Techniques

The following facilitation techniques should be incorporated in TDEs:

1. The art of asking questions
2. Teaching to objective
3. Briefing clear instructions

The Art of Asking Questions allows the facilitator to shape the dilemma that the student is expected to respond too. It requires the facilitator to incorporate two basic techniques:

1. Active listening
2. Questioning

Active listening is important in that it prompts the facilitator to ask questions, asking and answering in a productive way, and explains how to defer questions or bounce them off the rest of the group.

Questioning involves the TDE facilitator probing the player's thought process and forces the player to explain their rationale. Use questions to prompt thought in the student. The facilitator should avoid leading questions. Here are some examples and suggested alternatives:

Example: "Wouldn't this have been a more effective course of action?"

Alternate: "Did you consider any other alternatives?"

Example: "Do you really think that will work?"

Alternate: "On a scale of 1 to 10, what do you think is your probability of success?"

Example: "So by using air support, you really think that you can still use direct attack on this flank?"

Alternate: "What would you do if the air delivered munitions missed the target?"

Example: "Don't you think that hill is too steep for a dozer?" Alternate: "What information did you use in choosing a dozer for this assignment? Is there anything else you should consider before using a dozer?"

Objective focus describes the facilitator's primary responsibility is to ensure that the exercise and discussion do not stray away from the purpose of evolving toward adaptability. Additionally, the facilitator should refrain from lecturing and allow the participants to teach each other. To meet these two requirements, the facilitator should use provoking questions prepared to stimulate activity and limit discussion. The following guidelines can assist the facilitator:

1. Guide the discussion.
2. Focus on the objectives in a logical sequence.
3. Avoid detailed examination of events not directly related to major training objectives.

Teaching to the objective involves TDEs being set up with specific learning outcomes in mind; it is the facilitator's responsibility to ensure that the exercise and discussions do not stray from the purpose.

Refocus the objective to ensure that the objective of the TDE is decision-making. A TDE is not an academic test, it is an exercise in thinking and the application of information—a means of improving the decision-making process. The questions selected to prompt activity should help the player clarify that information inputs are consciously and subconsciously important to them. Additionally, the player should be able to rationalize how the information was used in the decision-making process.

Teaching Is Second to Commanding/Leading

In the end, scenario-based learning provides an educational approach for building a student's strength of character. Past curricula that dealt with leader development used process and task training to dictate to potential officers "what to think." Today, the Army is beginning to realize that the foundation of an effective future officer corps must begin early; the Army wants to create leaders who are adaptable and know "how to think" to sharpen intuition.

The ACM embraces the idea that every moment and event offers an opportunity to develop adaptability. Every action taken by a student in the classroom or in the field is important to the process of inculcating a preference for solutions. If a student errs while acting in good faith, they should not suffer anything more than corrective mentoring. Constructive critiques of solutions are the norm in an ACM, but more important in this model are the results of a student's action, and the reasons for taking that action. This mindset will spread throughout the Army culture once implemented by the ACM.

8

Creating Outcomes and Measures

Traditional training and education may not meet all the needs of an expeditionary Army; as appropriate, training and education must adapt to the needs of a new operational environment.... For example, outcome-based training and education is supposed to develop individuals and organizations that can think and operate in complex environments. . . . The focus is on the total outcome of a task or event rather than on the execution of a particular task to a standard under a given set of conditions. Given operational expectations, it is supposed to develop tangible skills such as marksmanship and intangible attributes such as creativity and judgment.

—GEN. MARTIN DEMPSEY, Commander TRADOC

An outcome, as it relates to training and education, is different than training or a learning objective, even though an outcome is part of the definition of the training objective. Just as a commander's intent states the broader purpose for the operation, an outcome provides a broader purpose for the training or instructional topic.[1] As Chad Foster describes, "An outcome, on the other hand, provides a broader purpose for the training event. Conceptually, it fills the same role as training as a commander's intent statement in a tactical operation. By articulating a desired outcome(s) for a training event, the commander can provide guidance on results he expects the training to achieve, regardless of any constraints that might emerge."[2]

Outcomes include intangible behaviors that are difficult to measure (objectively) but are easily observable in practice by more experienced observers such as teachers, trainers, and instructors. Whereas learning objectives and training objectives depend upon, indeed require, action-oriented words to frame assessment for objective measurement, outcomes provide a broader, and from a military perspective, more useful definition of the end state. OBT&E (ACM and CATC) focuses on teaching students to understand the "why" behind any problem; its primary purpose is to teach "how" to think. This is taught in an environment that encourages learning through mistakes: it is okay to falter from time to time.[3]

OBT&E does not focus only on tasks, conditions, and standards; it must also include the necessary attributes required by individuals, teams, and organizations to carry out any task. Successful OBT&E events include: a clear criterion of success or standard of performance (the intended end) that guides both instructors and learners, and a variation in the time and number of opportunities (critical means) that learners might take to achieve the standard. Without defined boundaries in time and effort, as well as measurable standards or tactics, techniques, and procedures that serve as the baseline or core competencies required, the outcome effectiveness is at risk. Let's review the definition of OBT&E given by CSM Morgan Darwin:

> OBT&E looks for results; it puts the burden of professionalism more on the shoulders of the student and lets the instructor decide how to get results, much like mission orders or mission tactics where the how to is left to those executing the mission with little or no oversight from higher up. OBT&E is best described as "developmental training"—development of the individual within the training of a military task. Students are held accountable for what they should already know and bring to the next course.[4]

OBT&E also focuses on developing students over time by exposing them to experiences designed to enhance attributes such as confidence, accountability, and initiative, as well as such associated capabilities as awareness, discipline, judgment, and deliberate thought.[5]

Input vs. Outcome—Example: Warning Orders

Traditional "Input-Based" Approach

Task: Issue a warning order (from STP 21–24 SMCT).
Condition: Given preliminary notice of an order or action that is to follow and a requirement to develop and issue a warning order to subordinates.

Standards: Within time allotted, develop a warning order and issue it to subordinate leaders. Issue order so that all subordinate leaders understand their missions and any coordinating instructions. Issue it in the standard operation order (OPORD) format.

Performance Measures   GO   NO GO

1. Student said, "Warning order"
2. Used standard terminology
3. Used five-paragraph format
4. Gave all available information

OBT&E Outcome-Based Approach
Desired outcomes of a warning order:
1. Subordinates *understand* and can *explain*, the nature and purpose of the upcoming mission.
2. Subordinates know what preparations they must accomplish for the upcoming mission, *why* they must complete those preparations, and *when* those preparations, must be complete.
3. Subordinates *have maximum time* to prepare for the upcoming operation.

These outcomes do not restrict the trainee in terms of methods or techniques that they can use to achieve "success" other than the requirement that they are *appropriate within the context of the current situation and the higher commander's intent.*

A friend of mine applied the ACM training approach to a local youth football team he coached in the fall of 2012. The teams consisted of seventh- and eighth-grade students. At first, he coached the team in the proper way to tackle the ball carrier by having two players show an example of a tackle, then the team discussed the techniques that were carried out correctly and those conducted incorrectly. With the incorrect techniques, they discussed the proper technique that should have been applied.[6]

After the discussions, the players were partnered with each other to execute the tackling drill. After the coach felt that the team was grasping the concept of tackling another player, he put them in situations that would train them to develop their problem-solving abilities. He used a blocker to demonstrate different types of blocking techniques. The defender would have to read the blocker and execute the appropriate tackle. As a coach, he used the game of football to develop the intangible problem-solving attributes.

The intangible attributes he was seeking from his players were those that would make them better students and overall better citizens in their community: discipline, initiative, hard work, and perseverance. As the team became more competent and began to understand the game of football, he introduced training designed to increase the players' deliberate thought skills. The coach increased the stress level by showing the defense different offensive schemes. He then executed different plays associated with that offensive scheme. This type of training would develop the players' situational awareness. This would also train them to be critical thinkers. At times, he would run this type of drill when the players were already fatigued.

As the players became exposed more to the Adaptive Course Model (ACM) training approach, my friend noticed that their knowledge of football grew tremendously. As weeks passed, he continued to raise the standards and expect more from his team. The team did not back down from the challenge and rose to meet his expectations. At the end of the season, he did not yell as much as he did as a coach. He could tell that the new training approach was working when a handful of the player's parents approached him stating that their son's grades had improved throughout the season. They also stated that their sons were taking more initiative in doing their household chores.

Leaders (all leaders are trainers) are already very familiar with assessing intangible attributes. The officer evaluation report (OER) and noncommissioned officer evaluation report (NCOER) depend upon the ability of an experienced rater to make judgments about objective competencies, skills, values, and other qualitative attributes, but also largely upon subjective aspects of individual performance within the context of a mission-oriented environment. OBT&E/ASLT&E creates a similar assessment environment.[7]

An outcome, when related to training and education, is slightly different from a training or learning objective, even though outcome is part of the definition of training objective. The difference is similar to the difference between a commander's intent and the concept of the operation. Just as intent states the broader purpose for the operation, an outcome provides a broader purpose for the training or instructional topic.

Outcomes include intangible attributes and competencies of individuals that are difficult to measure directly—they provide a snapshot of individual performance. The influence of intangibles on behavior is, however, easily observable in practice by more experienced observers, such as trainers and instructors.[8] Whereas learning and training objectives depend upon action-oriented words to frame assessment for objective measurement, outcomes provide a broader, and from a military perspective, more useful measure of effectiveness.[9]

OBT&E/ASLT&E is a good way for commanders to apply mission command concepts in training. The mission command operating concept depends upon trust, confidence, and mutual understanding while employing disciplined initiative within the commander's intent.[10]

One of the values of OBT&E/ASLT&E is that it forces all elements associated with the training and education activities to remain focused on the outcome, instead of being distracted or confounded by the inherent limits imposed by schedules, facilities, and other diminishing resources. This aspect includes the following:

Principles of Outcomes

- The commander's stated outcome becomes the top-level metric. It is written like a good and concise commander's intent: "What is my vision of success?"
- Teachers derive from that the knowledge, skills, and attributes that must be evident in order to claim success.
- Teachers then determine the indicators that support those claims (these may be performance or behavioral indicators).[11]

Teachers so equipped can now be purposeful in their planning efforts. Regardless of the time, equipment, or facilities available to them, they know what outcome must be achieved and will lay out a method to achieve it. This empowers the trainer and encourages flexibility in thought and action, while similarly preempting rationalizations for low-quality training because of minimal or absent resources.

As resource availability can frequently change, so too will the plan to achieve desired outcomes. This is the case for all participants and influencers in Army training and education. Combat-seasoned soldiers, for example, will not require the same approaches that might be appropriate for initial-entry training. While the outcomes may be identical, the methods to achieve them could be entirely different. OBT&E provides the trainer a focus to navigate the differences.

It is important to point out that just as mission command depends a great deal upon trust and confidence, the same is true of OBT&E. If the stated outcomes are accurate reflections of what is required, success is only apparent where those requirements are employed. Traditional measures of performance in training and education usually tend to measure the execution of methods employed, rather than whether any actual learning occurred.

In the case of OBT&E effectiveness won't truly be known until the personnel performs in combat, but evidence of learning and development of efficacy (the foundation or capacity for effectiveness) will manifest itself in ways that allow meaningful assessment of both the soldier (and unit) in training and the trainer in execution. It also provides for explicit or implicit self-assessment and the development of a sense of self-efficacy in both trainers and their soldiers. ("I know when I am performing well and I know that I can perform well.")[12]

Teaching the How-To of Outcomes

The teacher takes each student's or cadres' potential outcome from the current class they developed or teach, and develops an outcome with the entire class. The teacher starts out by saying, "Okay, what is it we want this student to leave with when they finish this class or course?" "An example is when we rewrote the outcomes for the Special Forces Qualification Course [Q-Course]; we began by saying, 'what does an A-Team Sergeant (Platoon Sergeant) want his new member just out of the Q-Course to be able to do?'" Another example is from the Army Reconnaissance Course: "What does the Army want from a graduate of ARC?"[13]

The teacher will mark down some suggestions on the white board. It is painstakingly detailed and takes a long time, but has to be done to demonstrate that this first task in course or class creation cannot be taken lightly. For example,

A graduate of the Special Forces Q-course will be a leader that possesses the strength of character to seek and strongly desire responsibility and making bold decisions. The graduate will become an expert in irregular warfare and the planning and executing the mission of the A-Team in an irregular warfare COE. He will demonstrate competence and confidence in leading small unit operations. In order to do this the Soldier should have an understanding of other cultures and languages beyond the mere fundamentals of learning another language. He will understand them in the context of another culture. Additionally, the graduate will understand the fundamentals of battalion and below operations in order to teach them with an understanding by foreign nationals. The graduate will also possess the confidence to demonstrate proficiency on the small arms carried and used by most of the world's militaries. Finally, the graduate will demonstrate the combat physical fitness that will enable him to endure days of stressful operations under all conditions.[14]

Writing this outcome took four hours with a room full of Special Forces officers and NCOs. This was only a draft used to demonstrate to them how to develop outcomes followed by measures of effectiveness to guide their teachers under their watch. We worked a full day on this outcome, but once created and agreed upon by the room full of leaders, we went ahead and developed outcomes for each face, which fed back to the above overarching or final outcome. With all the outcomes developed and agreed upon, we then decided on measures to help guide the teachers.

Hopefully, the teacher can walk a couple of students through their outcome for their class or course. Once the room of Special Forces leaders agreed with this outcome, we developed outcomes for each phase of the Q-Course. As we developed the smaller supporting outcomes, they became easier to the group. Once the group was pleased and agreed to all the outcomes, we then developed the measures of effectiveness (MOE) for each outcome.

Using Outcomes to Design Training and Education

Just as a commander or chief in the Operating force must visualize, describe, and direct to effect battle command, a commander in the Generating (training and development) force must visualize the desired result of the training or educational activity. Current Army training doctrine relies upon established standards for approximately 19,000 tasks that describe all the activities and functions of a soldier in the various branches and occupational specialties. Army established standards describe the *minimum acceptable level of performance* for a particular task. This performance floor is an essential requirement for the Army to be assured that soldiers and units can, within certain constraints, accomplish missions in any future combat environment.[15]

A performance floor is not consistent with either excellence or mastery, both of which are desired goals of Army training. Commanders desire that their units demonstrate excellence and want their soldiers to demonstrate the pursuit of mastery in the tasks that they routinely perform. A commander's expression of such an outcome becomes the starting point for designing training and education. The continual pursuit of mastery, including learning to learn, is critical because otherwise it is unlikely that the minimum acceptable level of performance measured at a point in time will be maintained, let alone exceeded, later and when it is needed for mission accomplishment.[16]

Well-defined outcomes help trainers and training developers deliberately create learning activities that motivate and direct future behavior toward desired outcomes. This is very different from using the achievement of a baseline performance standard as the measure of learning or mastery of the task. In practice trainers using outcomes might follow this approach as described with these principles of outcomes:

- The Army describes a particular requirement to provide its members with the key knowledge, skills, and attributes they require to successfully operate in any environment.
- Needs analysis and feedback from the operational domain identify more needs than there is time available to address.
- Prioritization of needs and allocation of scarce resources become a challenge of how many hours to devote to a particular task or subject.
- With an outcome in the form of an intent, the soldier (or unit) during training has the freedom and flexibility to prioritize learning opportunities and make good trade-offs about what to do so they will be more likely to contribute to mission accomplishment.
- Trainers and developers now are able to design activities focused on the outcome and develop ways to adapt to constraints imposed by time, trainer to student ratios, and other aspects of training and education that are commonly seen as obstacles.[17]

Planning Training Using Outcomes

Trainers so equipped can now be purposeful in their planning efforts. Regardless of the time, equipment, or facilities available to them, they know what outcome must be achieved and will lay out the method to achieve it. This empowers the trainer, encouraging flexibility in thought and action, while preempting rationalizations for low-quality training because of minimal or absent resources. In sum, well-developed outcomes provide an aiming point for instructors, directors, and commanders, and the commander's stated outcome becomes the top-level metric. From this, trainers derive the knowledge, skills, and attributes that must be evident in order to claim success. Trainers then determine the indicators that support those claims (these may be performance or behavioral indicators).[18]

As resource availability can frequently change, so too will the plan to achieve desired outcomes. This is the case for all participants and influencers in Army training and education. Combat-seasoned soldiers, for example, will not require the same approaches that might be appropriate for initial entry training. While the outcomes may be identical, the way to get there could be entirely different. OBT&E provides the trainer a focus to facilitate the differences.[19]

Just as mission command depends a great deal upon trust and confidence, the same is true of OBT&E/ASLT&E. If the stated outcomes are accurate reflections of what is required, success is only apparent where those requirements are employed. Traditional measures of performance in training and education tend to measure the execution of methods employed rather than whether learning occurred. In the case of OBT&E, effectiveness won't truly be known until the soldier performs in combat, but evidence of learning and development of efficacy (the foundation or capacity for effectiveness) will manifest itself in ways that allow meaningful assessment of both the soldier (and unit) in training and the trainer in execution. It also provides for explicit or implicit self-assessment and the development of a sense of self-efficacy in both trainers and their soldiers ("I know when I am performing well and I know that I can perform well").[20]

Training and Education with an Outcome Focus

Because today's operating environment is so demanding, with little regard for where or when operations may occur, soldiers are expected to have the ability and agility to perform all things well. The increasing complexity of combat creates an intense competition between the need for specialization and the general capabilities required for agility.

This tension can be resolved by outcomes that motivate task direction and organization within a broadly defined scope of training and education that guide the adaptive definition and execution of specific training events. An exhaustive task list that meets—but only meets—an expedient interpretation of a standard encourages a checklist mentality in which the meaning of completing one training task is justification to move on to the next training task. OBT&E, on the other hand, forces the trainer to focus on principles and fundamentals that are applicable in all but the most unusual circumstances. In this context, the meaning of completing a training task is that one had made progress toward a developmental outcome.

Focusing on enduring fundamentals and immutable principles does not, by itself, produce durable learning, or encourage adaptive thinking and creative problem-solving. It does ensure a basis for individual or collective understanding of the purpose of training, the approach to training, and the connection between training and more complex situations in future operating environments. Service members and units that can understand the implicit and explicit inter-relationships of the myriad systems comprising our Army and Marine Corps' war fighting capability (as well as the more complex problems confronted by law enforcement), from the basic level up through the various unit echelons, significantly improve the agility of the force as a whole. For this to occur, a consistent and developmental approach to learning must be practiced in all phases of training and education.[21]

Well-designed outcomes in OBT&E/ASLT&E promote conditions to allow soldiers and units to demonstrate agility, show initiative and creativity, grow confident and competent in ambiguity while fostering a climate that encourages freedom to try different solutions to challenging problems. These conditions rarely emerge in training that only seeks attainment of momentary performance standard as the objective. With outcomes serving as the purpose of training, performance is not limited or constrained, and the trainer can revisit a task or sequence of tasks as often as necessary under varied conditions with increasing complexity.[22]

Constant repetition, through variations on a basic theme, is less onerous on the training audience than the contrived retraining of a particular task to the previously demonstrated standard of performance. Training that ignores a soldier's existing knowledge or experience, that requires achieving a standard of performance that is seemingly arbitrary, or is excessively procedural has little chance of maintaining a soldier's attention; it depends almost exclusively on some form of artificial extrinsic motivator—none of which increases the likelihood of learning or durability.[23]

Rather than a view of task mastery that treats all tasks equally and in isolation, OBT&E considers task mastery within the broader context of the intangible attributes and competencies required in a mission setting. Neither soldiers nor units accomplish a single task and move on to another task in the execution of a mission. In task-based training, the task is isolated as an end unto itself. Condition statements are, by design, supposed to establish a framing context for the soldier or unit but rarely do. In OBT&E/ASLT&E, the totality of soldier or unit performance becomes important.[24]

The soldier comes to understand the relationship between an individual and the unit as well as the linkage among tasks. How well the mission is accomplished is more important than specific procedures; constraints such as time are not confused with criteria for mission success. Mastery evolves from repetitive exposure to both competence and opportunities for improvement (i.e., the capacity for efficacy) in essential tasks in order to solve the current problem within the constraints at hand. This concept applies equally from an individual-level response to a problem as it does to a unit-level response to a mission.[25]

From these smaller outcomes, always linked to the larger course outcome, we then created MOEs.

Measure of Effectiveness (MOE)

What is an MOE? It is not a checklist!

Colonel Haskins states that the outcomes must "specify what each graduate should be and be able to accomplish."[26] These outcomes also required more than a book test to ensure mastery. The outcomes shape three points: the credentials or license acquired if the student was successful in demonstrating their mastery, the tools that would be used to assess soldier-student performance, and how the teacher-trainer would design the instruction to ensure that the outcomes were understood and mastered.[27]

Practical, authentic, or live demonstrations (versus) a paper test were used to demonstrate that the soldier-student could demonstrate mastery of the outcome. Unlike most academic evaluations, the person being evaluated is not penalized for making mistakes. The intent is for the soldier-student to become confident. Finally, soldier-students are encouraged to move at a speed that best suits the individual. Training events are driven by mastery of the particular skill and not blocks of time.[28] Here are some examples of MOEs supporting outcomes:[29]

Outcome: How Students Are Able to Go Beyond Mere Regurgitation of Information from Higher HQ by Effectively Analyzing the Enemy Threat for an Operation.

- Students can estimate enemy strength, composition, and capabilities based on information and analysis from higher headquarters as well as their own common sense and knowledge of the area.
- Students can identify enemy weaknesses that can be exploited by friendly forces during an operation as well as enemy strengths that must be avoided or neutralized.
- Students can formulate an educated guess about the enemy's course of action based on that enemy's capabilities, limitations, and past patterns as well as an understanding of the effects of terrain, weather, and all other pertinent factors in a given situation.
- Students can explain why they believe the enemy will take the actions that they outline in the enemy course of action, or ECOA.
- Students understand and can explain how an anticipated ECOA is just informed conjecture, and describe how that supposition can be used as a starting point for tactical planning.

The outcomes-based model is also used by West Point's Academic Affairs Division to develop objective MOEs designed to "produce graduates who can anticipate and respond effectively to the uncertainties of a changing technological, social, political, and economic world."[30]

Outcome: Students Are Able to Develop Simple COAs That Ensure Unit of Effort by Their Subordinates and Adhere to the Higher Headquarters Commander's Intent.

- Students can clearly define a successful end-state for an operation that adheres to the higher headquarters commander's intent.
- Students can assign tasks to subordinates that make sense in terms of accomplishing their intended end-state for the operation.
- Students can effectively "link" the efforts of their subordinates by explaining why each element is performing their assigned task and how that supports their overall plan.

The academic outcomes ensure the students have developed the necessary cognitive skills required for their assignment as a junior officer immediately following graduation while also creating a solid foundation for success as a captain and major in the next five years. Although it remains to be seen if the OBT&E model is used by the instructors in the classroom, the evidence suggests that this model can be used effectively in unique environments such as the USMA.[31]

Teacher preparation is of even greater importance than for task- or objective-oriented training. This does not necessarily require more time in teacher preparation. It does require a better understanding of what it means to be prepared for instruction. Teachers must understand how to operate within the commander's intent in a learning environment. Experience, knowledge, imagination, and creativity are the key criteria for selecting trainers. Most significantly, they need to believe that their efforts to promote learning in training and education have command support and are underwritten.[32]

Curricula and training developers need constant reminding that the outcomes are most important in design. Their requirement is to generate learning activities that promote many opportunities to reach the outcomes in a sequential and developmental fashion. Ultimately, the intent of lessons should be to provide constraints and guidance as opposed to limitations and prescriptions.[33]

Outcomes shape the assessment measures and their associated instruments. The focus is bifurcated in that assessment; it considers the performance and behavioral indicators of the training audiences as well as the means used by the trainer to achieve them. The two must be linked for the commander to have any meaningful data for analysis.[34]

How Were These Created? Where Did They Come From?

When developing outcomes, of course the first thing you do is ascertain your higher commander's desired outcome, as you would do with a commander's intent. What does your higher expect from you? The commander will use examples from the ACM briefing to highlight how the MOEs were created and how they evolved (see previous excerpts from Lt. Col. Chad Foster's briefing) to flow from the outcome. The teacher will go over how to create these with key players. This way, your organization is involved and takes ownership of the outcome for your organization or unit.

The commander or leader starts out by saying, "Okay, what is it we want this student to leave with when they finish this class or course?" For example, "when we rewrote the outcomes for the Special Forces Q-course, we began by saying, 'what does an A-Team Sergeant . . . want his new member just out of the Q-course to be able to do?' "[35] Another example is from the Army Reconnaissance Course (ARC): "What does the Army want from a graduate of ARC?" The old or linear form of teaching using the *competency theory of education* would create a long list of tasks, without linking them in context to the environment or demonstrating them collectively in context to a particular environment.[36]

The teacher shows this on an overhead and then facilitates the discussion; he may want to not show this until the students create their own conclusions based on the outcome for that specific period of teaching.

With a current list of outcomes, the teacher then creates MOEs for each outcome for one class or course. Let us refer back to our earlier draft outcome for the Special Forces Q-course:

A graduate of the Special Forces Q-course will be a leader that possesses the strength of character to seek and strongly desire responsibility and making bold decisions. The graduate will become an expert in irregular warfare and what that means when planning and executing the mission of the A-Team. He will demonstrate competence and confidence in leading small unit operations. In order to do this the soldier should have an understanding of other cultures and languages beyond the mere fundamentals of learning another language. He will understand them in the context of another culture. Additionally, the graduate will understand the fundamentals of battalion and below operations in order to teach them with an understanding by foreign nationals. The graduate will also possess the confidence to demonstrate proficiency on the small arms carried and used by most of the world's militaries. Finally, the graduate will demonstrate the combat physical fitness that will enable him to endure days of stressful operations under all conditions without serious degrad[ation] of performance.[37]

We will use our outcome for the Special Forces Q-Course to demonstrate how MOEs are developed. As I said earlier, after we agreed upon the outcome for the entire twelve-month-long course, we then developed outcomes for each phase (but instead of me leading it, the respective battalion or company commander and sergeant major led the work). The leaders discovered while we were creating these that each smaller outcome easily flowed from parts or sentences of the larger outcome. Some of the outcomes had to be demonstrated in almost every phase (such as physical fitness).

Below are the outcome and measures of effectiveness (MOE) for physical fitness as part of a Q-course graduate. Again these were created by the leaders of the course, which included the company commanders and sergeant majors, as well as cadre: "The graduate will demonstrate the combat physical fitness that will enable him to endure days of stressful operations under all conditions without serious degradation of performance."[38]

Physical Fitness MOEs for Q-Course

Students will be able to conduct a twenty-mile tactical foot road march with seventy pounds of equipment (standard fighting load) over mixed terrain (roads, trails, and cross-country) in six hours.

Students will be able to negotiate the combat obstacle course with tactical equipment, including rifle in two hours, while negotiating each and every obstacle without failure.

- Students will be able to conduct a 10km run in physical fitness uniform in 40 minutes.
- Students can conduct back-to-back missions for five-day durations with as little as four hours sleep a night without falling out.
- Students will be able to do 10 pull-ups.
- Students will score a 290 or above on the APFT.[39]

With the outcomes and MOEs drafted and agreed upon, we can then outline the course and classes to support the learning necessary to meet the outcomes within real-world resource and time constraints. What we don't want to do in our lesson plans and courses is tell our teachers how to teach. We simply hold them to the outcomes, while measuring this outcome through our agreed upon MOE. As training developers, we should be prepared to hold an AAR of this class and course, and we should be prepared to continue to evolve each based on what we learned.

Remember that an outcome is the result you want, MOE is the test for that result, and people train for the test.[40] It is now up to each teacher on how he achieves this outcome guided by the MOEs for that selected outcome. He or she may adjust their lesson plans based on this in order to achieve the outcome. They are held accountable for the result, not how it is done.[41]

Implementing OBT&E/ASLT&E

Commanders, leaders, trainers, and training developers seeking to create learning opportunities based on outcomes should consider that the crawl–walk–run approach to training remains a valid methodology in the context of OBT&E. Every iteration is viewed from a military or law enforcement personnel developmental perspective.

The task deconstruction and step-wise method of training or teaching complex tasks remains equally valid as an approach to promote preliminary learning, but OBT&E provides a different perspective on what the steps can be. In particular, it stresses that the way one achieves a particular step in training, not just the achievement, is important with respect to one's capacity to progress *at* the next level not just *to* the next level.[42]

Training or education that requires only rote repetition or evidence of declarative learning has marginal value and is highly perishable. Such training or education does not promote thinking, adaptive capacity, creativity, initiative, or accountability, and only moderately affects confidence—all things that leaders value in their subordinates. Instructor preparation is of greater importance for task- or objective-oriented training. This does not necessarily require more time in instructor preparation.[43] It does require a better understanding of what it means to be prepared for instruction.

Trainers must understand how to operate within the commander's intent in a learning environment. Experience, knowledge, imagination, and creativity are the key criteria for selecting trainers. Most significantly, they need to believe that their efforts to promote learning in training and education have command support and are underwritten.

Curricula and training developers need constant reminding that the outcomes are most important in design. Their requirement is to generate learning activities that promote many opportunities to reach the outcomes in a sequential and developmental fashion. Ultimately, the intent of lessons should be to provide constraints and guidance as opposed to limitations and prescriptions.

Outcomes shape the assessment measures and their associated instruments. Assessment considers the performance and behavioral indicators of the training audiences as well as the means used by the trainer to achieve them. The two must be linked for the commander to have any meaningful data for analysis.

The Army fundamentals remain valid and any training or education that fails to achieve these minimums deserves no further support or resources. However, the standard is only the starting point and without elaboration, has little value to the student and trainer. Tasks, for their personnel in training or in education, are missions— which are problems that need to be solved, problems that become

increasingly complex by altered situations that demand greater application of cognitive ability (although not necessarily application of a
greater cognitive ability).[44]

Personnel in training (and trainers) will make mistakes. Any training
or education that is devoid of mistakes in execution should be suspect
as not promoting learning. Constant, short, sharply focused AARs are
of greater value than carefully scripted activities that mimic perfection
but require inordinate time to practice and are unrealistic. They have
greater value because they directly influence the capacity for improvement, the capacity for becoming effective, and one's understanding of
these capacities.[45]

Commanders should be ready to contest regulations and practices of long standing that may impede OBT&E. This is no less than
commanders would do with restrictions that impede performance
in combat. Many such restrictions were designed to marginalize the
possibility of errors by attempting to impose artificial controls that
would be absent in the execution of a real mission. By applying pru-
dent measures, commanders can do what commanders are expected
to do—prepare soldiers and units to accomplish difficult missions in
combat.[46]

Time for an Evolution

Much is expected of the soldiers who secure our nation. Their values and strength of character help make the United States the most
capable land power in the world. The training and education we provide must sustain that capability. We must also field the most capable training cadre in the world. And the training that is designed to
achieve that standard will not assure excellence in execution, nor does
it account for the enhanced confidence that follows achieving a level
of mastery in executing a mission.

The Army standards are a necessary guarantee to the people and our
government that soldiers, leaders, and units can perform as designed
and expected. Training to a determined level of competence and proficiency can consume significant resources. To both achieve and sustain this level of capability, training should aim beyond competence
and proficiency.

Leaders are held accountable for mission accomplishment with the resources available to them. Soldiers are accountable for their actions at the point of decision. Training must therefore flow from the leader's vision of how they will accomplish the mission and must generate confidence for the soldiers who execute the mission. OBT&E/ASLT&E empowers leaders by fostering initiative and accountability, it empowers trainers to produce meaningful results, and it empowers soldiers by arming them with knowledge and confidence.

9

Tactical Decision Games or Exercises

You warned us about calling them Tactical Decision Games. As soon as the USMA academic review board saw the name that included games, they said it could not be called that because it sounded fun. So we [Department of Military Science] changed the word game to exercises. Thus, they approved the change to our curriculum with the use of Tactical Decision Exercises or TDEs.

—MAJ. CHAD FOSTER TO DON VANDERGRIFF, 17 NOVEMBER 2008

Tactical decision exercises (TDEs) are situations, both combat and noncombat, employed with an array of different tools to create conditions that encourage adaptability in participants. This process over time is referred to as "evolutionary adaptability." Each TDE emphasizes one or more of the traits of adaptability. TDEs come in many shapes and sizes (instructor selection of the tools and methods employed is of the utmost importance).[1]

A Little History

Cognitive development (CD), or how to solve problems, should occur early in a person's learning (as early as grade school), because it is more complex and imparts a longer-lasting lesson through difficult shared experiences. Some of these experiences occur during training, but again, when individual commanders and leaders understand that training requires expensive resources, it is easier for them to change course and focus on developing the intangibles. Correctly done, *training* is resource intensive, while *education* is intellectually expensive; it takes much experience and well-prepared teachers to effectively use their resources. By "intellectually expensive," I mean that TDEs put demands on the instructor that go beyond most "ease on instructor" or "turnkey" curricula used today. There is an art to teaching. It requires a teacher who understands war, is proficient in the technical aspects of the profession of arms, and who is a good leader.[2] Training and education combine to yield knowledge development (KD)—the acquisition of knowledge or information—which is one aspect of experience. Experience leads to more adaptability when developed using the TDE tool as one of many learning tools.

TDEs are but one tool that promote an individual's development of adaptability. TDE is a cheap tool, but an intellectually expensive centerpiece of any ACM-based POI. (One last important asset: As we discovered in previous chapters, the teacher must have a active imagination. With these ingredients, the teacher will find many ways to use the TDE to teach decision-making and to build character. It is important to understand the history behind TDEs. TDEs are used to teach leaders how to think while reinforcing established ways of performing a task. The technique can be traced back at least to the Chinese general and military theorist Sun Tzu, who advocated for their employment more than 2,500 years ago.[3]

Ways to develop officers who could make rapid decisions in the chaos of the battlefield were at the heart of the reforms led by Gerhard Scharnhorst shortly after the destruction of the Prussian army at Jena in 1806. Prussia's military education of its officer cadets was based on an approach developed by a Swiss educator, Johann Heinrich Pestalozzi. In the late 1700s, Pestalozzi developed his theory that students learned faster on their own if allowed to "experience the thing before they tried to give it a name." More specifically, the Prussians used Pestalozzi's methods to teach leaders to identify the core of a problem and deal with the centerpiece of the problem without "wasting time working their way to finding a solution."[4]

The new education system, along with other radical Scharnhorst reforms such as the strenuous selection of officers from a broad base of the population, gave the Prussians what they sought—a professional officer and noncommissioned officer corps. Being situated in the center of Europe, surrounded by several potential enemies, Prussia had to be able to mobilize rapidly. Its officers had to prepare hard in peacetime to be ready when war began.[5]

From the very beginning of a Prussian (later German) cadet's career, TDEs were used to sharpen the students' decision-making skills and to provide a basis for evaluating them on their character. Prussian cadets had to solve problems with many variables under different conditions and explain their decisions to the instructor and class. The problems a cadet was given were complex and sometimes dealt with units three levels above his own (in the case of cadets, a company, battalion, or regiment).[6]

The instructors wanted to find out what the cadet would do when presented with a complex problem. They were not concerned with what the cadet had already learned, but with the cadet's willingness to present and solve the problem. These scenarios were timed; when time was up, the cadet presented his solution. Instructors and peers evaluated decision-making ability, not how tasks were accomplished.

The TDEs introduced the cadets to the unknown, with the result that cadets wanted to know more and therefore asked questions. They also sought to answer for themselves what they did not know. Also, the students were given orders that conflicted with the situation on the board and were forced to resolve the conflict between the two.

Another technique used by the Prussians to teach decision-making was to change the original situation or the orders while the cadet was preparing his solution to the initial problem. This forced the student to either challenge the original order because it was out of date or accept the old order and live with the consequences. Most of the time, the TDE was also presented under limited time, creating even more stress. But it was when the cadet briefed his solution that the major part of the learning took place, not only for the cadet but also for his peers. "It is not so much 'training' and 'pretraining.' That is to say, they serve to develop habits that are conducive to the use of all sorts of other methods, to include more elaborate simulations and field exercises, to study tactics."[7]

The cadet would have to present his proposed solution in front of his peers, instructors, and (sometimes) visiting officers. The great von Moltke, chief of the Prussian General Staff from 1858 to 1888, frequently visited corps-level district academies (where the Germans produced cadets) and would sit in on these games. He would even frequently oversee the instruction, present the situation, and guide the discussion afterward.[8]

The Prussians went beyond using TDEs to teach, they also used them in their evaluations. Weak performance on graded TDEs was grounds for failure on an exam or for expulsion from the academy. Signs of weak character, too, were grounds for failing an exam; repeat offenders were expelled from the course. The inability to make a decision or defend one's decision in the face of adversity resulted in the cadet not being commissioned.[9]

Short of performance on an actual battlefield, there were several measures that demonstrated what type of character the cadet possessed. If he changed his original decision to go along with the solution recommended by the instructor, he was seen as having weak character and was thus judged a failure. Weak character was also demonstrated if the cadet stayed with a poor or out-of-date decision from higher authority because that is what the instructor (the higher authority) told him to do. The worst thing a cadet could do was to make no decision at all.[10]

The "How-To" with TDEs

Today and in the future, TDEs will assume more importance in developing and sharpening a person's problem-solving skills without an extensive and expensive commitment of resources. To be sure, experience is one of the most valuable aspects of teaching and training, but it is also costly. The Adaptive Course Model should also encompass military history, essays, and varied education techniques, which carry over easily to the field. A new curriculum combined with a new operating environment and training philosophy will provide an opportunity to learn from the successes and failures of earlier warriors. Surveys of cadre taken by the author (2000–2004) garner similar responses regarding the use of TDEs: "There is no task-condition and standard";

"How can I grade this?"; "The cadets need to be taught more before given this [TDE]"; "This is something they should learn later [after they are commissioned and later in their careers]."[11]

When thinking how to use the TDE, cadre can also consider it a tactical exercise without troops. The cadre are only limited by imagination. There is a lot that can be done with the TDE. The cadre can use it in a written exam, like writing an operations order to plan for the scenario for a test. Along with the written portion, there will often be a sketch or plan that a student is required to do in developing his or her own plan. The scenario should also define who you are, why you are there, what your assets are, your mission or objective, and the threats.[12]

The teacher can change or adjust all of these based on what he or she wants to achieve and the students' level of proficiency. Although cadre at an ACM-based course will want their personnel to "experience the thing before you try to give it a name," give your personnel problems they can manage. By exposing your students or personnel to too complex a problem, a program may discourage them early on from taking risks and thinking boldly about their solutions.[13]

The author teaching a map exercise using Kriegsspiel rules to a group of Fort Benning instructors.
Author's collection

The Adaptive Course Model POI encourages cadets to seek more knowledge when they ask pertinent questions. The instructor will now do this through the student or personnel brief-back of their solution. Personnel or students give their solutions to their peers, who will in turn evaluate their decision. The instructor is there to guide the discussion and encourage the theme of classical education. Because of this session, cadets will seek to gain more knowledge on their own.

The teacher is also the referee, adding reality to cadet solutions with comments like, "Not possible" or "In reality, this is what this so and so can do for you in this type of terrain." Or the instructor asks probing, Socratic questions such as, "Is your course of action in keeping with the spirit of the commander's intent?" or "What caused you to change the mission you were given by higher?" These repeated sessions build character—adaptability and intuition—over time. Maj. Mark Sonstein discovered the value of this approach when teaching cadets in 2010:

> An extremely useful training method is the separation of information during the exploratory phase of instruction. By giving the Cadets small pieces of information and allowing them to establish acceptable solutions based on the limited information they have. This can only be done early in the class and is useful in teaching the importance of mission analysis. For example a fellow instructor told me, "I may give the Cadets a mission, with no further guidance. After the Cadets complete a course of action for the mission I have given them I then give them an enemy COA, and they realize that they must change their plans to compensate for this new information. After analysis, they are next given terrain and weather data. This teaches them the importance of conducting good mission analysis." I have not actually used this method as described, but have accomplished similar results with comparable methods.[14]

The primary benefit of this type of education is that your students can be put into situations that are either impractical or too expensive to enact in the field or in an electronic simulation. Students can go over hundreds of scenarios without ever leaving the classroom. This establishes a solid foundation in understanding decision-making prior to moving to the field and more costly training. This is not a substitute for free-play force-on-force exercises but acts as a useful adjunct. If you find a particularly relevant scenario, you can enact it live.

The POI of the ACM-based course puts into context when and where education and training fall. There are three other factors that must work together to produce learning synergy:

- How the teacher facilitates.
- Does the student understand or try to understand what is being taught?
- The most important factor, mentorship (either individual one-on-one or through an after-action review).

The teacher must sit down with the leader and their team, both together and separately, and go over what was just learned. With the team this can resemble the AAR, and with the individual, it is similar to counseling—but both are conducted in a two-way forum.[15]

TDEs are situational-based where individuals are required to exercise mental agility to meet the demands of the situational stimuli while implementing a problem-solving solution. A TDE can take the following forms:

How to deliver scenario-based training.
What form should it take?
- Listening exercise where instructions are translated from paper media to a situation given orally to students by the teacher. The students are given limited time to write the instructions down and give them back to the teacher.
- Seminars
- Computer-based virtual war games
- Staff rides
- Terrain board exercise
- Tactical decision exercises (TDE)
- Free-play, force-on-force exercises

The purpose of TDEs is to provide opportunities to gain experience. Through multiple participation, either as a leader or team member, students gain breadth in experience and skills in decision-making to meet a specific set of circumstances.

TDEs that employ the proper tool provide cadets and students with supplemental information that can be converted to experience when a situation presents itself. It must be noted that these scenarios and the prescribed teaching approaches shown later are not a substitute for true real-world experience.

TDEs benefit personnel by:
- Improving pattern recognition skills
- Exercising the decision-making process
- Improving and practicing communication skills
- Increasing leadership potential

The Terrain Board Exercise (TBE). A terrain board exercise is one of the most effective ways of delivering a TDE. The terrain board exercise is a training device that employs a three-dimensional terrain model with various props to represent assets or liabilities. Assets are items that can be utilized to develop a solution or optimize performance in some manner. Terrain boards or similar training support items benefit the students by creating "top sight," which is the ability to see how the pieces of the problem fit together.[16]

Advantages of TDEs

Another way to understand scenarios that enable adaptability is by the use of historical case studies to facilitate learning.[17] These are sprinkled throughout the scenario wherever the instructor sees fit to enhance learning. Every training application has benefits and limitations, as training can only *simulate* the operating environment and the mettle required to function under combat conditions.

The TDE is no exception, while all scenarios enable a student's ability to think critically in conjunction with some level of situational awareness and analysis, the generalized benefits of conducting scenario enabling are listed:

The benefits of TDEs are:
- Interactive training
- Hot-seat thinking
- Experiential learning
- Command experience
- Learning organization

The benefits of the TDE are summarized below.

Interactive training uses the seminar approach to scenario enabling that creates an interactive learning process. This can be highly effective. The instructor can project training focus and integrate experience into the TDG/TDE while providing immediate feedback to cadets on their solutions.

Hot-seat thinking describes a situation in which a student is put on the spot and has to make decisions, then deal with the outcomes just as they would in a real situation. Soldiers take great pride in performing well in any application they are assigned. The ability to perform in front of peers can generate the motivation to develop greater proficiency or diversified skills. In order to create this positive learning environment, the instructor must use judgment to create a challenging level of stress during the scenario and adopt a mentoring approach to the after-action reviews.

The combination of leadership finesse and mentorship will build a more cohesive leadership team within the unit, since hot-seat thinking leads to proactive leaders.

Experiential learning allows students to learn through the experiences of others. The learning can come in the form of after-action reports, case studies, or actual observation of an event. They own their experiences in the learning environment; they take ownership of their learning. This is key to getting students on the road to adaptability and critical thinking.

Command experience refers to tactical decisions being expressed in the form of combat orders. The students must understand and be able to give "frag" orders based on initial conditions with the scenario and subsequent changes as the scenario progresses. This builds confidence and presence.

Learning organization in this context describes a scenario and how it is applied; so that it can be designed as a rewarding way for students and leaders to expand skills while creating a positive environment in which training and the associated learning are both fun and practical. The ability to create new skill sets affects leaders in much the same way that qualifying on their weapon affects soldiers in basic training and advanced individual training (AIT). A given scenario and how it is implemented provides a great team-building and mentoring forum that builds tactical and technical proficiency through decision-making.

Limiting Factors of TDEs

Understanding the limitations of TDEs allows the adaptability instructor to link the training objectives with the appropriate tool when using the TDE.

The limitations of different tools that TDEs use are:
- One-move TDEs
- Difficulty in simulating operating environment

One-move TDEs represent a "snapshot in time" that requires players to make only a single move. These TDEs do not capture the ongoing interactive nature of tactics or decision-making.

Difficulty in simulating operating environment is important to develop mental agility and critical thinking skills; the decision execution is the primary difficulty and often becomes the limiting factor of TDE. While the TDE can enhance critical and creative thinking skills, it is almost impossible to simulate the friction and uncertainty of the operating environment.

Difficulty in applying to special operations. Sometimes operations that require specialized personnel, intricate planning, and large quantities of detailed technical information and intelligence are too difficult to facilitate TDEs, no matter what tool is used to implement them.

TDE Design

While the TDE has viable applications at every level, it is most effective at the company level because of the enhanced number of variables and limited perspective of the scenario. When TDEs are used at higher or lower levels, they are more difficult to design. At higher levels, the decision-making cycle takes longer and the scenario must generally describe a situation developed over time. At lower levels, a terrain model might better serve the TDE or detailed micro-terrain details.

Designing a TDE and choosing the appropriate tool to employ them can be a challenge. Instructors using TDE need to incorporate critical thinking and decision-making skills in order to improve the performance of their cadets and themselves. This section focuses on how to design scenarios that are conducive to learning.

The TDE is only as successful as the design and the tool selected to deliver it. During and after the development of a TDE, the facilitator should try to incorporate as many of the following elements as possible for TDE play when determining what tools and methods to employ. The following principles should be taken into account when designing and facilitating a TDE:

- Generate interest
- Appropriate level of challenge
- Level of detail
- Granularity
- Multiple interpretation and solutions
- Avoid a solution approach
- Role-play
- Limiting information
- Limit time
- Create a dilemma
- After-action review
- Simplicity of design

Remember, the employment of a TDE should *generate interest*. In order to accomplish this, the teacher has to focus on quality and application reality. A mission that reflects the possibilities of the operating environment will build interest. Gaining interest is the first step in developing an infectious desire to learn and excel.[18]

Developing a TDE with the *appropriate level of challenge* requires the instructor or facilitator to continually monitor the skills and abilities of the students involved. Pushing the limit on a student's tactical and technical ability is fine as long as it does not minimize interest and learning opportunity.

The *level of detail* for each TDE will be different and will also drive the decision of which tool should be used to deliver it. For example you may have the resources to do a TDE involving a squad through the force-on-force free-play, while a company or higher TDE would be appropriately delivered with a TDE. The facilitator must present enough information allowing the player to act. The right level of detail keeps the TDE participant from getting bored or overwhelmed. Ideally, creating a situation that amply shrouds the dilemma in the "fog of war" without overwhelming or boring the participants creates the maximum benefit for the players and facilitator.

Granularity refers to the level of information in proportion to the level of the game. Squad-level games should set squad- or platoon-level objectives and have appropriate maps and details. Granularity can be achieved by using the systems approach to training.

The systems approach to training is an orderly process that helps you work smarter and train better. The first phase of the process is analysis. In the analysis phase, you should look at the situation and the needs of the participants to determine what each specific training exercise must include. The analysis can be exhaustive and include written surveys of all participants and thorough document reviews. On the other hand, it can be as simple as a few phone calls or informal questions asked of the likely participants. The key benefit of a successful analysis phase is ensuring that every training session you offer meets the needs of the target audience. Additional benefits include: the ability to engage your audience and build investment prior to the training, increased attendance at training exercises because the sessions are relevant to participants' needs, and the creation of deeper trust between the training organization and participating organizations.

Multiple interpretation and solutions describes how the TDE should present a dilemma that is open to scrutiny and free thinking, one that will generate multiple reasonable solutions. For example, when using a seminar with multiple players to deliver the TDE, the multiple options create opportunity for discussion and interactivity.

The *avoiding a solution* approach is where the TDE and tool provide the solution. The TDE and appropriate tool should present a problem or dilemma, not a solution reverse engineered into a problem. Contrived situations with a "canned solution" limit interest and the decision-making opportunity.[19]

Role-playing refers to the perspective from which the TDE is designed to view the dilemma. For example, a squad leader may have to capture the perspective as the company commander, which could significantly change the play of the problem. Role-playing expands the perspective of the battle space and the requirements for mission accomplishment or solution.

Limiting information in a TDE requires the player to critically analyze the information that is provided, then apply it as creatively as possible for the maximum solution with minimum time requirements.

Limit time in TDE requires the players to focus on adaptability while economizing the information flow to critical information requirements only. Decision-making under mental duress hones the player's ability to make decisions in real situations where the operating environment may be hostile.

Create a dilemma is when the TDE starts out as a basic problem. The problem and how it is delivered should be appropriate for the level of experience and skills of the personnel, students, or cadets participating in the TDE.

The *after-action review* allows the facilitator to draw out lessons learned from the TDE play. Reviewing the chosen course of action or reasoning behind the decision-making process can be beneficial for all parties. Building the experiences and reinforcing lesson learned is an essential part of the decision-making process.

Simplicity of design often has greater effect than complex TDEs. Simplicity requires intuitive thinking and focuses on basic or universal concepts. Universal concepts can be altered slightly for unique situations quickly and effectively. The TDEs should infuse fog and friction to create a situation that has no one clear solution. The ability to cause friction gives the simple TDE magnified value through discussion and decision-making potential.

Designing original TDEs from scratch can be a great challenge. After defining the objective of the TDE, the facilitator may be able to draw a workable scenario from another source. Some of the possible sources are listed below and should be considered by instructors developing TDE and what tool to use to deliver them.

A historical battle can provide a useful basis for a TDE. The teacher can update the scenario by using modern weapons and the organizational structures. The scale of the battle can be adjusted, as necessary, to meet the TDE objectives. When the seminar leaders brief the historical situation and outcomes pre- or post-TDE, they should be careful to not present the historical solution as the "right" solution. The focus is on developing decision-making capacity and capabilities.

Personal experience can be converted into TDE, but the teacher should focus on the decisions generated rather than the actual outcome. If the personnel, students, or cadets involved all share common core competencies, this particular approach is particularly effective.[20]

Specific dilemma:
- Mission
- Enemy
- Size
- Disposition and activities of enemy
- Disposition of friendly forces
- Terrain and weather

Random engagement focuses on a specific piece of terrain with relief, vegetation, and other features. The instructor then makes the enemy and friendly forces appear in different locations and multiple directions, as the scenario requires. The situational factors should be filled as appropriate for the skills and abilities of the students participating in the TDE.

In general terms, a TDE can be designed in one of two methods. These methods are: *situation-based* ("Here's the mission") or *solution reaction-based* ("Now what?").

Situation-based TDE focuses on a particular situation that is given to the player in a mission order format.

Solution reaction-based TDE focuses on taking the initial situation and moving one situation forward in time. The situation should be considered in three-dimensional terms, so that the instructor can select the best option to feed to the students.

Enhancements can be used to modify a TDE to achieve different adaptability objectives, and develop a larger experienced base. The instructor can implement any number of the following suggestions to increase the decision-making opportunity, and minimize the amount of time required to negotiate the TDE.

Reverse scenario is where the scenario is flipped and players have to rethink the dilemma from the opposing perspective. It is mainly used with either a TDE or seminar approach. If time and resources allow, though, free-play force-on-force can get exciting when the winner now has to assume the role of the opposing force they just defeated. A player has to create an analysis of how an opposing force would execute an operation on the same piece of terrain that was either being defended or assaulted. This is an excellent method to war-game a scenario to identify strengths, weaknesses, opportunities, and risks that fortified or weakened the previous scenario.

Modify terrain perspective is where the TDE can change drastically by simply modifying terrain perspective. Using a map, terrain model, or sand table, and rotating the perspective 90 degrees can totally change the way decisions have to be made and implemented. This is even the case when using a free-play force-on-force tool to deliver the TDE. During the after-action review, which is conducted by the instructor, focus should be placed on how the TDE dynamics and decision-making rationale changed by rotating the terrain.

Variable modification is where TDEs slightly change the problem analyses and decision processes, which alters the solutions significantly. For example, the instructor could change the TDE scenario in one or more of the following ways:

Variable modifications:
- Daylight to nighttime operations
- Foot mobile forces to mechanized or heliborne forces

- Changing climatic or terrain factors, such as desert operations to woodland operations
- Modifying the size of the enemy forces
- Changing it from a noncontact situation to a contact situation

In order to be successful using variable modification, the instructor must be intimately familiar with the capabilities and the students in their group. Challenging the mental processes and procedures is the goal, but care must be taken not to overwhelm the cadet to the point that they no longer wish to participate.

Examples of TDE Lesson Plans

The following three TDEs are baseline infantry-centric TDEs. But TDEs can be of any type dealing with a wide array of missions, unit types, and force structure levels. The Department of Military Instruction at West Point and the *Marine Corps Gazette* possess hundreds of TDEs of all types and sizes to employ in your classroom or in "hip pocket training." The following three outlines are presented to give a teacher and course developer ideas on what should be on a TDE lesson plan.[21]

Example 1: Lesson Plan for TDE
1. Scope:
Tactical Decision Guide: To Ambush or Not to Ambush? (See supporting map [figure 1] and narrative.)

References: *Raising the Bar*, chapter 3; "Swiss to Swift: Tactical Decision Games in their Place in Military Education" by Donald Vandergriff; and Chad Foster articles in *Armor*, *Cavalry Journal*, and *Assembly* (USMA) magazines.

2. Learning Objective
Students become familiar with how to conduct and use a TDE (or to teach a lesson). Students are continually exposed to facilitation techniques as well as how to conduct an effective AAR.

Measure of Effectiveness: Students fully partake in discussion by providing courses of action during exercise and will defend their COA against peer and teacher criticism. (The teacher should be the least engaged and should only facilitate the discussion.) On day five students will demonstrate their understanding of a TDE when they prepare and conduct a problem-solving exercise to meet a class outcome. The exercise is considered a success if the students do the majority of the talking. Several COAs should be displayed and examined in order to push the point that more than one solution, well understood and communicated, is appropriate.

3. Learning/Activity:
- Method of instruction: art of facilitation
- Instructor to student ratio, 1:5
- Time of instruction: unspecified
- Media: classroom with dry erase board and markers
- Laptop computer (for map)
- Student reference(s): guidance to this Lesson Plan

4. Conduct of Lesson:
A student leader is given the opportunity to put himself in the enemy's shoes in several of these TDEs. A student can "turn the map around" and look at the same tactical situation from the enemy's point of view. This provides the leader with valuable insight into how the enemy might view the situation differently, conceptualize his actions and outcomes, deploy his forces, control them in battle, and ultimately identify what the enemy considers victory during and after an engagement.

Through the methods used in *Adaptability Handbook* and *Raising the Bar* (chapter 3), students will be challenged to think like their enemies, better understand rapidly changing situations, and determine courses of action that take into account not just the kinetic fires, but also non-kinetic fires and civil–military relationships. Often in counterinsurgency, the immediate tactical situation is not difficult to solve. The problem is that solving it by force often has negative consequences. The challenge to students that the exercise seeks to address is to determine what COAs will undermine the insurgent's credibility and desire to fight while increasing our standing and respect in the eyes of the local populace.

While displaying this map, the teacher reads the following to the students: "You are the 1st Squad Leader, 1st Platoon (PLT), Company F, 2d Battalion, 7th Infantry. TF 2/7 is the ground combat element of the 3rd BCT that has landed at the port city of New Zeda in the country of Zedastan. The established government is struggling with counterguerrilla insurgency, and there have been numerous high-profile kidnappings, bombings, and assassinations in the past month. Conditions have deteriorated to a point requiring international intervention. The city is home to more than one million people, most in need of humanitarian relief. The main enemy force, the Zedastan People's Army (ZPA), retreated from the city upon the arrival of the Marines. ZPA is a large, but untrained, army with mostly small arms, machine guns, and a few mortars. They do have access to modern communications such as cell phones and global positioning systems. The PLT is the security element for both U.S. and international aid organizations that are feeding the estimated 300,000 refugees. Company F has been tasked with ensuring that ZPA forces do not return to the city to interfere with humanitarian efforts. Your platoon has been tasked with conducting security patrols outside the city approximately two kilometers to the northeast. The terrain is heavily wooded with rolling hills. Your squad has been on patrol for over an hour. The BCT perimeter and city outskirts are approximately two kilometers to the south. Your point man spots what appears to be an enemy patrol armed with small arms moving south toward your squad. You decide to establish an ambush and set your squad into hasty ambush positions oriented to the northwest. You radio higher headquarters and inform them of the situation. Just as you are about to initiate your ambush (with a closed-bolt weapon), the 1st Fire Team leader points out another enemy unit moving toward and behind the platoon. He counts at least six enemy soldiers with more following. He's not sure how many. The team leader also notes at least one RPK (Soviet) medium machine gun. It is now 1730 and end evening nautical twilight (EENT) is ten minutes away."

"What now, sergeant?" (Student is in squad leader role.)

Allow no questions and give the students sixty seconds to write down their COA, then say "Stop!"

Note: It is important that the teacher reads all four parts to this lesson plan before its conduct.

5. Teacher Notes:

This TDE introduces the student to *intuition*. This scenario is hypothetical, but based on actual historical events that occurred in Somalia in 1992.

- The unknown enemy force is a large squad of thirteen enemy soldiers; they also have an 82mm mortar at the rear of the column that your team leader does not see.
- The enemy objective is to disrupt the humanitarian relief efforts.
- The enemy plans to set up in the open area by your squad traveling in two columns to minimize detection.
- Tactical command of ground forces remains a complicated endeavor. There is some science involved in this process, but command mainly applies human talents through developed faculties, all habitually artistic. Watch the students for the following:

  1. Who made a quick decision, who delayed?
  2. How did they explain their rationale?
  3. Did anyone try to split their squad and ambush both enemy elements? This leads to trying to do everything or really not making a decision at all.

- Choose a written method in order to judge all students' answers, or use the "hot seat" method in a seminar where one student is put in the hot seat. If you are in a classroom, you can use the written method or allow them to actually simulate lying in an ambush. Pick a student to be the squad leader, then read them the scenario at the end pointing the direction of each enemy element.

6. Additional Notes:

No questions are allowed until after you have read the instructions and during execution of the TDE.

- The following techniques are recommended:
  1. Choose the student to present the solution using the hot seat method.
  2. Enforce the time limit rule, holding the students to a set time limit. They must act quickly. Time compression creates stress, which is normally part of the decision-making process especially under operational conditions.

- Possible questions during the discussion phase of this exercise:

  1. What was your reasoning for that action?
  2. What was your overall estimate of the situation?
  3. What would you have done if . . . ?
  4. What were your assumptions?
  5. What was the biggest concern about your plan?
  6. How good was the enemy?
  7. What are your platoon, company, and task force trying to achieve? What are their missions?
  8. Explain the term "hasty ambush."

- Key student issues include:

  1. Stay focused on the larger mission (this is early, but someone may show an ability to think holistically). The enemy cannot get close enough to the city to threaten food distribution.
  2. There is no choice but to engage, withdrawal now exposes the student's squad to dealing with two unknowns.
  3. The key aspect is that enemy forces are inexperienced and poorly trained.

- AAR focus is on *pattern analysis* (there are no wrong answers but there are *better* answers).

  1. After the time limit, take down each student's COA (this is why you have them write their COAs down so others cannot borrow a better-sounding COA).
  2. Write down each COA in brevity; did they ambush or withdraw? Did they ask to call for fire? Did they go into hiding (not ambush) and let the enemy go by them?
  3. Ask the students, "What are the facts of the mission?" (Did they listen initially?) This may include:

     a. Humanitarian mission
     b. Enemy is ill trained, but well equipped
     c. Enemy is trying to disrupt the humanitarian mission

  d. Was there a commander's intent (secure the humanitarian mission)?

  e. How far is the city from you?

  f. What is the friendly situation?

 4. Ask the students to deal with assumptions. What is an assumption? Ask them to define an assumption. Then list some
  assumptions from the mission.

 5. List the assumptions beside the list of facts, and then have the
  students revisit their COAs.

 6. Did any student change their COA?

Example 2: Lesson Plan for TDE

1. Scope:

Tactical Decision Guide: To "Attack or Withdraw?" (Introduction to
"house of cards") and group TDE.

 References: *Maneuver Warfare Handbook*, chapters 2–3; How to facili-
tate a TDE reference, "No Solutions in Asymmetric Warfare," by Chad
Foster; and "Swiss to Swift: Tactical Decision Games in their Place in
Military Education," by Donald Vandergriff.

2. Learning Objective:

Introduce "friction" as a way to teach adaptability and mission command. Students will be familiarized with the use of friction in the classroom and in the field as a way to promote the teaching of adaptability.

 Measure of Effectiveness: Students will demonstrate using different
tools to use friction to induce learning and evolve into adaptability;
these include problem-solving games, TDEs, war gaming, and free-
play force-on-force exercises with the use of friction-inducing stress
on the students to see how they solve problems.

3. Learning/Activity:

- Method of instruction: art of facilitation
- Instructor to student ratio, 1:5
- Time of instruction: unspecified
  - Media: classroom with dry erase board and markers
  - Laptop computer (for map)

° Computer projector with screen (include a CD with TDE map)
- Student reference(s): This lesson plan will be given to the students after they complete this exercise, not before.

4. Conduct of Lesson:

"Students this will be a group and planning exercise. You will get a certain amount of time, figure out the problem, and present a COA of how to solve the problem. You are to work as a group, but designate a representative as your briefer. At the end of the time period given to solve the problem, each group will be asked to come up and present and defend their COA to the rest of the class."

The teacher then reads the scenario on the following pages to the class. After the first group presents their plan, the teacher will change the conditions and the enemy situation and give them limited time to present their fragmentary order to the changing conditions.

Teacher, you read the following narrative to the students (this is a group/planning TDE), while displaying the map above:

"You are a rifle platoon leader. What do we do?

"You are assigned to 1st Platoon, Team Charlie, Task Force Shield. You are currently engaged in stability and support operations in the country of Grapeland. Coalition forces have routed organized enemy resistance, but there are still numerous 'dead-enders' who operate in squad-sized units.

"These units use Soviet bloc small arms to include AK-series assault weapons, light machine guns, rocket-propelled grenades, and 82mm mortars. They are mostly former regime military officers augmented by terrorists from other countries. Their actions are well thought-out, rehearsed, and usually effective. Hostile threat is high, but you have not been engaged in any manner in the fourteen days you have been there.

"Your Task Force is in a defensive perimeter at a run-down air-field located within city limits of Cartonville, Grapeland. Your rules of engagement state that you are only to fire if fired upon or if hostile intent is positively identified. You are to use the least amount of force necessary to gain fire superiority. There have been restrictive fire measures emplaced as well. In any situation, collateral damage is to be kept to a minimum. Your platoon has been tasked with a security patrol in the city. You have two machine gun teams and two assault teams attached to you. The platoon has a standard combat load of ammunition (squad automatic weapon, M203 grenade launcher, M4s), and each squad has one AT-4 rocket as well. You have no direct or indirect fire support due to the restrictive fire measures. Illumination is your only asset from your supporting weapons platoon and company.

"There is a section of AH-64 Apaches armed with 30mm chain gun and Hellfire missiles, as well as a dedicated medevac bird (on twenty-minute strip alert at a nearby forward operating base), that are within a five-minute flight of you once they launch. It is one hour before dusk, and your patrol exits friendly lines.

"Your patrol is spread out about four hundred meters long and staggered on both sides of the road. As you come to the intersection in the city square, you see that two of the avenues are now barricaded with trash, vehicles, and wood and are impassable for your patrol. There are very few people in the streets as well. At this time you halt the patrol to look at your map in order to coordinate new routes. You are hit from the front by small arms and machine gun fire. The machine guns seem to have interlocking fire, and the small arms are in sporadic positions within the buildings. All of the buildings in the square are two floors or higher and made of heavy concrete. (Fire Team A, 1st Squad, is pinned down and taking casualties.)

"As the patrol advances toward the contact, mortar fire begins to fall in behind your position, pushing you toward the kill zone. Fire Team B of 1st Squad and a machine gun team move to join Fire Team A on their own initiative upon enemy contact. 2nd Squad takes up hasty defensive positions upon contact. 3rd Squad moves into a reserve position between two buildings to the east or right side of the street, and all are awaiting orders.

"What do you do?"

Requirement: If using seminar or TDE in a classroom, provide the following:

- In a time limit of five minutes, come up with a fragmentary order for your squads and your attachments; include scheme of maneuver, commander's intent, and signal plan. Provide an overlay for your scheme of maneuver.
- Also prepare any reports that you would send to higher headquarters, along with any requests for support.

5. Teacher Notes:

"House of cards" technique. (Refer back to the information briefing on ACM.)

House of Cards Technique

- Let the first group brief their plan as they would their subordinates. (Teachers should always sit with the students.)
- Let the groups brief their plan, and then execute it. As the second group begins their plan, add enemy forces of platoon size, light infantry, off to the west coming into the tactical picture.
- Possible questions include:

  1. Is the order clear?
  2. If I were a subordinate commander receiving this order, would I understand the plan and my role in the action?
  3. Is the order complete?
  4. Are any key pieces of information missing?
  5. Is the order flexible?
  6. How well would a leader who received this order be able to exercise his initiative and react to changes in the situation?
  7. What is the decisive point of your operation? (Where and when was the most important decision and action to achieve success taken? This is often referred to as a "decisive point," or Schwerpunkt in the mission command concept.)

6. AAR Guidelines:

The after-action review is the key part of the entire learning process. A great AAR is one in which the facilitator (the leader) talks as little as possible. It is a great AAR because the facilitator guided the students to admit and take ownership of their mistakes, and learn from them. The process is a conundrum—on the surface, you are teaching the students to be innovative and adaptive by solving a stream of problems that should become more complex and ambiguous as the course progresses. Yet at the same time you are still teaching through facilitating each student's strengths and weaknesses in being creative and adaptable. You let them find their strengths and weaknesses by providing undeniable feedback; for example, if their plan fails, no one has to tell them it failed because it is obvious to them and everyone else. Your feedback must be swift and undeniable, so that they take it on board or own it. Only when they identify and take ownership of their weaknesses will they take the necessary steps to do something about them.

Issues for consideration include:

Examples of Facilitated AAR—Questions to Ask
- What does "clear" (doctrinally clear means every inch of a zone is free of the enemy) mean when given as a task to an infantry unit?
- How large an area must be cleared to make an airfield completely safe from enemy small arms fire? From RPGs or anti-air missiles? From heavy machine guns?
- What does it mean when you receive mortar fire? How do you deal with indirect fire? How do you avoid being targeted?
- Did you use all three squads to search a wide area or did you keep one back to be able to respond to enemy contact?
- What caused most of your casualties? How could these casualties have been reduced?

7. Tactical Themes:
Examples provided in the highlighted box deal with questions the facilitator may ask in games dealing with tactical problems.

Examples of Tactical Questions to the Students
- Movement to contact by bounding overwatch?
- Bounding overwatch by teams within the squad. Bounding overwatch by squads within the platoon. The measure of success is the number of units immediately able to fire on the enemy when contact is made.
- On contact, a squad envelopment is a two-team base of fire and team assault. A platoon envelopment is a two-squad base of fire and assault.

8. Main Point:
The facilitator finally gets to the main point of their critique with, "what was the purpose of the mission?" "To find the enemy and then use supporting fires to engage them." "Once you discovered the enemy was too strong, why didn't you chose to withdraw?" "Is that a tactical option?"

What Does This All Mean?
Finally have fun with TDEs.

There is no "right" answer, only better ones. All responses have some benefit, and highlight your perception of the problem. There is nothing to stop you from coming up with more than one response. Recognizing, however, that there are many ways to approach a problem, we did not limit the student to one pass-or-fail school solution.

This is hard when using the scenario through the TDE, for example to evaluate decision-making ability during an examination, but it can be done.

Questions to Ask When Grading the TDE Exams and Quizzes:
- First and foremost was a decision made?
- If so, we jump to two, how was it communicated to their subordinates effectively? And in a timely manner?
- Then we ask was the decision made in support of the commander's intent (long-term contract), and mission (short-term contract)?

A fourth question, the teacher asks himself was the student's, cadet's, or personnel's solution based on changing conditions that made it a viable decision even if it violated the original mission but supported the intent?

Failure in the TDE occurs when the cadet cannot make a decision. Or, in the course of briefing their course of action, or while the instructor is assessing the TDE, the cadet changes their decision because the instructor challenged the cadet's choice. Here, the student, cadet or personnel demonstrates the need to go along with the instructor ("higher"). Even if the teacher feels that the student's decision is a sound one, they may challenge or test the student's character in the face of adversity, to see how much self-confidence the student possesses.

In the end, scenarios executed through the right tool (mostly TDEs) provide the best educational approach for building strength of character. Current Army course POI uses process and task training to teach a potential officer on "what to think." In World War II, with the U.S. Army coming in late, after the Germans were bled down and almost beaten, it made it appear in the "glow of victory" that our system of officer production was the right one.

10

War-Gaming

The ability to do this [intuitive decision-making] is not some mystical power, it is the product of work—of prolonged study, extensive practice, repeated analysis of . . . combat situations.

Few Marines take the time or expend the effort to achieve a high level of competence in the art of tactical decision-making.

True tactical skill . . . comes only to those who have invested heavily in their own self-development. Tactics are at the very heart of the Marine profession, and Marines deserve leaders at every level who have made . . . the investment in tactical expertise.

—JOHN GREENWOOD, "Intuitive Decision-making Properly Understood"

A war game can serve to validate or disprove a course of action or current doctrine, while developing students in decision-making. A war game should consist of a given area, with friendly and enemy forces, each given specific missions and commander's intent, followed by free-thinking play-by-play on both sides, only limited by reality. A judge should be present who possesses a strong grasp of tactics and technical aspects of the scenario to present friction, to resolve combat, to decide if a player's moves are realistic, and to provide each side with a limited picture of what the enemy is doing based on their own side's forces, what they have planned in terms of reconnaissance and surveillance, and if that is successful.

Computer-generated war games alleviate the need to manage fire combat results, friction, and record keeping; they also eliminate the need for a judge (as well as the need to set up a huge map and hundreds, perhaps thousands of play pieces). The guide should still be present to observe the actions of both players, in order to facilitate the AAR. The teacher may also want to introduce the students to the history of war-gaming, asking them questions that lead to the following summary.

History of War-Gaming

Drawing inspiration from chess, Ludwig Hellwig, master of pages to the Duke of Brunswick created a battle emulation game in 1780. According to Max Boot's, *War Made New*, sometime between 1803 and 1809, the Prussian General Staff developed war games, with staff officers moving metal pieces around on a game table (with blue pieces representing Prussian forces and red pieces for those of the enemy), using dice rolls to indicate random chance and a referee to score the results. Increasingly realistic variations became part of military training in the nineteenth century in many nations under the moniker of *Kriegsspiel* ("war game"). War games or military exercises are still an important part of military training today.[1]

The first set of published rules was created in 1812 and named *Instructions for the Representation of Tactical Maneuvers under the Guise of a Wargame.*[2] It was originally produced and developed further by Lt. Georg Leopold von Reiswitz and his son Georg Heinrich Rudolf von Reiswitz, both members of the Prussian army. These war games were implemented by Helmuth von Moltke the Elder, chief of the Prussian General Staff. Moltke made several reforms to the Prussian military with the backing of Otto von Bismarck. These reforms, including Kriegsspiel, were the first of their kind in military education. As a result, this methodology allowed Prussian (and later German) officers, to become more flexible, independent, and responsible.[3]

After its initial development, this particular style of war-gaming became very popular among the Prussian army officer corps. After numerous successful Prussian campaigns in the late 1800s, Kriegsspiel was adopted by many militaries.

Germans playing a Kriegsspiel (war game) in the late 1880s.
NARA

Kriegsspiel is still played today in both its original format and more freestyle games, as proposed by Verdy du Vernois in the 1890s. The original 1824 rules by Reiswitz, the supplementary 1862 rules by Wilhelm von Tschischwitz, and several ancillary products (such as maps) are still published in English by *TooFatLardies*, a British war games publishing company. Much of the renaissance enjoyed by Kriegsspiel is due to Bill Leeson's translation of the original German text in the early 1980s and his promotion of the system in the hobby press.

Modern war-gaming originated with the need to study warfare and to reenact old battles for instructional purposes. The stunning Prussian victory over the Second French Empire in the Franco-Prussian War of 1870–71 is sometimes partly credited to the training of Prussian officers with Kriegsspiel. These first war games were played with dice that represented *friction*, or the intrusion of less than ideal circumstances during a real war (morale, weather, the fog of war), and an umpire who used his own combat experience to determine the results.

After World War I, the German army increasingly used war games for training because it was impossible to conduct large field maneuvers. Due to their wide use, the quality of these games improved considerably. To avoid regimentation, no instructions were issued by official sources. Yet in the spirit of professionalism, a clear winner and a clear loser were designated by an official. In the German army, the term "war game" was used to describe many types of exercises: war games, map exercises, staff or command post exercises, training trips, tactical walks, and sand-table exercises.[4]

Before proceeding with computer-driven simulations, you and your cadre should conduct a Kriegsspiel without a computer, on a map or terrain board or outdoors. What follows are rules and guidelines for this type of gaming drawn from post–World War II interviews with German generals.[5]

Types of War Games
How to Conduct War Games—from the German Rules

War Games train leaders in *estimates, decisions,* and *issuing orders.* The main emphasis is on the concise presentation of ideas. Two sides compete across a map table. A director supervises and serves as the higher headquarters and umpire. In all branches, in every unit, at all garrisons, and especially in officer schools, a large portion of the instruction consisted of war games. This continued even during the war.

"Many sources of friction and wrong measures were detected and rehearsed on maps that saved the lives of our soldiers. Knowledge gained in war games never replaces experience, but does aid in recognizing the demands of warfare. A secondary purpose is that war games give commanders an opportunity to observe their subordinate officers for fitness, knowledge, and strong and weak points of mind and character."

The director of the war game is critical. He must have knowledge, credibility and experience. Junior officers learn to direct war games in small groups under the coaching of an experienced officer. The director and the senior officer present should always establish an atmosphere of friendliness and camaraderie aimed at instruction rather than examination. The choice of the situation depends on the purpose of the war game.

The commander of each side should not be given more information than he would receive in actual warfare. Uncertainty is required. Orders destined for a unit in a war game should be crafted with particular care and must be exemplary in all respects. The situation should include a general setting and a specific mission. It is dangerous to conduct a war game based on an actual example from military history. Examples from history are best used to elaborate principles—the influence of an individual, responsibility, misunderstanding, fatigue, and other factors that are impossible to represent on a map.

One side starts. The commander states his estimate, decision, and orders. The director challenges the commander with objections to test his resolve and clarify unclear points. During games with advanced students, the commander is then released and the other participants, acting as subordinate commanders, give their orders without consulting their commander. This technique however, takes time.

The director dismisses the side, moves unit markers, and then covers them with a sheet. The opposing side is then called in. Any updates to the situation caused by the initial move are briefed by describing impressions, actions, or reports. The commander then states his estimate, decision, and orders. The director and assistants resolve actions and update the map. The game progresses turn by turn in this manner. The final move is often made in the presence of both sides. This move is concluded with a request for a new decision. In every game, efforts should be made to confront each commander, and ideally at least one subordinate commander, with at least one critical, ticklish situation which forces a difficult decision. This increases the value of the game for all participants.

After a pause to allow the participants and directing staff to make notes, the final discussion by the director should not exceed thirty minutes. The director does not describe the game, but picks out interesting aspects, comments on decisions made, clarifies the goals of the exercise, and issues praise and criticism. Approval should be expressed as freely as disapproval.

Although the director may present his own decisions, there is no standard solution. A war game with two sides requires three rooms—one main room and two adjacent rooms for each side. Scales are needed to measure distance. Manuals should be available. For a war game with two parties, four or five hours are required, or an entire afternoon plus evening. Two days are not unusual.

Map Exercises train leaders on tactical concepts. The emphasis is on making decisions on *weapons* and *unit employment*. Conducted by one side on a large scale—1:5000 or larger—map board, the director plays the opposing force to maintain focus on the subject of the game. A well-prepared map exercise may be conducted in three hours, including thirty minutes for the final conference. Before the campaigns of 1940 and 1941, all officers and NCOs trained on map exercises to become familiar with plans. Difficulties were recognized and corrected with field experiments. "As a division commander, I conducted a map exercise every four weeks. All regimental, battalion, and primary staff members participated. I acted as director and represented the actions of the enemy."

Staff Exercises or *Command Post Exercises* train the participants in teamwork and the command and signal system of a *staff in combat*.

These are usually conducted by one side. All the staff, from commander down to drivers, participates. Command decisions are relegated to the background. The command post is set up in the field or in garrison. The director and his assistants simulate various headquarters sections, adjacent units, and subordinate units. The staff is deluged day and night with messages, intelligence summaries, rumors, adjacent unit reports, aerial photographs, prisoner interrogations, supply problems, and higher headquarters orders.

This forces the staff to quickly recognize what is important. Friction can be introduced by assigning casualties. Full military measures, ground defense plans, and activities of the headquarters commandant should be exercised. Staff exercises are conducted before major exercises or when new staffs are formed. Special exercises to test new orders of battle, supply arrangements, or tactical principles can also be executed as command post exercises.

Training Trips are war games held outdoors to train leaders in *estimates*, *decisions*, and *issuing orders*. The main emphasis is on the concise presentation of ideas. One or two sides compete on actual terrain for several days, sometimes a week or more. Multiple types of training trips exist.

A tactical training trip was a series of tactical terrain discussions. An operational training trip focuses on the command of large armies. Supply trips train leaders on the practical problems of the supply and medical services. Training trips are useful to train General Staff officers, select school instructors, gain impressions of an officer's fitness for future employment, provide training, and test proposed military operations.

The trip is preceded by a take-home problem and selected leaders need to submit their first major decisions before the start of the game. Large groups are broken up into groups of twelve with a separate director for each group. It is advisable to change directors in the middle of the exercise. Participants of training trips test plans and gain insights in how long a campaign may last.

During the war, top-level headquarters had ample opportunity to study problems of troop assembly and initial deployments in war games, map exercises, and training trips. Training trips do not proceed as a continuous game, but as a series bounds to focus on controversial problems. The situations are briefed anew at each location. Every participant is required to submit his estimate, decision, and orders. The director then determines the commanders whose solutions he will use.

The final conference of the day should announce tomorrow's situation and set a deadline for submitting decisions and orders. This shows how officers can work under pressure. When two sides play, the director alternates between locations. It may take half a day to play through the moves of one side. The final conference, conducted on suitable map boards, should last half a day.

Training trips require several days, but subject matter should not be condensed to save time. During training trips, it is not advisable to occupy all participants every evening with written problems. Visits to nearby historic sites or natural features provide relaxation and prevent the monotony of excess technical instruction. Attendance at dinner is mandatory.

Tactical walks train the participants in *commanding small units* in combat. One or two sides execute the tactical walk on actual terrain in the vicinity of the garrison or school. At schools, the tactical walk can replace the indoor game, generally once per week.

Participants train in judging terrain, developing an eye for weapons employment on terrain, making decisions in respect to space, and quickly briefing a military appreciation of given terrain. The director selects interesting terrain that supports the purpose of the exercise. The defense of a defile or the struggle for a river crossing requires that specific type of terrain. For a two-sided game, each side moves out of earshot when not briefing. A tactical walk lasts four to six hours. The final conference, of no more than thirty minutes, should offer a good view of the area.

Sand-table exercises train small units, from battalions to squads, in *tactics*. Estimates, decisions, and orders are issued, terrain is analyzed, and weapons employment and maneuver are discussed.

Notes for Directors

To direct a war game is an art. This talent cannot be developed without practice, knowledge, ability, and experience. Every game should be made as realistic as possible through the efforts of the director. The director needs to maintain control of the game no matter what decisions the commanders of the two sides make. The director must insist on concise clear-cut answers. Long-winded answers should be cut off abruptly. Speech discipline, important in actual warfare, is thus developed.

Every exercise is driven by a training purpose. It is not sufficient to designate the topic vaguely as "attack" or "defense," but specifically: "A division advancing in two columns is attacked in its flank and is temporarily compelled to defend itself." The director may diagram the mission independently of the terrain. Each situation should be simple and involve no larger scale than is absolutely necessary.

The mission of the next higher headquarters must by clear. Nothing occurs in war independent of adjacent units and higher headquarters. The situation should be kept secret before the game unless preparatory work is required of the participants. The level of a game should be one echelon higher than the headquarters conducting it. A game conducted at regimental headquarters should be at division level.

Participants should command the same size and type unit that they actually command, or the next higher one. General staff officers and division commanders are appointed without regard to rank or seniority. The disposition, composition, value, and condition of the units should be clearly spelled out. In critical situations, these conditions materially influence the commander's decision.

The terrain selected should allow the participants to make a decision. Where only one river crossing site, one reverse slope, one road, or one hill is available, the decision is already made. The director needs assistants. If the problem involves artillery or engineer-specific problems, assistants in these areas should be included. Exhaustive preparation on the part of the director and the staff lessen problems from rearing their heads during the exercise. Command post exercises require a large directing staff. The cost of the exercise repays itself, as participants take home information to train their own troops.

The director should not try to cover too much subject matter in any one exercise, no matter what type. Every veteran of World War II will concur that a detailed description of visual and auditory combat impressions is needed. Higher headquarters and adjacent units must feed impressions. The director should keep a large number of messages, telephone calls, and reports available to edit and dispatch when needed. Commanders should ask for reports from adjacent units when none are forthcoming. Every commander must have an opportunity to announce his decision. The director may require important decisions be recorded in writing.

The Value of War Games for Training

After World War I, Generaloberst von Seekt repeatedly encouraged war games as an indispensable element of training until every last unit commander was convinced of their value for training officers and men. Company commanders and their NCOs conducted sand-table exercises and training trips were conducted by all commands, including the chief of the army command, and all schools.

War games are excellent for training unit commanders of all ranks. The value of any game is directly related to the skill of the director.

Games confront commanders with large varieties of situations in quick succession. Commanders improve their grasp of tactical conditions. War games test a commander's ability to make estimates and decisions, support their decisions with concise reasoning, adhere to decisions without being stubborn, and modify them as situations change.

The necessity of giving prompt offhand answers without assistance in front of a large number of people and in the presence of superiors develops a person's confidence, bearing, and skill at extemporaneous speaking. War games are an excellent chance to test the knowledge and ability of all participants and measure qualities of temperament and character. One should not draw too many conclusions about a person after having witnessed only a single performance, but an experienced superior will always gain valuable impressions. In judging a person's fitness for the general staff, as chief of staff, or as an instructor, the impression gained in several tests during a training trip will prove sufficient. The conditions in judging a person's fitness for a command position are similar.

Continuing with the comments drawn from the postwar interviews, we find these practical guidelines for cadre umpires:

- Keep up the mystery. We normally put a couple of players in each room, as there is no reason why they should not chat—as long as it's not about the game. But don't tell them which side they are on, let alone which characters each play. We normally put players from different teams together, and preferably those operating on different parts of the map. That way there is no possibility of collusion (although no Kriegsspieler would be capable of such infamy!) and less chance that they will pick up information that will be useful to them. You can sometimes only maintain this for so long. If two players from the same side meet on the map, they should obviously be allowed to converse freely for as long as they remain together in game terms, so some relocation may be needed.
- The umpire's word should be final. I suggest you be very firm on this from the outset. As well as the players frequently not knowing the full situation, any debate about umpiring decisions will slow the game for all other players. Any discussion of this nature should be left until after the game; we habitually finish with a debrief

session over tea and biscuits. By that time, a lot more will have happened in the game, and most problems will have diffused of their own accord.

- Take all major umpiring decisions away from the players, preferably in a separate room. If you need to throw dice, do not let them witness the throw. If someone has lost a combat against the odds, you can soften the blow (to their ego) by remarking that they were unlucky, but on no account go into details of how the results were calculated.

- Do not spend much time on resolving combat. A detailed treatment may be more accurate, but will slow down the game, and not all players will even be involved in that combat. As someone pointed out earlier, when the game was originally used as a training tool, there were plenty of officers to handle the administration. They also needed to record the results in some detail so that proper lessons could be learned. We do not have a pool of officers, and are playing the game for fun, so we can cut corners. In particular, we have moved away from recording exact casualties, on the basis that it takes time, and such detailed information would not be available in the heat of battle anyway.

- Resist the temptation to call players to the umpire table too often. All players are understandably keen to loiter here, because this infrequent sight of their part of the umpire map is the most detailed view of the game they get. To prepare the map (for example, covering all those areas they cannot see) takes time, and for as long as they linger, the game is on hold and there are the other players to consider.

- Wherever you can, extend the turn length beyond the two-minute minimum. Most of the time you can work in much larger time increments if you have a general idea of the player's intentions (fifteen or twenty minutes seems to work). If the opposing forces are some way apart at the start of the game, you can move the clock even faster than that—perhaps until the first reports from patrols start coming in.

- *General Course of Play*: (The teacher may deviate any way he wants based on his own experiences and that of the players, but try to maintain realism.)

180 | Chapter 10

General Course of Play

The teacher starts by reviewing the desired outcome and writes down two key points to discuss during the AAR. The teacher assigns positions to each side after reading their mission and the commander's intent from higher without the other side hearing what these are. The teacher may hand them a piece of paper with orders and locations as well, but this is a good memory and note-taking drill. One side should defend and one side attack, another good mission is a movement to contact. Make sure each side is always out of sight of the other side with major terrain features between each side. There can also be stationary units to represent screening or units they must pass through.

1. A good way to start is to have a task force–size unit start in an assembly area somewhere on the map away from their given mission (giving them something else to worry about).
2. Gives each side time to make plans (around five minutes).
3. The teacher/umpire decides which side moves first; this side will make a move that spans from one to five minutes (time spans are up to the teacher). The first side shows the umpire all of his or her unit's moves and places unit markers or draws with a pencil the route they take. The teacher makes an estimate on how far the players can move their units. The teacher also communicates what they see before and while they are moving, while looking at the other side, and lets them know what they may be seeing and what actions they will take, if any.
4. The teacher continues this back-and-forth process (like chess, but neither side sees exactly what the other side is doing unless informed by the teacher/umpire) until it is determined that the exercise has achieved the desired outcomes.
5. If more than one player is involved on each side, the team must designate what role each player plays before the exercise begins or the teacher designates a role player for each unit. For example: There can be a battalion commander and three team commanders and a fire-support officer. On the opposing forces side, there is a reconnaissance commander, two motorized rifle company (MRC) commanders, and a fire-support officer as well as the commander.

If playing with more than one player on each side, the players can only communicate with each other as if they are on the radio, unless the players' units are collocated with each other.

6. The teacher/umpire assesses casualties/losses, damaged vehicles, and impacts of indirect fires as he tells each side what they see. Players then must react as they would in combat. For example, your lead vehicle is coming around the bend in this road and is hit by direct fire, but the fire from this hill does you no harm (it is a BMP 73mm against an M1A1 tank). The teacher does not say, "What do you do now?" as in a TDE, but lets the action play out for AAR purposes. Each player tells what his actions are as events are thrown at them by the teacher, but the teacher does not prompt them to do something, it is up to them to describe their actions.

7. The teacher then conducts an AAR emphasizing one or two main points, as has been done on all the previous exercises.

Practical Example

This is an example of the war game I use in the "Deciding under Pressure and Fast Workshop." The teacher conducts the war game using the "one-sided method" of war-gaming, meaning that he (the teacher) will play the enemy while a student plays the friendly forces. Refer to pages 98–102 of the *Maneuver Warfare Handbook* for giving of orders and starting this war game.

The teacher reads the overall scenario and assigns the students their missions, then gives them five minutes to develop their plan. The teacher then chooses a student to brief their plan to the rest of the class.

The teacher may quiz the student on the commander's intent from battalion and brigade. What is the enemy situation?

At this point, the teacher conducts a "house of cards" method of war-gaming. Once the student has briefed their COA, the teacher begins to change the situation by adding enemy forces coming off the eastern edge of the board. First, the teacher tells the student company commander, "Okay, your company is here now, and scouts to your east report an enemy mechanized company of four tanks and ten BMP-3s attacking into Centreville. What do you do?"

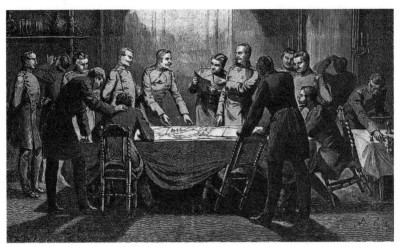

Prussian officers playing a Kriegsspiel, 1890s.

NARA

The teacher lets the student explain the disposition of forces, moving them to their new positions on the map. (The teacher estimates how far the student company commander could move his or her forces in a few minutes and places them in their new positions. If they make contact, the guide will tell the student the results.)

After the student explains his or her actions, the teacher jumps in and points out that more enemy forces, possibly a battalion, are beginning to attack the screening forces to the southeast, about ten kilometers away. Additionally, a 122mm SP battery has moved to the north side of the Muddy River and is setting up. The teacher turns to the student company commander and asks, "What now?"

The teacher allows the student commander to reposition his or her elements and justify that decision. Most students will rush their tank company to the east, usually a platoon at a time, to relieve or assist the screening forces and battery that are south of Centreville. As the student describes their orders using a colored marker, they also plot where they would move their subordinate units on the map or board. The teacher conducts an AAR focused on the outcome (reason) for engaging in the war game, as well as highlighting the two main points determined at the beginning of the AAR.

Wrap Up with a Good AAR

Before the AAR, the teacher knows two good points that he or she wants the students to emphasize as they discuss their events. This is where the learning takes place. There is plenty of literature on compiling a good AAR, so the following is just some initial food for thought:

Lesson 1: Numbers Exercise

1. References:

The Art of Facilitation worksheet; *Adaptability Handbook*, "How to Conduct an After Action Review (AAR)"; and *Raising the Bar* (chapter 3).

2. Learning Objectives:

Outcome: Familiarize students with how to conduct an effective AAR.

Measure of Effectiveness: Students gain an understanding of how to conduct a proper AAR by focusing on two key aspects of an exercise and how to link the AAR to encourage learning and ownership of learning through the art of facilitation. They will be introduced to the power of the imagination—how to use a simple exercise as a powerful teaching tool.

3. Learning/Activity 1:

- Method of instruction: art of facilitation
- Instructor to student ratio, 1:20
- Time of instruction: unspecified
- Media: classroom with white board and dry erase markers
- Reference(s): guidance to this Training Plan

4. Conduct of Lesson:

The teacher determines the class size before class begins. The teacher then designs a game in which the class picks numbers from one to nine; these numbers form a goal. For example, the goal is seventeen, but a class of twenty students randomly picks numbers one through nine. The teacher then says, "Self-organize into groups of seventeen. You have one minute!" If the class is smaller, adjust the total number sought based on the class size. The point is to make the class think through how to solve a problem with little time to do it.

When one minute has passed, the teacher orders, "Stop where you stand!" The teacher goes to each group that is formed and asks them to add up to the total number sought—in this case the number is seventeen. Did any groups get to seventeen? How many did not?

The teacher should determine two points that must be emphasized during the AAR; the teacher guides the students toward these points during the discussion (note: use command and control, and communications). How did the students organize themselves? Did anyone take charge? If so, who? How did they communicate the organizational changes or how did they organize tasks to solve the problem? Finally, the teacher should discuss the difference between the legacy method of instruction and the "Art of Facilitation" handout.

Lesson 2: Self-Organize Exercise
1. References:
Adaptability Handbook, chapters 1–2; *Maneuver Warfare Handbook*, chapter 1; and "Misinterpretation and Confusion: Can the US Army Do Mission Command?"

2. Learning Objectives:
Outcome: Students become familiar with a non-lecture technique in teaching to an outcome. Students are also exposed to another example of how to conduct an AAR.

Measure of Effectiveness: Students begin to understand how to use non-lecture exercises to teach to an outcome. Students spend 70 percent of the AAR talking about what they learned from the exercise. Students may use this technique for their own exercise on day five of the ACM.

3. Learning/Activity 3:
- Method of instruction: art of facilitation
- Instructor to student ratio, 1:20
- Time of instruction: unspecified

- Media: classroom with white board and dry erase markers
- Student reference(s): guidance to this Lesson Plan

4. Conduct of Lesson:

Students are given a limited amount of time to organize themselves into groups for further class exercises. This is another example of something legacy instructors normally do when they want to conduct group exercises. Take thirty minutes (one minute for the exercise, twenty-nine minutes for the AAR) to organize. This is another small way to encourage adaptability. The teacher first determines the size and composition of the class; for example, how many females, what rank is each student, what race, are they civilian or military, and such before giving instructions to the students. The teacher predetermines this in order to give clear guidance or an end state on what they want to be achieved at the end of the time allotted. It divides the resources equally so each group formed has to have similar or the same composition.

Once the class composition is determined, the teacher tells the students, "You now have one minute to organize yourselves into four equal groups (if there are twenty students, they will self-organize into four groups of five students each). Each group must have equal numbers of ranks, race, gender, and civilian and military. At the end of one minute, you must also appoint the junior member of that group as the leader for the remainder of the week, as well as having adopted a group name. No questions? Go!"

After one minute the teacher orders, "Stop where you stand now! Okay, let's see what we have? Did anyone get into their groups by the standards presented? Who did not?" The teacher will go to the white board and take input from the students on what they just experienced. Most students will first say, "You did not give us enough time." In response the teacher says, "Enough time for what?" Let the students try to answer. "What was the standard?" "Was there a standard?" "Did anyone take charge?" You will be amazed at the amount of discussion this simple game will generate, particularly toward the old culture.

11

Free-Play Force-on-Force Exercises

Providing practice without effective feedback accomplishes little.

—GARY KLEIN, "Team Decision Training"

Free-play force-on-force exercises offer the greatest opportunity for the development of leaders and their units, while also being the most intense in terms of time and resources. The U.S. Army has been doing free-play force-on-force exercises since the Louisiana Maneuvers in 1941, in which judges using binoculars determined casualties and battlefield effects. Later, in the 1980s, the U.S. Army moved free-play force-on-force exercises to a new level with the ones they conducted at the National Training Center, Fort Irwin, California, as well as later at Joint Readiness and Training Center (JRTC) at Fort Polk, Louisiana, and the Combined Maneuver Training Center (CMTC) at Hohenfels, Germany. With the age of simulation software and computers, war games can be a great asset to enhance decision-making and understanding of war fighting. Even more so, they can assist with determining promotions and selections if used correctly.

OPFOR

An opposing force—OPFOR (the term used in the United States and Australia) or enemy force (as it is called in Canada)—is a military unit tasked with representing an enemy, usually for training purposes in war game scenarios. The similar concept of an aggressor squadron is used by some air forces.

At a basic level, a unit might serve as an opposing force for a single scenario or it may be semi-permanently tasked to perform this role. OPFOR differs from its "opponents" in its objectives; it may be outfitted and equipped to represent a particular enemy, depending on the training environment and the availability of resources. To avoid the diplomatic ramifications of naming a real nation as a likely enemy, training scenarios often use fictionalized versions with different names but similar military characteristics to the expected real-world foes.[1] The Army emphasizes the use of OPFOR in free-play exercises: "OPFOR will be included in training events as part of scenarios developed by various training activities and units. OPFOR will also be included as part of a specified OE incorporating a range of variables appropriate to the desired training experience. OPFORs and scenarios used in Army training events will be structured for maximum free play, including an opportunity to 'win' the fight. OPFOR should be permitted within the scope of the events training objectives to capitalize on the results of blue forces (BLUFOR) tactical decisions."[2]

At higher levels, opposing forces can also coincide with "red teaming" activities. Once the Analytic Red Team develops adversary tactics, techniques, and procedures it will be the OPFOR that makes use of those TTPs in war games and exercises. The Army and the Marine Corps have pushed red teaming in the last few years, establishing an excellent course at Fort Leavenworth, Kansas, called the University of Foreign Military and Cultural Studies. This institution prepares personnel to conduct red teaming.

Defined loosely, *red teaming* is the practice of viewing a problem from an adversary or competitor's perspective. The goal of most red teams is to enhance decision making, either by specifying the adversary's preferences and strategies or by simply acting as a devil's advocate. Red teaming may be more or less structured, and a wide range of approaches exists. In the past several years, red teaming has been applied increasingly to issues of security, although the practice is potentially much broader. Business strategists, for example, can benefit from weighing possible courses of action from a competitor's point of view.[3]

While units are training at their home station, course developers and organizations develop their scenarios while creating the opposing forces from their own organizations. The Department of Military Instruction at West Point uses different cadet class levels to represent the OPFOR against higher-level classes in free-play force-on-force exercises; these exercises were implemented under Col. Casey Haskins in 2008 and continue to this day. "It was great, but tougher than previous training summers to go against a thinking enemy who had some say in how you conducted your mission," a rising senior stated during his summer training at Camp Buckner.[4]

Some dedicated opposing forces may fight using the likely enemy's doctrine, weapons, and equipment. They may wear uniforms similar to those of the likely enemy, or nondescript outfits distinctly different from U.S. uniforms. Even their vehicles may be the same or similar to those of the potential enemy force. All these measures help to enhance training realism and provide useful lessons.[5]

Blank ammunition, smoke grenades, and artillery simulators are often used by both sides in the exercise to simulate the fog of war complete with the noise and smoke of battle. A simulation system such as the Multiple Integrated Laser Engagement System (MILES), recently replaced with Simunition (proprietary non-lethal training ammunition), may be used. MILES is based on an attachment that mounts on various weapons and is zeroed to the sights of the weapon. When a blank round is fired, the system sends out a laser beam that scores "kills" or "injuries" on any soldier or vehicle in what would be the path of the weapon's projectile. These laser beams are detected by receivers on harnesses worn by the soldiers, or on the vehicles. The Simunition system fires a variety of non-lethal marking rounds through a drop-in conversion kit attached to the subject weapon.[6]

Alternatively, paintball weapons that look like real weapons, or simulation rounds such as plastic bullets may be used. Usually, controllers follow the training troops to help score additional kills, such as when a simulated grenade is thrown. They may do so with the MILES system using a controller gun. All these measures help to emphasize the importance of aimed fire, and cover. These concepts, while obvious, are often neglected in ordinary one-sided training exercises because the soldier does not suffer the consequences. Just like the other development mentioned earlier, a free-play force-on-force exercise, no matter at what level, is not complete without a good, rank-blind AAR.

Conducting a Free-Play Force-on-Force Exercise

The following is an example that many of my former soldiers know all too well. I was the chief of reconnaissance for OPFOR at the National Training Center from April 1989 to June 1990 where we conducted large-scale free-play force-on-force exercises followed by thorough AARs. I also conducted free-play exercises in both of my armor and headquarters (HHC) commands, as well as in the Reserve Officer Training Corps (ROTC). Additionally, we conducted a free-play force-on-force exercise in each week of the four-week Sergeants Leaders Course for the Baltimore Police Department.[7] The participants in these exercises always gave positive feedback on the learning that took place. Free-play force-on-force exercises accomplish one of the key objectives of ACM, which is to provide real-world examples of good and bad ways to develop and nurture adaptability to share with others through the proper AAR process.

Part 1 is an introduction of a free-play exercise. When I was the operations (OPS) officer and executive officer (XO) of the Georgetown ROTC program, we conducted many free-play exercises. The one that most of my former cadets remember was the fall semester field training exercise (FTX) that centered on a twenty-four-hour free-play force-on-force exercise. In this exercise, we did a lot of things that people said could not be done. I must add that during this time, both of my bosses (professors of military science, or PMS) were supportive and active participants as cadre, tactical officers, or observers. This example is given in five parts, an overarching scenario that includes our objectives, terrain, and scenarios, and an overview of what was done.

Part 2 offers a discussion of the blue forces' (BLUFOR) mission.
Part 3 is a discussion of the OPFOR mission.
Part 4 reviews cadre preparation.

Part 5 is a summary of what happened (we did this exercise several times over a five-year period, so I will try to highlight key points from all).

Before giving an actual example of how one exercise was conducted, you should discuss the following with the students:

- When should free-play force-on-force exercises be introduced to students—at what point in their career?
- How are these exercises critical to the development of adaptability?
- Why doesn't the U.S. military use them more?
- What do these types of exercises encourage?
- How often should they be conducted?
- Is there anything else someone wants to add?

The five parts of a free-play force-on-force exercise are:

Part 1: Introduction

Our program's objective was to develop adaptability as well as a strong foundation of competence and confidence. Emphasis was on troop leading procedures (planning and preparation), small unit tactics, and leadership. We would do this with stress and little sleep while performing under simulated combat conditions against a thinking enemy. We trained on rough terrain (Fort A. P. Hill, Virginia) which included low hills and small valleys over terrain crisscrossed by streams and swamps, cut by small roads, and heavily forested in many parts. Weather at this time of year was cool to cold at night, and included occasional rain. Both sides carried only what was dictated by standard operating procedure (SOP). Weapons included small arms with blank ammunition (I later used Simunitions with Law Enforcement organizations, and it worked better).

The scenario began with the OPFOR setting up their patrol base, simulated and manned by all our vehicles and logistics. They operated out of this site for all their missions, and it provided an aiming point for the BLUFOR. The OPFOR were then given specified missions by their "front," which included ambushes and combat patrols, as well as pulling security for their base. The mission would end if the BLUFOR found the base, and the BLUFOR was given a new mission to conduct a raid on the site, while the OPFOR would displace. From that point they were given another new mission to move to an extract point and move out of the area of operations.

At the same time, the OPFOR were given a final mission to pursue the BLUFOR. Along the route of egress to their landing zone, the BLUFOR were given another fragmentary order for a new mission to conduct an ambush on the pursuing OPFOR after a Predator drone identified them and verified their pursuit (there was no fire support available for this mission). Each phase of the exercise was bridged by an AAR where the OPFOR representative reviewed their plan, and the BLUFOR discussed what they learned (facilitated by a senior and a cadre member).

Part 2: Friendly Forces Mission

Cadets who were preparing to go to the Leader Development and Assessment Course (LDAC) at Fort Lewis, Washington, were juniors who were in their Military Science Year III (MS III). They would act as a small BLUFOR infantry platoon conducting a simulated night air assault to identify and gather intelligence on an insurgent base of operations; in the process, they would also link up with allied forces.

Their previous two-and-a-half months of classes and field training centered around tactical decision games and small unit operations (squad and platoon) with cadets rotating through leadership positions, as well as small-arms proficiency and physical training. At the start of the semester, cadets received a packet that built on the scenario they would be conducting in November at Fort A. P. Hill. All classes and field exercises built toward this end with different scenarios and varying conditions. Canned lanes and lectures were not used.

Leading up to the free-play exercise, there were constant propaganda events promoting clean competition between the BLUFOR and OPFOR. Both sides got into the spirit and spent extra time outside their requirements in our course preparing for the event, such as holding tactical seminars and rehearsing simple SOPs.

Prior to the force-on-force beginning on Saturday afternoon, cadets conducted two other exercises—a land navigation course and a leader situational exercises using the sixteen-event Leader Reaction

Course (LRC). They began the weekend with a formation at 0530 hours at Georgetown, with their own student chain of command responsible for their preparation (individual and unit) for the event. After loading all their equipment and unit supplies, the unit made the hour-and-a-half trip to Fort A. P. Hill and headed straight for the land navigation exercise. From there, all cadets moved to and conducted the LRC, while eating on the move. After the LRC, the two sides were issued their weapons and any special equipment required, and moved out to begin their first mission.

At the beginning of the free-play force-on-force exercise, the BLUFOR squads conducted air assaults at different points. Their second mission was to move and link up as a platoon and then occupy a patrol base (at night). From there, they were issued fragmentary orders (new missions) that centered around finding and observing enemy activities. Once they discovered the enemy base, the BLU-FOR received a new order to conduct a raid (which had been covered in previous TDEs and rehearsals). After completing their AAR for that mission, the new chain of command (which changed after each major mission) was ordered to move out quickly and link up at a pick-up zone (PZ) to move out of the area. Along the way, the chain of command was informed that the enemy was in hot pursuit and they were to conduct a hasty ambush to destroy them. After the AAR for this event, both sides reunited and conducted a short road march to their ground transportation for the trip home.

Part 3: Enemy Forces

This is where the chain of command above ROTC battalion levels (brigade, region, and cadet command) were shocked that these young people could conduct the missions they were given. The enemy OPFOR was composed of MS Is and IIs (freshmen and sophomores) who were organized in a small two-platoon light infantry force and given an OPORD from a higher command. They were overseen by MS IVs (seniors) and cadre (officers and NCOs).

The OPFOR chain of command even conducted their own preparation that included a company order (given by their own command) and rehearsals. The OPFOR was led by MS Is and IIs who were picked by the seniors based on their leadership potential and how well they had performed to date. The cadets saw this as based on merit and it drove them hard because many of them would get to lead fellow cadets for the first time under simulated combat conditions.

Part 4: Cadre Preparations

Prior to the start of the semester, cadre officers were expected to go over their class materials and discuss the contents of each FTX to culminate by mid-November with this exercise. Cadre also oversaw the development of the seniors who were allowed to run as much of the program as possible, including issuing OPORDs, conducting briefings, and the preparations of both sides (actual MS IVs were given tactical responsibilities for both sides early on so they could begin to work with the appropriate side).

Two weeks or so out from the exercise, the cadre conducted a rehearsal at the actual site, and a daylight walk-through of all the missions. They also tested their communications through small handheld radios to facilitate passing along observations and locations of each side to be used in the AAR. This is a key safety feature; it also facilitates the smooth communcation of information that allows the TAC observers to maintain a holistic view of the unit they are observing in the context of the larger picture. These rehearsals were preceded by map exercises to go over the checkpoints to enhance the passing of player locations. This eased the TACs' job of facilitating the AAR. Finally, to make the exercise run smoothly, the cadre reviewed the logistics plan down to the smallest detail—who, what, where, and when, both during the map exercises and the full-up rehearsals.

Finally, the cadre were operating off a timeline that reflected a cadet timeline to ensure cadet leaders were given guidance in a timely manner, as well as when the cadets were expected to backbrief their progress.

Part 5: Summary

After the first year, this became the cadets' favorite exercise. We would post lessons learned and conduct overall AARs in the classroom upon our return the week after Thanksgiving. Also, throughout the spring semester, we would continue to build off the lessons learned in the culminating fall exercise. We found that the cadets would continue to think about missions that seemed too hard to outsiders, and also we built pride in the cadets by allowing them to conduct missions considered by many others as being too hard (such as moving into and occupying a patrol base at night). This occurred time and time again when our cadets talked to cadets they knew from other programs who were doing canned STX lanes.[8]

The only snag pertained to safety. The cadre was "smoked" after doing this exercise with the cadets but would still have to ensure that the drivers of vehicles got adequate sleep before returning to Georgetown University from Fort A. P. Hill (sixty miles). The cadre also had to oversee the return of weapons to the 3rd Infantry at Fort Myers; they also had to drive and park the vehicles and turn in equipment upon their return.

What Does This All Mean?

Why was Panzer Corps Guderian (XIX Panzer Corps) able to move through the Ardennes Forest and across the Meuse on a one-page order? Because it had practiced Auftragstaktik from the time its officers were cadets. They had war-gamed this scenario several times, so they understood what they had to do when ordered to execute. War-gaming was pursued as a free-play force-on-force exercise at all levels. The enemy, as we like to say, has a vote.

Think about moving 41,000 vehicles (1,200 of which were tanks) and 300,000 soldiers through the Ardennes on three parallel roads in three days on orders that were only a half-page long!

The pace continued even as they encountered the French; German commanders were left to improvise how they were to move forward. For example, the French 5th Infantry Division (Motorized) had set up its overnight bivouac on the road to Avesnes, leaving its vehicles neatly lined up along the roadsides. At this stage, Rommel's tanks dashed right through them, firing to both sides with all guns. Within minutes the French unit disintegrated into a wave of refugees; they had been overrun literally in their sleep. But Rommel's pace did not even slow that night. When he reached Avesnes, he continued the assault pace by launching a sprint through Landrecies and on to Le Cateau. He was forced to halt there only because of ammunition and fuel shortages.

Why was Rommel successful in his bold gambit? Because he and his subordinates had war-gamed this scenario several times using a free-thinking opponent. They had conditioned themselves and were mentally prepared for a variety of courses of action that could have been driven by the enemy.

12

Combat Physical Fitness

Expanding battlespace increases ... uncertainty and ambiguity ...This is why greater autonomy at lower levels ... is necessary to overcome the fog and friction of future war.

The tasks that ordinary soldiers are being asked to perform now involve decisions which previously would have been made by officers ... they will only make the right decision if they are trained, selected, and encouraged to do so.

—DOUGLAS MacGREGOR, *Breaking the Phalanx*

One of the principles of an ACM is that "every moment of the day, every task, offers an opportunity to teach adaptability, how to think, in places you never imagined." One of the most glaring downfalls of most existing leadership programs is that they fail to treat physical training time as an opportunity to develop adaptability.

The author conducted an analysis of thirty-nine ROTC programs throughout the United States from September 2004 to May 2005 as part of the "Raising the Bar: Creating Adaptive Leaders to Deal with the Changing Face of War" study. I was asked by Col. Robert Frusha, commander of the Eastern ROTC Region to study how programs did their Army Physical Fitness Test (APFT) and if there were ways to improve it. I received physical training (PT) plans and schedules from

ROTC programs as well as other Army courses. I found that the tasks conducted in physical training are effectively addressing most of the physical readiness components.[1]

However, promoting adaptability in an ACM, as well as motor efficiency and mobility, were almost nonexistent in these programs. Analysis of a warrior-leader's combat tasks revealed that in asymmetric warfare, they would execute complex tasks in more than one plane of motion that require a high degree of mobility and coordination. Unquestionably, developing motor efficiency and mobility, alongside mental adaptability, is essential. Poorly defined fitness objectives and means of assessment exasperate this discrepancy. My study revealed that leader development programs do not consider the need to develop adaptability during their PT time. An analysis of the study includes:

- Units run too much, but they are not focusing enough on developing aerobic endurance. Running and foot marching are the only events being used to build aerobic endurance. They are not working incrementally, varying tactical foot road marches and using different weights and a variety of real or simulated equipment.
- Physical fitness events conducted in sequential order remain task-centric (such as foot marching). Physical fitness training is not structured in the context of a problem.
- Lack of weight training does not mean that unit programs are not developing muscular strength.
- Courses are very focused on those events leaders use to define their fitness objectives and assess physical fitness readiness.[2]

ROTC and Army schools' programs revealed surprising similarities:

- Cadre at these courses believe that preparation for the APFT replicates doing more of the three events. This means in preparing for the test cadets or students run four miles to do well at two miles, do multiple sets of push-ups and sit-ups in order to do well at the two-minute push-up and sit-up events during the test.
- If there was any leader development at all, it consisted of "your turn to lead PT." If it involved the student tasked to develop a

PT plan, it consisted of "replicating and perfecting what has been done" (at this point, it becomes task proficiency with cadets or students using a checklist as they go through the PT regime).

- If innovation is involved with a PT event, it is seen as exceptional, or as a "fun day" that occurs monthly or quarterly.

Specifics to Findings
The APFT is a three-event test that only assesses muscular endurance and cardio-respiratory fitness. The Army culture also narrows leader development in physical fitness to the APFT score. It has become so obsessive that at some courses, such as the ROTC Leader Development Assessment Course, the results of the APFT on day three of the thirty-two-day course usually determines (in the minds of the cadre) how well the cadet will finish.

Running: There are a number of injuries associated with running. These include a prevalence of foot pain, knee pain, and shin splints. The three primary reasons for running related injuries are:

- Poor progression
- Too little recovery between runs
- Running too hard or too long on a given run

The "Raising the Bar" study revealed that most leader-centric programs ran three days a week and foot marched once a month (for ROTC programs this became more frequent the spring semester or quarter before MS III attendance of LDAC). The distance covered on an average run was three-and-a-half miles. This means the average run, conducted at an eight-minute-per-mile pace, required twenty-nine minutes to complete. Though not examined in "Raising the Bar," research suggests that providing recovery between PT events that stress the same body parts in the same way goes a long way toward reducing injury.[3] The study reveals that the lower extremities of warrior-leaders are taking a beating in programs that adhere to the warm-up, push-up, sit-up, and run approach to PT. Too much running, especially in younger potential leaders not conditioned to the distances or frequency with which runs are executed, can lead to higher injury rates.[4]

Leader and adaptability development: Feedback from cadre and students revealed frustration with current approaches. While most agree that they get in better shape from their respective programs, most also found their programs to be rote and boring.[5]

What does it mean to develop physical mobility and agility? There are three planes in which the human body moves. In the *sagittal plane* of motion, the body is divided into right and left. Walking, nodding, and reaching overhead all constitute motion primarily in the sagittal plane. In the *transverse plane* of motion, the body is divided into upper and lower. Swinging a baseball bat, twisting open a jar, and turning the head to the right and left all replicate movement in the transverse plane. Lastly, movement occurs in the *frontal plane* of motion. In this plane, movement is divided into front and back. Common movements in the frontal plane include the side straddle hop and putting the hands on the hips.[6]

Though movement can be defined in three planes of motion, most human movement and most battlefield tasks occur across multiple planes. As a result, physical fitness programs must be more geared to this reality, and must be mobility oriented. The emphasis on Army physical fitness, which tests events (pull-ups, sit-ups, and two-mile run) that occur predominantly in the sagittal plane, detracts from more mobility-oriented physical training.

Along with FM 21-20, *Physical Fitness*, I assert that among other exercises designed to increase mobility, guerrilla and grass drills are considered some of the most challenging and functional means to train for combat-related skills. Mobility is a component of fitness that is essential in combat and cannot afford to be overlooked in the development of physical training programs.[7]

Recommendations

These recommendations pertain to both the Army and leader-centric programs, as well as to units' orders to train for adaptability along with physical fitness:

- Develop a "Combat PT Adaptability" assessment that will allow commanders the opportunity to accurately assess the physical readiness of their cadets, students, and soldiers.

- Educate leaders on the importance of adaptability in unit physical training programs. This includes formal education at all NCOES schools, the infantry officer basic course, infantry officers advanced course, CGSC, and the Army War College. A change in programs will not be realized until leaders—especially senior leaders—are educated on the topic and understand the overall benefits.
- Significantly increase the amount of leader development and collective tasks conducted in leader-centric programs. Combat PT TDE integration increases the frequency of doing collective and individual tasks during course physical training while under mental and physical stress. Again, PT can be performed in the context of a problem.
- Reduce the frequency and distances that cadets and students are running (replace with combat-loaded terrain walks avoiding trails and roads; start short at first and increase weekly—instead of monthly foot tactical road marches, conduct these marches two to three times a week).[8]

An analysis reveals that aerobic endurance has a minimal impact on the successful execution of combat tasks. Additionally, by reducing the frequency and distances being run, more time will be available to develop other physical readiness in conjunction with adaptability.[9] As a study conducted in 2012 found:

Road marches are an excellent aerobic activity. They also help develop endurance in the muscles of the lower body when soldiers carry a heavy load. Road marches offer several benefits when used as part of a fitness program. They are easy to organize, and large numbers of soldiers can participate. In addition, when done in an intelligent, systematic, and progressive manner, they produce relatively few injuries. Many soldier-related skills can be integrated into road marches. They can also help troops acclimatize to new environments. They help train leaders to develop skills in planning, preparation, and supervision and let leaders make first-hand observations of the soldiers' physical stamina. Because road marches are excellent fitness training activities, commanders should make them a regular part of their unit's PT program.[10]

ACM Combat PT

The hour or more used for PT during duty days or during an ACM-based course is just one more opportunity to develop adaptability as well as develop physical fitness.[11] Leaders must make better use of those events that build and enhance a soldier's mobility, agility, and coordination.

With ACM, emphasis in how to think through adaptability education adjustments to existing physical fitness programs requires little time and resources. The mental aspect may be taxing. Take for instance a unit that decides to do a circuit as a part of physical training. The students conduct the standard formation warm-ups, and along a three-mile run route, they stop along the road or trail at designated areas to do push-ups, pull-ups, crunches, flutter kicks, sprints, etc.

A workout of this nature improves muscular strength, aerobic and anaerobic endurance, and muscular endurance. However, the development of adaptability is lost. These tasks are physically demanding, but executed in a single plane aligning with task proficiency. A small adjustment to Combat PT of ACM integrates the development of adaptability with physical training focused on combat. In an ACM, a student leader identifies a cross-country route and at designated stations instead chooses to conduct a vertical rope climb, low crawl, zigzag rush, saddle back carry, monkey bars, broad jumps, three- to five-second rushes and a fireman's carry, all performed as fire teams. Cadre are positioned at the start and finish with stopwatches to time each team, so they can reward the winning team and work with the slower teams.[12]

There is a significant difference between these PT programs in terms of developing adaptability, physical agility, and mobility. Like the first circuit, this circuit also improves muscular endurance, aerobic and anaerobic endurance, and muscular strength. The advantage to the second circuit, however, is that it also develops adaptability, agility, and mobility—both physical and mental. Additionally, it very closely replicates many individual and small-team warrior tasks without significantly changing the PT session.[13]

Combat PT TDEs

Cadre and cadets at Georgetown ROTC from 2001–5 successfully executed all the Combat PT TDEs mentioned below several times.

Do not limit your programs or units to these TDEs. Develop the ones listed here further, or make up new TDEs.

"You're It!" TDE Uses a Squad-Level Casualty Evacuation

1. Conducted as a squad-level exercise, in this case with nine cadets per team. (In this scenario there were eight teams.)
2. You will need a lane of terrain a mile long from start to finish; hills and forests are preferred. The cadre should determine width of training lane based on variables of avenues that can be chosen to get to the objective.
3. Cadet squads are lined up in groups along a start line (in this case a wood line), and in front of each squad was placed the following materials:

   a. Poncho liner
   b. Nine rubber M16s
   c. Each cadet has arrived in PT outfit, but were told to bring LBE and rucksack with their SOP packing list, which includes a map of that area and a protractor.

4. Cadre gathers all squad leaders and reads them a fragmentary order or FRAGO: Prepare to copy. Enemy contact is not likely. Though fighting continues two miles behind you. Mission: You and your squad are to move (when you reach your squad after I read you this FRAGO, at my command "Go!") a casualty (designated by another cadre member from your squad—in this case the biggest person), with a gunshot wound to the thigh, to this grid in order to be evacuated by helicopter (actually a van) no later than (NLT) [a specified time].
5. Squad leader returns to his squad and faces the cadre running the event.
6. Once all the squad leaders face the cadre, the cadre orders, "Go!"

Game Rules and Goals:

1. Fastest team that loads casualty in van wins. We will determine what you win once all teams have arrived.

2. If you don't have your map, improvise (cadre outlines perimeters of exercise area).

3. You can use the materials in front of you and anything else in the area, but not from your cars (parked behind them, to get to PT some cadets had to drive).

4. You cannot use any motorized vehicle. You do not have to use any materials if you so choose.

5. You cannot issue your plan from this FRAGO until after I say "Go!"

6. Time begins when I say "Go!" You have only one hour after I say "Go!" to complete this exercise. If you are short of the finish and reach one hour, a cadre or cadet officer will tell you to stop and all members continue hastily to finish point.

7. After I say, "Go!" you can issue your order, but you must also treat the casualty's wound with the materials you have now. A casualty card will be given to you after I say, "Go!" Once you assess that the casualty is treated and wound bandaged correctly, tell the TAC "casualty ready." The TAC will tell you to continue if you properly treated the casualty. If you treated the casualty wrong, then the TAC will have you stand in place for five minutes, after which he will tell to continue with mission as if the casualty was treated correctly.

8. If you drop your casualty at any time after I say "Go!" your accompanying TAC will make you stay in position for two minutes, then allow you to begin again.

9. Time stops when you successfully lay the casualty in the van, and you can account for all equipment and personnel.

10. No questions allowed, now head to your squad and as soon as you get in front of them, face me.

"Three's Company" TDE Uses Team-Level Casualty Evacuation

1. Conducted as a fire team (four-man) casualty exercise. (In this case, fifteen fire teams existed.)

2. Recommended course length, no more than a mile due to the difficulty of the task.

3. Teams are lined up at a start line with LBE, M16, Kevlar, and rucksack (weight determined by cadre).

4. Teams lined up with casualty on the ground, handed a casualty card (all teams the same), must treat the casualty and evacuate them to an objective (becomes a team race).
5. First team that treats the casualty right and evacuates them to the finish line, wins.

"Take a Stroll" TDE Uses Tactical Movement

1. Conducted at squad, platoon, or company as a tactical movement across a wide spectrum of environments—dense jungle, open terrain, built-up areas, and mountainous terrain.
2. Cadre determines what load over a long distance the student can handle within the time allotted for the PT session. Roads and trails are avoided, if crossed; students must be shown how to cross a linear danger area.
3. Student leaders select movement formations based on the likelihood of enemy contact, and this impacts the rate at which a unit moves, the chain of command determines their formations and passes this down using the appropriate hand and arm signals. Cadre will pass down varying situation reports to gauge student leader reactions.
4. Student units conduct tactical movements with all mission essential equipment, to include load-bearing equipment (LCE), Kevlar helmet, rucksack, and assigned weapon.
5. The TDE lists the demanding individual tasks that support the exercise:

   a. Move tactically
   b. Move under direct fire
   c. Move over, through, or around obstacles
   d. React to indirect fire while dismounted
   e. Move as a member of a fire team
   f. Perform movement techniques during Military Operations in Urban Terrain (MOUT)

Note: The cadre or student chain of command determine how students should be familiarized or taught these tasks before or during the TDE.

"Shoot and Move" TDE Uses Move under Direct Fire at the Team Level

1. Conducted as a fire team. Students simulate moving under direct fire using those individual movement techniques a soldier employs once under direct fire from the enemy.
2. Any field or strip of land wide enough to conduct a fire team movement can be used with varying terrain. If all that is available is a flat field, obstacles can be emplaced to simulate cover.
3. The cadre may choose to show a demonstration once of "what right looks like" of the conduct of the exercise.
4. The student, who is moving as part of a team, either simulates fires in support of another team member's movement, or moves forward to the next covered and concealed position as his team moves to defeat the enemy. As the student begins to move, he must select a route that provides the best available cover and concealment without masking the fires that are covering his movement. Based on the viability of the route, the student must be prepared to:

   a. Conduct a three- to five-second rush (very good covered and concealed route)
   b. Execute a high crawl (moderately covered and concealed route)
   c. Execute low crawl (very poorly covered and concealed route)

5. This exercise is conducted while wearing Kevlar helmet, LCE, and carrying a weapon, but without the additional burden of a rucksack.
6. TDE lists demanding physical tasks:

   a. Three- to five-second rush
   b. High crawl and low crawl

   The three- to five-second rush requires a soldier to rise up from a prone firing position, rush forward to the next covered and concealed position, stop and plant both feet, then fall forward—rolling onto the non-firing side of the body. This must be done as quickly and efficiently as possible, remembering that the enemy is actively attempting to engage the individual with direct fire. The high crawl requires the soldier to keep his body off the ground, resting the weight on the forearms and lower legs. The weapon is cradled in the arms with the muzzle off the ground. The knees are kept well behind the buttocks so it stays low. The student advances forward by alternatively advancing the right elbow and left knee, then left elbow and right knee. When low crawling, the soldier keeps his body as flat and as close to the ground as possible. The weapon is carried by grasping the upper sling swivel, then allowing the handguard to rest on the forearm with the butt of the weapon on the ground. The soldier moves forward by a combination of pushing and pulling movements with the arms and legs.

"Obstacle, Up and Over" TDE Uses Moving over and around Obstacles

1. Students move as a fire team or squad over, through, or around obstacles addresses negotiating various obstacles and danger areas that are encountered when conducting a tactical movement.

2. In negotiating obstacles and danger areas, students must be prepared to execute this task while carrying all of their assigned equipment—to include rucksack.

3. As defined by the cadre, these obstacles and danger areas may be natural (streams or open areas) or man-made (walls or wire entanglements).

4. When crossing a man-made obstacle, the cadre directs checking the obstacle for booby traps, then making one of three decisions regarding negotiating the obstacle—crossing over it, cutting through it, or crossing under it. Crossing over the obstacle requires a mat or piece of material that protects the individual from the wire. If in his possession, the soldier places the mat on the wire, and then crosses by walking or falling over onto the mat. To cut through the obstacle requires a tool (i.e., wire cutters or bolt cutters) that can cut through the object impeding movement.

5. Crossing under the obstacle requires obstacles that provide some clearance. If this clearance exists, the student is instructed to slide on his back, push his weapon forward against the wire to prevent it from catching on his skin or clothing, then push with his legs

and heels while maneuvering the shoulders. This movement is almost identical to the low crawl, except it is executed on the back, not the stomach.

6. When crossing an upright man-made obstacle, the cadre directs the students to climb quickly over the top, then rolling over the peak quickly to prevent silhouetting the body.

7. When crossing an open or danger area, the cadre directs crawling (high or low crawl) up to the edge of the danger area, observing the far side carefully before crossing, then running rapidly, but quietly, across the area.

TDEs "Shoot and Move" and "Obstacle, Up and Over" lend themselves to having the student teams carry something from one point to another as part of their problem-solving exercise. In examining a task like carry, one begins to understand the importance of motor efficiency in the tasks that a soldier executes. Very often, calisthenics focus on the repetition of one muscle group (i.e., push-ups or sit-ups).

However, carrying anything requires a great deal of tasks coming together successfully. Soldiers carry many things on the battlefield—sandbags, ammunition, but most importantly, casualties. An unconscious casualty, regardless of weight, is incredibly difficult to balance and lift, especially considering the need of the "lifter" to maintain his own balance. All these things must happen to successfully pick up the casualty, but the lifter still has a responsibility to move and evade enemy fire, while evacuating the casualty. The result is a task that requires a great amount of muscular strength, anaerobic endurance, and motor efficiency.

The need for strength is obvious. The simple task of lifting a casualty may be the most physically strenuous task a soldier, Marine, or law enforcement officer is asked to perform. To successfully evacuate the casualty, while evading fire, requires anaerobic endurance, as the soldier bounds from positions of cover to protect himself and his casualty from direct fire. The need for motor efficiency has already been discussed. Once again, another example is presented where several tasks must be completed successfully to accomplish the mission.

"Sand Castle" TDE Uses Building a Fighting Position

1. Students can be in two-man teams, or a fire team.
2. Cadre will need a place where fighting positions can be dug. If sandbags are available, they should be used. The exercise also includes filling the hole back up. If not available, then the exercise can use rocks or piles of sand to fill up the sandbags. The students will then be tasked to build some type of barrier (the cadre assess that is appropriate with the time and materials they have).
3. They are required to begin construction of fighting positions and are given standard pioneer tools or use their assigned entrenching tool (e-tool).
4. To achieve a hole that is armpit deep, the average soldier must dig a hole to at least a depth of three to four feet and at least the same distance wide.
5. Additionally, the standard for frontal and overhead cover is generally achieved by the massing of sandbags.
6. To prevent compromising an individual position, leaders direct that soldiers disturb the terrain as little as possible around the position so that the natural foliage assists in camouflaging the position.
7. As a result, soldiers fill sandbags behind their positions, then carry the sandbags forward to fortify their defensive positions.
8. TDE demanding tasks: dig, carry. The primary component needed in digging is muscular endurance. Digging is characterized by repeated submaximal muscular effort that places a great demand on the biceps, abdominal muscles, shoulders, and back. Additionally, it requires a moderate amount of muscular strength, aerobic endurance, anaerobic endurance, and motor efficiency. Strength is demanded in the lifting and throwing of the dirt. Though digging looks simple, the act of digging itself stresses different parts of the body. A soldier uses his arms and abdomen to thrust the shovel into the soil, uses the back and biceps to lift the shovel from the soil, then uses the arms, back, and shoulders to throw the soil from his position. These intermittent events, executed at a high intensity, represent an anaerobic demand on the body. Aerobic endurance is required because the series of actions needed to dig, when conducted continuously, place a cardiovascular stress on the body.

Combat PT, non-TDE Events

The Obstacle Course. Conducting the obstacle course as a team competition is another excellent example of an event that builds motor fitness, enhances mobility, and can exercise other components of fitness as well. FM 21–20 states, "Success in combat may depend on a soldier's ability to perform skills like those required on the obstacle course."[14]

Foot March

1. Foot marching is the basic staple of the warrior-leader and Marine Corps. Future operations will require some form of movement by foot. Foot marches are performed by students with load bearing equipment (LBE), Kevlar helmet, individual weapon, and a rucksack with a varied load. In total, this weight may be anywhere from thirty to ninety pounds.
2. Student leaders must be prepared to perform foot marches in all environments and for long distances.
3. The foot march measures the local muscular endurance of the leg and back muscles.
   a. Additionally, because the road march is a continuous movement requiring submaximal effort, it also measures aerobic endurance.
   b. As a result, foot marching demonstrates a high demand for muscular endurance and aerobic endurance.

4. As discussed above, a soldier's load can be anywhere from thirty to ninety pounds. Lifting this load onto the soldier's back and then carrying it requires strength. It also requires motor efficiency. It is not enough that a soldier is able to get the load onto his back, but he must also be able to move efficiently with the load. This includes movements in a wide variety of environments—mountains, swamps, rolling hills, and deserts. As a result, road marching demonstrates low demands for motor efficiency and muscular strength.

Climbing

1. Cadre finds a place that students can climb. It does not have to be a cliff requiring rope and safety equipment, as well

as "certified" cadre. Climbing demonstrates a high demand for muscular strength, anaerobic strength, flexibility, and motor efficiency. When climbing, as a team, the students were often required to pull a combined weight greater than that of their body weight into an opening or up a rope (provide the tools but do not tell them how to do it). This requires great strength from the biceps and *latissimus dorsi* ("lat" muscles).

3. Because of the incredible stress placed on the muscles, soldiers are taught techniques for "locking" on a rope, and therefore, providing the arms with an often necessary break before the next pull and movement upward.

4. Warrior-leaders may be required to climb for a number of reasons:

   a. In an urban environment, soldiers are often expected to scale walls and fences, and climb into second and third story windows or balconies.

   b. In mountainous terrain, there are scenarios where soldiers are required to climb or scale cliffs.

   c. When crossing water obstacles, soldiers are required to perform a horizontal climb across rope bridges.

   d. Though in an urban environment it will not necessarily be a rope that a soldier is scaling, the intent is the same. The soldier provides maximum intensity as he thrusts upward until provided the opportunity to lock on a rope, rest on a windowsill, or rest on a new foothold. It is the movement itself that places the most stress on the muscles. Because of the intermittent nature of this movement and the fact that a soldier will often have to perform repeated or prolonged climbs (long rope), it requires a lot of anaerobic endurance.

5. Climbing is achieved by several skills coming together to perform a movement. It is the hands, feet, and arms all working together to scale an obstacle. When one does not work in unison with the others, the task is significantly more difficult and usually not successful.

6. Climbing requires a great deal of motor efficiency.

7. Flexibility allows the soldier to maximize his technique, and therefore lessen the chance of injury and reduce fatigue.

Team Sports

Sports are excellent team builders, and should be conducted at least once a week. For example, basketball requires the execution of complex motor skills to be successful. Many of the tasks required in basketball are multiplane. These tasks include rebounding, dribbling, shooting, defending, blocking, etc. Unless these specific tasks are trained, a person will not develop the skills necessary to excel on the basketball court. It is with this same mindset that military leaders must approach physical fitness training for soldiers. Ultimately, they are preparing soldiers for the complex, mobile, and fluid environment of combat. As a result, leaders must make better use of those events that build and enhance a soldier's mobility, agility, and coordination.

Combat Olympics

1. Combat Olympics includes a combination of mental and physical events.
2. This can be the most resource-intensive Combat PT session, but also one of the best at developing adaptability alongside physical attributes mentioned earlier. It easily becomes a major training event as the scope presented here, but in a leader-centric course with a hundred students, the scope can be narrowed to a few events conducted in a morning session.
3. Examples of Combat Olympics include:

   - One event consisted of a Law of Armed Conflict challenge, a Humvee pull, an obstacle course, a sniper fire land navigation event, and capture the flag.
   - 3rd ROTC Brigade Ranger Challenge: In spring 2002, I was tasked to make the ROTC nationwide Fall Ranger Challenge more realistic. The competition had consisted of teams of cadets competing in events that were individual-focused and task-centric (with the exception of the timed rope bridge). In addition, coaches and teams knew exactly what the "test" looked like, when and where they would participate in events, as well as the standards. This is not combat. The was course laid out over fifteen kilometers at Fort A. P. Hill in central Virginia amidst hills, swamps, and dense woods crisscrossed by roads

and trails. Brigade issued an OPORD set in a COIN environment. The OPORD also listed likely missions (tasks) the teams might encounter along their route. The order specified times to report at a start point, as well as reporting procedures to monitor each team's progress. Teams consisted of ten members (a squad). Each team was assigned a cadre TAC. During the conduct of the competition, teams received FRAGOs as they concluded an event on where to proceed next. Decision-making was constant throughout the day. The actual events consisted of mounted land navigation, tactical foot march, dismounted land navigation, chance contact (battle drill), obstacle course, rope bridge, an LRC, and a first-aid and litter-carry race. The competition concluded with a "commander's event" (only the brigade commander knew what this would be—one year it was a shooting event using M16 trainers, another year it was a series of sprint races with the team having to carry and perform tasks at the end of each sprint). A point system was created based on times and task performance. Events were run by committee while the RC assisted in each assessment and monitored times. During the competition, there were no administrative breaks or down times. Teams were issued three MREs to be eaten when they had an opportunity. Water was positioned along the course at each event. The event standard time to complete was eight hours forty minutes.

What Does This All Mean?

Combat PT is another chance to develop adaptability to succeed under Auftragstaktik. Combat PT in ACM and conducted according to the principles of OBT&E demonstrates how small unit leaders (officers and NCOs) lead by example in their unit physical training. ACM teachers lead by example and demonstrate ACM leader physical training performance expectations through the ways in which they structure and participate in student planned and led PT sessions. In units, NCOs plan innovative PT that helps develop adaptability to succeed under Auftragstaktik and officers participate fully in the activities the NCOs have organized.

ACM-based PT is used to reinforce fundamental skills, toughness, perseverance, and "muscle memory" under physical stress. Physically challenging land navigation problems, crew drills, and tactical foot movements all build practical understanding and ability. They also stress development of the critical leader attributes of character and resiliency.

OBT&E-based practical skill learning activities are designed to be physically challenging for students, not just limited to exertions during morning PT. Adaptive physical training events can be done at any time during the day, not just in the morning, and not just in PT uniform: periodically perform PT with students in the middle of the day, in the field, in ACUs, or with weapons and gear.

Adaptive PT events are limited only by cadre imagination and discipline to plan. They must be as well prepared and rehearsed as any other training. Cadre must physically rehearse the event and clearly understand all timings, locations, and equipment requirements. Events can be as simple as negotiating a confidence course or as complex as incorporating live fire on a range.

13

Evaluations

Proficient decision makers . . . use their experience to recognize a situation as familiar, which gives them a sense of what goals are feasible, what cues are important, [and] what to expect next.

Experienced decision makers deliberate more . . . about the nature of the situation, whereas novices deliberate more . . . about which response to select. . . . Training can be more productive by focusing on situation assessment.

—GARY KLEIN, "Strategies of Decision Making"

There is a widely held dictum that "you cannot manage what you cannot measure."[1] Resourcing decisions depend a great deal upon a degree of confidence associated with reports that describe readiness measured against a range of standards accepted as meaningful indicators of future performance. Unfortunately, those same standards can obscure the realities of military conflict and the associated impact of intangible human factors in solving complex problems.[2]

Our leadership doctrine does account for human factors and this is why performance appraisals focus on values, characteristics, and attributes subject to the judgment of an experienced rater. Though the officer evaluation report or OER attempts to make judgments of character in the absolute (yes/no), the noncommissioned officer evaluation report or NCOER is less demanding; in practice, raters rarely are so finite in their appraisal. The same is true when assessing training and education.

Assessment is and should be a leader's judgment of performance weighed against their knowledge and experience. The experiential basis for such judgments reveals the dangerously misleading and false dichotomy between subjective and objective assessment in this context. Training evaluations have their place but should never assume a degree of prominence greater than a commander's assessment. An approach that bridges this gap would seek both subjective accuracy/validity and objective precision/reliability.

When focused on naive objectivity (assessments that could be done by a novice), measures of performance can pervert the purpose of training and education. Without the currency and relevance that novices are incapable of considering, mere verifiability and repeatability are insufficient to assure the soldier's development. Evaluations tend to focus on specific aspects of the nominal "training and education" process rather than on the results.

Trainers, whose own performance evaluation depend upon these rating factors, begin to operate so as to maximize the arbitrarily observable aspects of their instruction and minimize the role of their own expertise as a soldier and instructor. On the other hand, if instructors focus on the outcomes in their students' learning, their experience as a soldier and instructor becomes a critical foundation for good training.

Consider establishing a range of performance that uses the standard as the baseline for performance while extending upward toward full achievement of the desired outcome. This would provide a measure of effectiveness that works as well for the training audience as for the organization providing the training. It does not diminish or negate the essential Army requirement to achieve a minimal level of performance ("the Army standard") but it does raise expectations for increasing levels of qualitatively improved performance. As a baseline, for example, a standard could be used to assess improvement or capacity for improvement instead of a particular level of performance, however achieved at a particular moment in time. Capacity for improvement reflects the intangible personal performance attributes that the Army, Marines, and law enforcement find valuable.

Leader Evaluation System (LES)

The ACM curriculum and Leader Evaluation System (LES) will use two criteria to judge whether students did well: the timeliness of their decisions, and their own justification for them. The first criterion will impress on the student the need to act quickly, while the second requires the student to reflect on their actions and gain insights into their own thought process. Since the student has to justify their decision in their own mind before implementing it, imprudent decisions and rash actions will be less likely.

During their coursework, the students' decisions are relatively unimportant. The emphasis is on the effect of the students' actions overall, not on the method they may have chosen to arrive at them. The ACM will create a learning environment in which there will be no formulas or rigid processes to achieve optimum solutions. This environment will solicit creative solutions.

The LES is based on the idea that undue criticism after the fact, of any student—who will be in a confused, dangerous, and high-pressure situation and who has the best command of immediate information—is unwarranted.

Anything beyond a constructive critique will only destroy the student leader's willingness to act and might even lead them to withhold adverse information or provide falsely optimistic reports simply to avoid a less-than-perfect evaluation report. An ACM will recognize there is little in adaptability that is systematic and will make allowance for it.

The heart and soul of Auftragstaktik—a theme that runs throughout an ACM—will be the desired result, not the way the result is achieved. Teachers of adaptability should reject any attempt to control the type of action initiated during a mission as it is counterproductive to do so. The ACM should instead concentrate on instilling in students the will to act as they deem appropriate in their situations to attain a desired result. The LES should be a "double loop" system defined as "the knowledge of several different perspectives that forces the organization to clarify differences in assumptions across frameworks, rather than implicitly assuming a given set."[3] Whether on an exam employing TDEs, or during training, teachers should use multiple tools to give students continual and detailed evaluations that will allow the cadet to evolve, improve, and prepare for the graded field evaluations. During these tests, students will be evaluated on their ability to lead, demonstrate adaptability, and make intuitive decisions under varied conditions. Evaluation criteria should consider the following questions:

- First and foremost, did the student make a decision? Was it timely?
- Did the student effectively communicate it to subordinates?
- Was the decision made in support of the commander's intent (long-term contract), and mission (short-term contract)?
- If not, was the student's solution based on changing conditions that made it a viable decision, even if it violated the original mission order, but nevertheless supported the commander's intent?

"Guiding actions" intertwine with the Army's core values when evaluating a student's leadership performance and potential. The stakes are high, as retired Lt. Gen. Walt Ulmer described it: "The Army needs to broaden its understanding of successful leadership from one that focuses almost entirely upon mission accomplishment; to one that includes long-term organizational health of the unit and its personnel alongside of mission accomplishment."[4]

In other words, the Army's current culture evaluates successful performance by determining whether a leader accomplished a specific mission; the focus is on the "bottom line." However, this method is shortsighted, and in the current leader paradigm it can produce "performers" rather than leaders. Measuring a student's potential, on the other hand, allows for an assessment that incorporates a student's ability to develop teams as well as subordinates, even in a classroom setting. This method can also include measurements of a student's loyalty, initiative, and risk-taking aptitude.

To create problems that will properly demonstrate a student's potential, scenarios must be used that encourage students in subordinate roles to take risks (that they can justify and explain) in accomplishing their mission. In the AAR, the student commander should praise good performance of his peers (in the subordinate role), while accepting responsibility for their failure. The idea is that students will eventually emulate this behavior over time and begin to realize their potential.[5]

Assessments should involve more than just cadre and student observations of a student's level of adaptability. Performance evaluations also occur in the classroom. However, this does not imply that the use of traditional, Industrial Age testing techniques should be continued, because those techniques only reinforce rote memorization. These negative techniques include "true or false" questioning, "fill in the blank," or "multiple choice" examinations.

However, cadre likes to save time by using these linear evaluation techniques. These techniques also provide quick feedback to the tested student, the cadre, and the chain of command when utilized for reports and PowerPoint slides. But these teaching techniques cheat the student because they focus on short-term results.

Since "knowledge" and "social judgment" are also part of the traits of adaptability, continual observations and evaluations of how a leader chooses to communicate decisions to subordinates or to inform the chain of command must occur. If leaders do not communicate decisions effectively to their subordinates or units, it makes no difference whether they are decisive or timely. This is why it is important that evaluations assess communication abilities, whether written or oral.

Thus, teachers should use essay-based evaluations in the classroom. The use of essays requires that teachers have a firm grasp of the English language (spelling, grammar, and style); essays take more time to evaluate, but in the end they provide a much deeper sense of the students' educational progress.

What should teachers look for in evaluating student leaders? A teacher should look for leadership failures that suggest weak character. For instance, if a student changes his original decision in order to go along with the instructor-recommended solution, or if the student stays with a poor or out-of-date decision from higher authority simply because that is what "higher" told him to do, teachers should mark these traits as a failure. The worst thing a student can do is to hesitate or make no decision at all.

Evaluations can be used to award and highlight superior performance. They are also used to serve as a record on which TAs might evaluate an individual's ability to become a leader. An effective organization should further reward students when they exceed the standards, while enforcing the standards themselves. Failure in timely enforcement of the standards that all students are required to follow degrades the effectiveness of the organization; in warfare, it undermines trust and endangers soldiers' lives.

As stated above, inability to make *any* decision is a failure in a scenario using any tool. Another sign of failure in a scenario would be if a student changes their decision simply because the instructor challenged the student's choice during the course of briefing. If that occurs, the student is demonstrating a common failing—the wish to go along with the instructor. Even if the teacher believes that the student's decision is a sound one, he may challenge or test the student's character in the face of adversity to see how much confidence the student has in their decision-making ability.

In the end, TDEs, case method, and the other tools listed earlier in the book provide the best educational approaches for building a student's strength of character as well as cognitive abilities. But as we will see in the next section, using a variety of tools is fine as long as the teacher grasps and has a thorough understanding of OBT&E and ACM. The need to develop teaching tools that help develop adaptability while steering clear of tools that involve more time and resources in procurement and operations or that distract from the main objective is the primary goal. Maj. Frank Brewster describes his use of TDEs:

> The TDE provides an effective mechanism for developing individual ability to make decisions under physical and mental stress. While TDEs are not the perfect substitute for actual training and experience, they do serve to sharpen individual intuitive decision-making ability. In today's military, constrained as it is by shrinking budgets, personnel shortages, and numerous missions, TDEs provide leaders at all levels an opportunity to hone decision-making skills during scenarios that place the student-leader in stressful situations. Recently, there has been a resurgence of the TDE variety of war games. Experiences in peace operations have rekindled interest in the merits of using these role-playing scenarios to develop decision-making skills.[6]

The How-To for Evaluations

The DMI at West Point perhaps had the toughest transition in getting OBT&E doctrine and ACM methodology accredited in the evaluation of cadets. This stands in stark contrast to previous evaluations at the DMI prior to Col. Casey Haskins taking over as director in May 2008. The OBT&E-based POI for the DMI was accredited in the summer of 2008 just prior to the 2008–2009 academic year at the USMA. As Maj. Mark Sonstein learned when teaching through OBT&E and ACM while at the Academy,

> When evaluating the Cadets, I often look at areas that they are not aware of. I try to design evaluations that show expertise in the training. In the past I evaluated the Cadet's knowledge of fundamentals by having them evaluate each other. While Cadets think the test is focused on them producing a tactical solution, and then fighting that solution on Follow-me, another Cadet is paired with them and writes a one page analysis of the strengths and weaknesses of their partner's solution. The evaluation is actually the critique, not the solution to the exercise. By having Cadets write a critique, it demonstrates true understanding of the concepts taught in the course, more than just producing another solution to a tactical problem. Through this evaluation I am able to more closely examine if the Cadets are working at higher levels of understanding. Here I am looking to see if they can analyze the information, as opposed to simply applying the knowledge they have gained from the course.[7]

There are several key points in this statement. Major Sonstein decided his evaluation of cadet performance would be based on the critiques from other cadets as well as his use of problem-solving exams. Again, cadre or teachers are given outcomes guided by MOEs that are determined before the beginning of the course or class; these are linked and support higher-level outcomes. It is up to the teacher to use whatever methods they think are useful to obtain these outcomes. Teachers are held accountable for producing the outcomes, and in return they are given the latitude to determine how their students will achieve those outcomes. The resulting elevation of morale and confidence of both cadre and students in using OBT&E is apparent in all the courses that I have been involved with. And it is not because it is easier; it is, in fact, in spite of the increased level of difficulty.

Major Sonstein also talked about the different tools he uses to evaluate student abilities and their progress of learning while achieving outcomes:

> Through the use of technology we are able to extend the learning and understanding of the lessons taught in the classroom. By using value-added learning equipment such as "Follow Me," a computer based video game that allows a Cadet to simulate being a platoon leader in combat, and the Engagement Skills Trainer (EST), a direct fire weapons simulation system, available at the WARCEN we are able to actively examine the cadet courses of action. Nearly all TDEs taught in the classroom are available to be executed on Follow-me, allowing the Cadets to act as a Platoon Leader and face an enemy. The key to using technology for this is that it reduces the resource requirements that would normally be necessary for a Cadets to control a platoon of soldiers, while providing useful feedback about their planning process.[8]

Evaluating in an OBT&E environment is not simple; it takes diligent work and preparation, beginning with the creation (or updating) of outcomes and MOEs by the cadre, and approved by all cadre that support higher outcomes. Then you have to calibrate the types of tests you are giving by the cadre to determine if they support your outcomes. Problem-based exams take time to grade as well, but as Dr. Robert Bjork stated, such exams are more than simply evaluations—they provide another opportunity to learn. After the cadre proofs the exams by taking them in practice, corrections are made, and the the exams are ready for students. After two years of teaching using ACM under OBT&E, Major Sonstein found:

> The key outcome that we are trying to reach is producing Cadets that can make decisions in an environment of ambiguity. We use

tactics to teach this, but it can be done in every learning environment. Cadets are presented exercises that do not contain all the information they need to make an accurate decision, and forced to develop a course of action, or answer, within a limit amount of time. This limited time and information produces the uncertainty that we want, and forces the Cadets to make a best effort decision.

By placing Cadets in an environment where they must make decisions, based on limited information and time, we are able to produce stressful situations. This helps us determine how Cadets can react to future stressors, in ambiguous environments. Additionally we have the Cadets brief their solutions to classmates, this test the Cadet's abilities to effectively communicate their plan to others, as well as evaluating the Cadets ability to stand by their decision when faced with differing opinions.[9]

What Now?

In the end, scenario-based learning provides an educational approach that builds strength of character. Past curricula that dealt with leader development used process and task training to dictate to potential officers *what* to think. Today, several courses in the Army reveal that the foundation of an effective future officer corps must begin early, and that to create leaders who are adaptable, fledgling officers need to know *how* to think in order to develop the necessary operational intuition.

The ACM holds to the idea that every moment and event offers an opportunity to develop adaptability. Every action taken by a student in the classroom or in the field is important to the process of inculcating a preference for solutions. If a student errs while acting in good faith, they should not suffer anything more than corrective mentoring. Constructive critiques of solutions are the norm in an ACM, but more important in this model are the results of a student's action, and the reasons for taking that action. Once implemented by the ACM, this approach will spread throughout the Army culture.

The role of mentoring and 360-degree assessments should be used to teach students that their future actions will make a positive contribution to their unit's success, no matter what the mission. ACM teachers will also place an emphasis on ensuring that students gain and maintain an instinctive willingness to act. In numerous AAR and mentoring sessions—during and after a variety of scenarios under a wide array of conditions—the teacher should analyze why a student acted as they did and determine the effect the student's action had on the overall operation. Establishing a blend of instructional technologies is critical to promoting growth in cognitive and emotional skills, and consequently knowledge development.

Current Army instructional approaches lack opportunities for experiencing the emotional trauma of failing within a safe environment—something that is needed to promote maturity. The ACM permits building richer and deeper understanding of the self and alternative worldviews, an understanding that will enrich one's own concept of self. The Army's highly technical war fighting capabilities and its mission to fight in a variety of uncertain and complex environments in the twenty-first century demand that emphasis be placed squarely on growing by "learning to learn" from the outset, and not merely cataloging information without the power to employ reason and intuition to make informed decisions.

14

Army Reconnaissance Course (ARC):
What Right Looks Like

The purpose of the Army Reconnaissance Course is to prepare commissioned officers and noncommissioned officers (NCOs) to perform effectively as leaders of recon platoons in the modular force. This is achieved through developing the fundamental tactical and technical skills and adaptive leader qualities needed to face current and future operations across the spectrum of conflict. Recon skills and leader attributes transcend the type of parent organization or platform. Leaders must be well grounded in fundamentals that allow them to adapt quickly to the operational circumstances that dictate why a particular type of brigade combat team (BCT), such as infantry, heavy, or Stryker, has been deployed.

—ROBERT C. PERRY AND KEVIN McENERY

C ol. J. W. Thurman, then chief of Armored Cavalry Tactics, developed the Scout Platoon Leaders Course (SPLC) to provide armor lieutenants the skills required to conduct successful reconnaissance and security operations in 1986.[1] The course continued to evolve over time and was opened to noncommissioned officers and combat support branches to identify the contribution that all ranks were bringing to the reconnaissance force. The course was later renamed the Scout Leaders Course (SLC). The SLC focused almost exclusively on the science of reconnaissance (evaluation of routes and obstacles, demolitions, and intelligence preparation of the battlefield [IPB]) with little development of the intangibles that lead to adaptability in soldiers in a command climate of Auftragstaktik.

The Armor School understood that there were shortcomings with the old model and in 2008–2009 elected to restructure the course focused on current needs identified from the force as well as the latest in learning theory. In 2009 the original model of SLC was retired, and it transitioned to the Army Reconnaissance Course (ARC). With the need to continue training reconnaissance leaders, TRADOC directed the development of a course that focused on developing confident and agile reconnaissance leaders that could operate in unpredictable combat environments within their commanders intent.[2]

The ARC led the way when it transitioned from the input, or Industrial Age, approach to training to outcomes-based training and education as discussed earlier. OBT&E would be renamed Adaptive Soldier Leader Training and Education (ASLT&E) in 2011, but the methodology has stayed the same. Mainly, ARC builds and evolves the traits of adaptability and independence demanded under a culture of Auftragstaktik.

Students conducting reconnaissance during the Army Reconnaissance Course at Fort Benning, Georgia.

Author's collection

Traditional methods teach soldiers and leaders how to apply approved doctrinal solutions to specific tasks. The previous SLC taught 230 individual leader tasks for 150 supported collective tasks (what units do) using 123 PowerPoint presentations over thirty-one days with only four of those in the field. Even the field problem was a series of "canned" situational training exercise lanes. The instructors were strictly told what to teach, when to teach, and how to teach the students, with evaluations consisting of true and false and multiple-choice tests, as well as canned school solution problems. The student simply had to follow a checklist, while the instructor evaluated the student from the same checklist. A student was required to score a 70 percent of approved solutions on each event to receive a "go" or pass for each test, as well as the course overall. The Army finally came around to realizing these deficiencies, and slowly began to do something about it in the way it developed its leaders and soldiers.[3]

As detailed in Chapter 6, the problem is that the traditional knowledge-based rote learning is no longer sufficient to produce the kind of adaptive soldiers the Army needs to confront today's complex challenges. Teaching along the lines of traditional methods, forces instructors to present, direct, and instruct, rather than teach, coach, and develop. OBT&E approach teaches soldiers how to frame and solve problems, focusing on the result rather than the methods. OBT&E simultaneously equips leaders with the fundamental skills and builds expertise in the ARC intangibles (critical thinking, judgment, problem-solving, initiative, agility, adaptability, and confidence). OBT&E is an integrated approach to planning, managing, and developing training, education, and self. The ARC course now follows this mindset.

The ARC student is an Army staff sergeant, sergeant first-class, first lieutenant or second lieutenant coming out of Armor Basic Course or assigned to a reconnaissance formation. Assignment is immaterial to the soldier's military occupational specialty. ARC student classes are predominately composed of Army personnel but also have students from the Marine Corps and international militaries. The ARC is a twenty-seven-day course divided into three training blocks. This consists of seventeen days in the field, eight days in the classroom, and two administration days. The content is not what is important, but how it is presented and in what context. Finally, the process by which students are evaluated is critical to the outcomes produced by the course.

The student body within ARC is varied; NCOs and officers intermix in small groups, providing the opportunity for insightful discussion. The OBT&E approach encourages student collaboration and teamwork during training. The emphasis on collaboration and teamwork creates an environment in which students understand the importance of delegation and trust in subordinates, which is vital for successful reconnaissance missions. They also see the strengths and weaknesses of their students or subordinates, points to strengthen and work on.

Those serving as cadre have to be a graduate of ARC in order to teach there. Then they still go through a strenuous validation by current cadre on how to teach and mentor under OBT&E (or ASLT&E) doctrine. Before a new cadre member is allowed to teach and mentor, he must demonstrate proficiency in each phase of the ARC course. Course sizes range from thirty-five to forty students per class in order to achieve a one to six ratio of cadre to students and in some events one to three ratios, which allows more interface and peer-to-peer learning.

The course is divided into three "blocks" or phases. Block I of the ARC focuses on individual competencies required for the reconnaissance leader. It covers land navigation, analysis of terrain, and introduction to the capabilities and limitations of different types of reconnaissance formations. Block I concludes with Operation Bushmaster, a four-day field problem in which students apply their understanding of land navigation, terrain, and weather to individual and team dismounted movements.

Block II of ARC training introduces students to area reconnaissance operations and observations, post establishment. Students gain technical training on surveillance target acquisition, night observation sensors, and the employment of communication systems including high-frequency tactical communication. Block II concludes with Operation Goldeneye, a four-day field exercise in which students conduct a platoon area reconnaissance of an urban environment.

Finally, Block III training focuses on execution of zone reconnaissance and security operations. Block III of ARC training also educates students on integration of additional assets, including air and ground integration and indirect fire planning in support of reconnaissance operations. Block III, and the course, culminates in a four-day field exercise, Operation Blackjack, in which the students conduct a platoon dismounted and mounted zone reconnaissance and security operation.

ARC graduates return to the force possessing several clearly identifiable talents required of junior reconnaissance leaders. They exhibit higher-level application of the fundamental skills in land navigation, reporting, assessing terrain, and assessing enemy and friendly capabilities. Graduates now have greater understanding of their commanders' informational needs and can communicate observations that are relevant to commanders' decision-making needs. Graduates are able to plan and execute operations without compromise through their abilities to anticipate enemy contact, anticipate the consequences of their tactical decisions, and apply assets to mitigate risks.

The student must demonstrate mastery of each outcome in each phase to move on to the next phase. The ARC outcomes are the skills and attributes that distinguish an ARC graduate from other soldiers and leaders. The outcomes below each have specific associated performance measures used in formal student counseling and assessments:

- Observably higher fundamental reconnaissance skills—land navigation, communications and reporting, and tactical analysis
- Better understanding of higher commanders' information requirements and how to find and communicate information
- Better planning and execution without mission compromise or loss of freedom of action
- Competence with employment of organic and attached support assets—air, ground, and technical
- Confidence in mission-relevant judgment, problem-solving, anticipation, initiative, and risk management

To increase student desire for lifelong learning, ARC students conduct independent research and self-development outside the classroom. Instructors introduce students to the professional forum maneuver net, and the students contribute their thoughts on several professional reading assignments. ARC students train in a variety of learning environments, including the classroom, the field, and the battlefield simulation program, "Virtual Battlespace 2" (VBS2). Because they have been exposed to a variety of training environments, the students develop the insight that allows them to continue their own development as leaders, as well as the development of their soldiers across training modalities.

Accountability and Adaptability

Before any student attends a course, he must meet criteria outlined in Army regulations.[4] The prospective student's commander is responsible for ensuring that the student meets these criteria. Under the old training methods, this was taken lightly all too often. The result was that most, if not all, students attending courses (with the exception of the Ranger School and the Special Force Q-Course), had to perform additional familiarization training or retraining on subjects that students should already have known how to do. This particularly applies to physical fitness. Students often showed up physically unprepared to successfully complete a particular course; someone from their unit signed a document saying they met Army physical fitness standards.[5]

Students are required by Army regulation to show up to their course in the physical condition that complies with U.S. Army standards as they apply to the student's height and weight. Yet, much valuable time is allocated to testing and validating these standards, normally at the very beginning of the course. Why is this so? If the Army is built on trust and a leader's word that these standards were checked and verified before the student left his or her last unit, why do they have to be checked again immediately upon arrival at the new course?

In a course or unit under Auftragstaktik, the student is held accountable for showing up prepared for that course so there is a smooth or seamless transition from one duty to the new duties—that is professionalism. The ARC is a physically and mentally demanding course, and students know they have to show up in combat condition, as well as knowing certain tasks that serve as the baseline for ARC missions. The ARC cadre are not going to retest or familiarize students with knowledge they should already possess or tasks they should know before they attend

ARC. Holding the students accountable for a baseline of knowledge allows the cadre to move to the next level of learning and maximize their limited time for more new learning as opposed to relearning or retesting. As Capt. Robert C. Perry and Kevin McEnery point out in their 2009 article, "Army Reconnaissance Course: Defining the Aim Point for Reconnaissance Leader Training": "The ARC is not an 'introduction to recon' course. . . . The ARC course schedule does not allocate time for re-teaching doctrinal reconnaissance information or refreshing baseline task standards already achieved in OES/NCOES courses."[6]

With this in mind, the ARC targets a student's character and accountability through the ambiguous design of missions. All orders that students are issued are written under the context of a reconnaissance push framework. This flexibility in the order provides students numerous opportunities to develop fundamentally sound courses of action, rather than scripted checklists. Student plans create conditions in which the students must operate, and they are accountable for adapting to those conditions. For example, a student must determine his own recovery and resupply plans. When poor planning leads to his platoon's inability to accomplish a reconnaissance mission, the leadership of that platoon is accountable for the platoon's actions.

Students do not receive packing lists for field operations. They are briefed by a fragmentary order on the type of mission and the expected duration of the field problem. The students must then assess weather forecasts and demonstrate their capabilities and limitations to develop a packing list feasible to accomplish the upcoming mission. With supervision from the cadre to ensure safety, the students' decisions on what to pack or not to pack lead to conditions under which the students operate.

During dismounted operations, for example, a student's desire to pack additional items may decrease their ability to maneuver for long durations. The improved outer tactical vest, the advanced combat helmet, eye protection, and gloves are essential for both the soldier in a combat environment and for the ARC soldier. Additionally, the soldier must use his professional judgment to arrange his ammunition and additional equipment to best accomplish his mission.

Accountability and responsibility at ARC occurs in every aspect of the course. The course development and evaluation leads to more adaptive personnel. This is carried over into physical fitness as well. ARC physical fitness events require problem-solving abilities as well as physical endurance. During one physical training event, for example, the students divide into teams of four or five students and are provided a map with three sets of points in a circular pattern. Red points, set along the ring closest to the start location, are worth five points each. White points, which are mid-distance from the start point, are worth ten points each. The third ring of blue points is set the farthest away from the start location, and each blue point is worth fifteen points.

Teams have five minutes to plan their routes and forty-five minutes to execute the course. Students are instructed to return before time expires with the most points they can accumulate; the route and points they run are based solely on the teams' decisions. During the event, the cadre is able to determine not only a student's overall level of fitness, but also, more importantly, how students conceptually solve problems. Students demonstrate how they are assessing their own abilities and the abilities of their teams to accomplish the mission. Yes, the students do run for forty-five minutes and conduct a physical fitness event, but the students' ability to problem solve, demonstrate land navigation skills, and persevere under physical and mental pressure builds a more comprehensively fit soldier.

Operation Bushmaster, Days Two through Six

The Army's standard land navigation training usually includes tasks, conditions, and standards. For example:

Task: Navigate from one point on the ground to another point while dismounted at night.

Conditions: During hours of darkness, on a land navigation course, and provided with a lensatic compass.

Standards: Locate two out of a possible three stakes by using dead-reckoning techniques, record the identification number at each stake, complete all performance measures within the specified time (two hours).

The input or Industrial Age land navigation exercise to which leaders and soldiers are accustomed generally fits into the task, conditions, and standards formula described above. There is a pre-test to prove the student can orient the map to the compass, convert G-M angle, plot an eight-digit point on a map using a protractor, identify terrain features on a map, and perform resection, modified resection, and intersection problems as well. Then the student is sent out to establish their pace count. They must locate four out of five designated points during the day and two out of three at night to receive a "go."

The problem is that soldiers often stare at a compass and walk on an azimuth as best they can for fear of getting off course. Once complete, the soldier is stamped approved at land navigation and everyone goes home. It is of no great concern to the instructors how they got to the points. They could've stumbled upon the stake, cheated by using roads, or some other method—as long as they did not get caught.

The cadre are often consumed with running the exercise instead of being able to walk with the students. Cadre success is characterized as all students completing the course with a "go" grade having met the minimum standard, while bringing everyone back to home base without any serious safety incidents or losing sensitive items (assuming students performed the course with weapons and combat equipment). The unintended consequence is that we teach a student that he can't train land navigation without owning the approved post land navigation course, or that training in itself is a risk to one's career.

What has he learned about himself, the capabilities of his equipment, and how terrain affects movement/maneuver? And what has he learned about himself?

He can pass a test.

If you replace this with OBT&E and you have terrain mastery in the ARC—Operation Bushmaster (three days) looks like this:

Mission: Achieve terrain mastery

Purpose: Develop intangible skills and confidence in all aspects of land navigation

Method: Four-day exercise in mounted and dismounted land navigation in which students are given the general guidance and tactical problems, are coached by cadre, and employ peer-to-peer learning to frame and solve these problems. They are taught how to use new tools, such as: stars, a watch, shadows, D-Street, and route planning—

all while they evolve from being cadre-led to being cadre-assisted using peer-to-peer learning.

Outcomes: Student demonstrates a higher level of fundamentals in land navigation and increased confidence and leadership.

A scout staring at a Force XXI Battle Command Brigade and Below (FBCB2)[7] friendly (blue) forces tracker, or a compass is not doing much reconnaissance, and a scout who cannot plan a route that avoids decisive engagement and who doesn't use the terrain to their advantage is useless.

ARC begins with dismounted reconnaissance fundamentals. At the same time, the ARC attempts to get at higher fundamental skills as demanded by Auftragstaktik.

As mentioned earlier, Operation Bushmaster is preceded the day before with the packing list problem. Students are not told what to pack, but are instructed to pack a thirty-five-pound ruck that will sustain them for up to ninety-six hours. The student must apply what they know about themself, but they should also conduct research to determine weather conditions or other factors that might influence what to pack.

Once at the training site, the cadre takes the students to some location and tells them they have five minutes to self-locate. Real learning continues with, "Where are they" without being told start points, or "You are here, and here are the points you need to find."

Now the true test is if they can apply resection, modified resection, and intersection to determine where they are in the world. This is often a wake-up call and a humbling experience because they have rarely had the opportunity to apply that skill other than in a classroom. The instructor now realizes that he must help them discover and learn how to apply skills, observation, and their senses to determine their location.

The cadre will stay with the small group through the duration of the exercise. Students do not come in for chow, hygiene, or sleep. Sustainment (how they are supplied with the essentials) is all on them. It is their collective problem to solve under the mentorship of a senior member of the profession. They quickly realized that humping five gallons of water all day was a really bad idea. Now they have to determine how far they can move in the time it will take before the next resupply will be needed. They also realize their own limitations with respect to continuous operations, and the value of a well-trained and cohesive team (even though it has not been together for but a few hours or a day).

How effective are they after so many hours on the move without sleep? It is on them to determine their rest cycle based on the mission context provided. This begins the process of developing the ability to assess friendly capabilities and the effects of weather and the terrain on movement and maneuver.

The ARC cadre teach them new skills, such as determining direction by the sun using the shadow-and-stick method, and drawing sketch maps; as students demonstrate proficiency in one method, they are challenged to demonstrate the ability to use another. In this way, they have the confidence and the judgment gained through three full days of practice to balance different tools to a different set of conditions, resulting in increased operational adaptability.

The skills that are developed in an individual, small unit, and dismounted context are built upon in subsequent days in the course. The student's understanding of the capabilities and limitations of their personnel and equipment in regard to sustained operations gained during Operation Bushmaster are the foundation for how they'll solve the similar, but more complex problems posed by different types of vehicles, platoon–sized operations, external assets, enemy threats, ammunition considerations, fuel, food, and so on.

Goldeneye and Blackjack

ARC imbues students with a sense of adaptability and initiative through the design of orders for Operation Goldeneye (days thirteen through seventeen) and Operation Blackjack (days twenty-two through twenty-five). Under a reconnaissance pull context, when the brigade is still developing its course of actions, limited information forces students to determine on their own what information is truly relevant to the brigade commander. Reconnaissance pull refers to the reconnaissance assets that pull the rest of the brigade through weaknesses in enemy defenses to exploit and attack an enemy vulnerability.

For example, when the students receive an order that directs them to conduct reconnaissance for the brigade focused on an enemy threat and no threat presents itself, each student must determine what additional information they should provide to assist higher headquarters to develop the plan. The student must show initiative and adaptability to make decisions when the mission variables change.

ARC trains adaptability through conducting student leadership changes during the mission. However, unlike most other U.S. Army and Marine Corps courses in which student leadership changes coincide with a pause of the operation and a new order, ARC conducts one mission order and expects each successive student leader to conduct a quality reconnaissance hand off to his peer. The oncoming student leadership has to show the adaptability and initiative to quickly analyze the current mission variables and his organization's capabilities, and then make a plan for the continuation of the operation. The ARC's approach to how and when student leadership changes improves confidence and initiative.

During the course's culminating event, Operation Blackjack, the students receive an ambiguous brigade order framed as a reconnaissance pull mission with an enemy military force moving south and a friendly brigade moving north on the attack. The ambiguity of the operations order comes from the lack of a clear timeline or well-defined enemy force. Students do not receive a timeline from higher headquarters or superiors to be on the objective or a clear enemy situation template. The lack of information forces the students to analyze their capabilities and terrain to determine when and where they need to be on the battlefield to conduct effective reconnaissance and security for higher headquarters. This method is a great forcing function to drive home critical thinking required to serve as a reconnaissance leader. The resemblance to a German-style education session on decision-making and war-gaming is remarkable.

Evaluations

ARC evaluations use the Army standard in tasks as the minimum during the various blocks, but performance in tasks is but one aspect of a student evaluations. Evaluations assess how a student is evolving and demonstrating confidence and competence. The ARC increases student communication skills through weekly self, peer, and instructor assessments. The 360-degree assessments require students to apply

236 | Chapter 14

professional judgment to their own abilities as well as to the abilities
of their peers. The subordinates of a platoon leader or platoon sergeant
do not take tests to prove their superiority. The leader's assessment of
his subordinates' actions helps to determine the strengths and weakness of his organization. ARC fosters the students' ability to articulate
intangible assets through written and oral reports.

ARC also conducts reconnaissance operations in which students
conduct debriefs of the reconnaissance to the troop, squadron, and
or brigade commanders (played by cadre members). This activity
forum provides students the opportunity to develop oral and written
communication skills. Clear and concise reports by reconnaissance
leaders, who often operate at the extremes of the brigade's boundaries, improve the overall effectiveness of the unit. During all these
missions, students are assessed by cadre and peers on how well they
communicated the order, their tactical proficiency, and their confidence. There are no check blocks; rather, there are written summaries clearly stating how the student performed in a given event. It is
clear throughout the course whether a student demonstrates reconnaissance proficiency or needs to be recycled or failed out of the
course.

Assessment of soldier attributes: During the conduct of the exercise,
instructors must be observant of the leader attributes that we are
attempting to foster including strengths and weaknesses. The criteria
are objective guidelines used to assess the leader attributes that are the
focus of this lesson. These criteria are not exclusive but each serves as a
key to the overall assessment. For example, the cadre uses these MOEs
during Operation Bushmaster to guide them in evaluating the intangibles of each student. With this in mind, here are some of the MOEs
as they apply to land navigation:

1. Problem-solving: solve problems by applying deliberate thought.

Exceeds:

- Able to integrate problem–solving, anticipation, adaptability, and
  risk management during mission planning and execution.

- Able to integrate navigation, commander's reconnaissance needs, and communicate relevant information to solve problems by applying deliberate thought during mission planning and execution.

Succeeds:

- Able to navigate and apply navigation to solve problems by applying deliberate thought during mission planning and execution.
- Able to understand commander's reconnaissance needs and apply understanding to solve problems during mission planning and execution.
- Able to communicate relevant information and apply the information to solve problems by applying deliberate thought during mission planning and execution.

Needs improvement:

- Able to navigate but unable to apply navigation to solve problems by applying deliberate thought during mission planning and execution.
- Able to understand commander's reconnaissance needs but unable to apply understanding to solve problems during mission planning and execution.
- Able to communicate relevant information but unable to apply the information to solve problems by applying deliberate thought during mission planning and execution.

2. Anticipation: foresees future requirements and conditions.

Exceeds:

- Able to integrate problem-solving, anticipation, adaptability, and risk management during mission planning and execution.
- Able to integrate navigation, commander's reconnaissance needs, and communicating relevant information to anticipate requirements and conditions during mission planning and execution.

Succeeds:

- Able to navigate and apply navigation to anticipate requirements and conditions during mission planning and execution.
- Able to understand commander's reconnaissance needs and apply understanding to anticipate requirements and conditions during mission planning and execution.
- Able to communicate relevant information and apply the information to anticipate requirements and conditions during mission planning and execution.

Needs improvement:

- Able to navigate but unable to apply navigation to anticipate requirements and conditions during mission planning and execution.
- Able to understand commander's reconnaissance needs but unable to apply understanding to anticipate requirements and conditions during mission planning and execution.
- Able to communicate relevant information but unable to apply the information to anticipate requirements and conditions during mission planning and execution.

The first thing that pops into the mind of the novice or some-one conditioned by the old checklist evaluation system is, "How do you tangibly measure with these measures of effectiveness (MOEs)?" The answer is vast experience and professionalism of the cadre allow for this approach. The ARC cadre represents senior members of the recon profession, who share hard-won experience and expertise with junior members of the profession, who will soon have the responsibility for training and leading soldiers in combat. Each day builds on skills, knowledge, and lessons learned that were developed during the previous day. The cadre has all been chosen and must pass a rigorous program to become teachers at the ARC. They have been developed to combine their experiences with the latest techniques in teaching, while understanding by the tangibles and intangibles of doctrine and how humans perform in combat.

The cadre already knows each mission that the students are undertaking. They have examined and war-gamed several ways the students can solve the problem they have been given. They also have listed all possible tasks the students may incorporate during the solving of the problem they have been given. The cadre knows how to perform each task to an Army standard. They have also done the problem they give to the students and have evaluated with other cadre the many ways to solve that given problem to succeed. This is called "calibrating the cadre." Finally, the cadre are open-minded enough to realize they also may learn from the students and discover a new way to solve a given problem.

Great courses or schools do this before a single student is ever given a problem. The cadre know each problem and each class inside and out; they know how it is tied to the outcomes, how it is measured, and what will be measured. There is no turnkey training at ARC, nor can substitutes come in, take a given lesson plan, and teach it. The cadre at the ARC represent the best of the best because they are well prepared to teach each student how to be the best reconnaissance leader.

OBT&E Institutionalized at ARC

Since the first ARC pilot program in June 2009, the OBT&E-based POI has been institutionalized. The question is, "How?" The answer is that despite resistance from TRADOC, the cadre took ownership of the program. The cadre embraced the program because they were entrusted with the program. Cadre built trust because standards were used to select the cadre, creating a brotherhood of pride in the program. While there are several hundred pages of TRADOC-generated lesson plans with all the tasks and how-to's, the development and preparation of the cadre is the key to success. The cadre are professionals who are certified to be able to guide the student to a given outcome as they are allowed the flexibility to impart knowledge of reconnaissance operations to the student as they train.

The biggest shock for most students as they arrive at ARC is that they are held accountable for what they are supposed to know on day one, based on previous courses and experiences. Additionally, they are not given prescriptive checklists regarding what they must do to pass. There is no road map that says, "Perform these exact tasks by the Army standard in order to pass." Once all military courses and schools hold students and teachers accountable and responsible, the foundation for developing for Auftragstaktik can be set, and student responses will always be along these lines: "In my life in public education, in college, and in numerous Army courses, I have never *experienced an education experience like I have at ARC. This course sets the standards for all other courses and how units should train their people for combat. I would also like to see this methodology applied to academic education."* [8] Another student added, "I have never experienced anything like I have at ARC. It is the only way to learn how to master complex tasks. ARC puts all other Army courses I have attended to shame."

These quotes are just two of the hundreds of similar feedback given by students about ARC.[9] The Army Reconnaissance Course sets the example for how to prepare leaders for Auftragstaktik.

15

J. S. Wood, the 4th Armored Division, and Mission Command

Burn 'Em! That's the last written field order this division prepares! Every order I give will be verbal, either eye-to-eye or by radio.[1]

—MAJ. GEN. EDWARD BAUTZ

After viewing his division's first written order in combat, Maj. Gen. John S. Wood, commander of the 4th Armored Division (AD), told his G3 (operations officer) not to issue any more. Wood believed the formatted, five-paragraph order taught to U.S. Army officers at the Command and General Staff College at Fort Leavenworth would only slow down his division's decision cycle in combat. The fact that Major General Wood could dispense with written orders while leading his division across France highlights the level of training, cohesion, and education that a unit would need to achieve in order to execute verbal mission orders.

The 4th Armored Division's "daring, hard-riding, fast-shooting style" was made possible through the execution of mission orders. But only by "throwing away the book," did the division accomplish the armored warfare envisioned by the writers of FM 17-100, *Armored Command Field Manual, The Armored Division.*[2]

The division was activated on 15 April 1941, at Pine Camp, New York, and stayed together and trained in the United States for thirty-two months before shipping out to England in December 1943. By that time, the division had trained in New York, Tennessee, the Desert

Training Center in California, and Camp Bowie, Texas. In July 1944, the division entered combat for the first time during Operation Cobra, the breakout from the Normandy beachhead, and from that point on led the rest of the Army across France and into Germany. The division offers valuable lessons in developing leadership.[3]

The 4th AD adapted many tenets of German maneuver warfare. The objective of maneuver warfare is to exploit firepower, mobility, and shock action through aggressive tactics and techniques. It optimizes the capacity to move, shoot, and communicate more effectively than the enemy. The 4th AD could do this because its commander and his subordinates modified or defied existing officer and unit personnel policies as they implemented an evolving doctrine. Employing the fundamentals of maneuver warfare to include a culture of mission command, the 4th AD exploited and pursued the Germans across France, and then carried out a mobile defense against a determined, well-trained, well-equipped enemy in forested terrain inhabited by an unfriendly population.

By the time the division entered combat, with none of its units bloodied, it was ready to fight. Wood had reason to feel that his division was ready to take the fight to the enemy because it had been preparing for more than three years, in snow, mountains, sand, and hard-scrabble plains. It is probable that no other outfit in our military history had trained together longer, more intensively, or in more varied terrain and weather than the 4th AD. It was ready to a fare-thee-well.[4]

As it fought, the division got better because its officers and soldiers could easily incorporate new lessons learned from the battlefield. This was the key to success. Flexibility became the division's watchword, and accepted way of doing business. Though according to its table of organization and equipment (TO&E), the division was divided into three subordinate brigade-size "combat commands," lettered A, B, and Reserve, the actions of Combat Command A (CCA) merit specific study, providing many examples of rapid and decisive decision-making, from the individual tank crew to the combat command commander. The 4th AD's offensive in Lorraine demonstrated speed, "not just speed of movement, which is important, but speed in everything."[5]

In several battles, the principles of leadership and cohesion held firm against the best the Germans had to throw at the U.S. Army. The division had to employ maneuver warfare to succeed because it faced longer-range weapons, manned by veteran German soldiers with some of the best technology of the day. The Germans had better tank sights and range-finding equipment, and larger main tank guns with more hitting power and longer ranges. Many of 4th AD's battles in France in 1944 would pit its smaller, yet well-equipped forces against determined German units, some of high quality, such as the Panzer divisions, and some of inferior quality, such as the *Volksgrenadier* divisions and the newly formed Panzer brigades (September 1944). In many cases, the division operated its combat commands over vast distances, yet the long experience operating as a team bonded them as they fought. They had trained and grown to think as a team, with a single mind.[6]

A long period of training and building cohesion enabled the division to perform at such a high level. The soldiers themselves were as confident as they should have been. One of their noted members, retired Brig. Gen. Albin F. Irzyk, remarked that, "We felt that we were destined for greatness, much the same feeling that a college football team must have when it senses the national championship."[7]

The entire division did not stay together as a team through its three years. The Army's poor policies stripped the 4th AD of many of its trained members to form the cadres of other divisions. In fairness, there was no choice: there were not enough trained personnel in the Regular Army at the beginning of the war to train the new divisions. In 1942, many members of the 4th AD were reassigned, yet a cadre of key leaders remained, allowing the division to remain effective. General Bautz described how the division overcame this: "Though many soldiers were taken away in 1942, many leaders and staff officers stayed. This cadre of individuals, particularly men like [Bruce] Clark and [Creighton] Abrams, allowed the division to retain its lessons learned. The learning and innovating did not stop as a large body of lower ranking men were pulled away to create other divisions."[8]

There were key reasons that allowed the 4th AD to remain effective despite the loss of several thousand personnel. First, the division retained

Maj. Gen. John S. Wood in eastern France, September 1944, conferring with a Frenchman about 4th Armored Division locations.

Library of Congress

its key officers. Another reason was the command atmosphere: Wood fought hard to create and sustain an atmosphere of trust during his tenure as division commander. He began training his division in a situation that was no different than any other division. His new officers, the men who would train the division for combat, and lead its men against the famed German Army, were no more than amateurs.[9]

J. S. Wood and His Officers

From the time of his youth, Wood was an individual of character and a natural leader. A graduate of the University of Arkansas, he then attended West Point, which had a strong interest in him due to his football reputation and his academic record. At the Academy, he excelled in both academics and athletics, particularly football, graduating in 1912. He became known as the professor, or "P," for taking the lead in helping tutor other students. As a Regular Army officer, Wood constantly showed his desire for independence and responsibility. In 1936, already a known advocate of maneuver warfare and a student of the writings of Charles de Gaulle, B. H. Liddell-Hart, and J. F. C. Fuller; Wood sought assignments that would give him experience.[10]

Despite the advice of friends, Wood turned down attendance at the Army War College and instead took command of the Army's only independent truck-drawn howitzer brigade, stationed in Des Moines, Iowa. It was during this assignment that Wood experimented with mechanization and mobility. In numerous exercises, Wood would use his initiative to move his howitzer brigade thousands of miles to separate firing points. He tested his unit's abilities, as well as demonstrating its mobility, not associated with artillery at the time. Despite Wood's noble efforts, he continued to be criticized by senior officers, even as he was reporting to become Patton's artillery chief in the newly formed 2nd Armored Division.[11]

Upon assuming direction of Patton's artillery in September 1939, Wood's character was once again called into question by senior officers because of his advocacy of maneuver warfare. Wood now attacked, verbally and in writing, the traditionalist views that advocated linear— or attrition—warfare. In numerous reports and articles, he stressed a familiar theme: "The motor offers one of the few hopes of securing surprise in modern war."[12]

Despite his warnings and recommendations, and the demonstration of the power of blitzkrieg as German forces overran Poland and France in 1939 and 1940, there was still resistance to an American armor force. It would fall on the shoulders of Wood to prove the value of his words with actions. At the beginning of World War II, the Regular Army had 14,000 officers and 120,000 enlisted men. Almost overnight, the officer corps expanded about sixty-fold. The war exposed Regular officers to responsibilities far beyond anything they had experienced and forced them to rely on subordinates who were essentially commissioned amateurs.

Most division commanders and their regimental commanders, who were largely prewar regulars, turned toward authoritarian, top-down methods of command. They issued detailed orders, insisted on unquestioned obedience, and used their staff officers to check on compliance. Reposing trust and confidence in a subordinate entailed the possibility that he might fail and embarrass his ambitious superiors with their eyes on one of the many commands being formed.[13]

Wood was the exception to this trend, taking the pain of creating autonomy that would allow his officers to learn from their mistakes. He won their loyalty and developed subordinate leaders not afraid to take risks in the face of German actions. Wood got the opportunity to combine the theories of maneuver warfare advocated by J. F. C. Fuller and Heinz Guderian with his own experiences when he was offered an armored division in 1942. Wood took over the division in June 1942, at Camp Pine, New York. He immediately brought with him simple, yet time-proven philosophies such as:

- Audacity (*de l'audace*)
- The indirect approach
- Direct oral orders—no details, only missions
- Movement in depth always. This allows flexibility and security of flanks.
- Disregard old ideas of flank security.
- Organization of supply (taking rations, gas, and ammunition in rolling reserve)
- Personal communication with commanders
- Never taking counsel of your fears. Never fear what they will or do, "they" being the same old bogie man—high officialdom or general opinion.
- Trusting people in rear to do their part, a trust sometimes misplaced, but not generally.[14]

It was said that "he would try anything once; he encouraged initiative."[15] With this fundamental outlook toward training, it was not surprising that many officers, such as Maj. Creighton Abrams (later Army chief of staff), and Lt. Col. Bruce C. Clarke (later NATO commander) became brilliant officers. The 4th AD did a lot of experimenting, and "Wood had ideas and was willing to give them without reserve."[16] One of these inventions was the use of the task force. At Pine Camp, the 4th Armored Division established the task force principle. One key derivative was that the building blocks of such task forces—especially the tank and armored infantry battalions—would not be permanently assigned to any higher headquarters (a combat command in an armored division), but rather tasked out to one or another such headquarters depending on the tactical situation.[17]

Wood speeded up decisions by using this ability to change task organizations to solve a particular tactical problem. From the first day of his command, Wood did his utmost to ensure that his commanders and their staffs were not focused on processes or formulas. Wood understood that over time, through constant training, officers memorized and verbalized a seemingly complex decision-making process. He was against these tidy methods of control and written prescriptions for ensuring control. He wrote, "Contrary to the practice in many other armored divisions, we had no separation into fixed or rigid combat commands. To me, the division was a reservoir of force to be applied in different combinations as circumstances indicated, and which could be changed as needed in the course of combat by a commander in close contact with the situation at the front. There is not time or place for detailed orders, limiting lines or zones, phase lines, limited objectives or other restraints."[18]

In order to create such flexibility, Wood stressed hard, realistic training. The division truly exemplified the phrase, "train as you fight." Constant maneuver training, in all conditions, enabled the commanders of companies, battalions, and the combat commands of the division to know each other as officers seldom do. The division trained on how to task organize for a particular mission, and then, on Wood's orders, reform the task forces while on the move to meet a new threat. Wood did this with no fancy briefings or lengthy rehearsals. He used the radio and face-to-face oral instructions to train his division to operate without written directives.

Speed was always on Wood's mind as he trained, not just speed of motion, but speed in everything the division executed. The training enabled the division's officers to do away with many standardized procedures that would slow down their actions, such as abiding by strict radio procedures.

For example, Wood's battalion commanders and the division command learned to recognize each other by voice—authentication by familiarization. This increased flexibility and translated into the ability of commanders to change directions more quickly, without worrying that the orders received were false. Rapid decision-making increased with operating procedures that eased the ability of commanders to make decisions. This translated into fluid tactics. When the division or its subordinate commands attacked, it was by flanking movements. The division practiced moving and attacking behind enemy lines. The spirit of such aggressive tactics infected the entire division.

Wood never let his standards drop, knowing that the Germans would never give the division a second chance. He kept his training intense and realistic. From physical fitness to collective training, there was never a break. In force-on-force battles, opposing forces fought with live .30-caliber ammunition slapping against "buttoned up" turrets. Maneuver, speed, and competence—the basic military skills—were taught and practiced over and over in varying situations.[19]

Wood exemplified the best in a senior officer. With a foundation established in the basics of soldiering and discipline, Wood created a command climate that was open to innovation. He believed loyalty was a two-way street, and continually stood up for his subordinates, especially when they followed his evolving armor doctrine). He had an intense, indeed fierce, sense of loyalty; he was ready to act as a shock absorber for all who served under him. But he had little toleration for rigidity, inflexibility, or stupidity. He could not condone them, even in his superiors; he felt his highest loyalty was to his country and the Army he served, not to any single individual, even one of superior rank.[20]

In the fall of 1942, 4th AD executed maneuvers in central Tennessee as part of Lt. Gen. Leslie McNair's methodical training plan to prepare divisions for combat. It was an opportunity for Wood to see what his subordinates could do with his premise of "I will let you decide what to do on the spot."[21] It also allowed Wood to shield them from his conservative superiors. An example of the fierce loyalty inherent in Wood's command style occurred after the division seized a bridge over the Duck River near Columbia, Tennessee. Wood went against guidance not to conduct movement at night. He seized the bridge after a surprise night march. The Second Army commander, Lt. Gen. Ben Lear, criticized the officers of the 4th AD for being too aggressive and going beyond established and risk-averse boundaries.[22]

At that time, as mentioned in the previous chapters, most officers adhered to the methods they had learned from the French army—rigid adherence to staying within designated boundaries, reporting locations, and being on time based on orders that were hours out of date and given from HQs out of touch with reality. To leave the boundaries, even to outsmart the enemy through maneuver, was breaking the rules of the game in the mind of General Lear.

Wood bore the brunt of the verbal attack, by jumping between Lear and the division's officers, then said to Lear, "You do not know what you are talking about, either as to the employment of armor or of the quality of people in my division!"[23] Such moral courage can be traced to Wood's background, which fostered independence and commitment to excellence.

Finally, it must be highlighted that while Wood enforced high standards in both competence and performance, he was not a "martinet or a 'spit-and-polish' general."[24] He enforced maintaining the proper uniform—keeping sleeves and shirts buttoned—and saluting, not merely to a higher rank, but as an informal "soldier's greeting." To Wood, discipline brought about pride, so essential in a good unit. While Wood knew discipline was important, he did not, as some leaders did, believe in "imposing your will . . . even by the martinet method."[25] Wood refused to transfer poor soldiers to other units, instead expecting his officers to train them. And as always, Wood exemplified the high standards he set by leading by example. He lived with his soldiers constantly, from the onset of his command until his departure in November 1944.

By the time the 4th AD entered combat in July 1944 in Operation Cobra, it was not only well trained, but capable of speed under the revised organization for armored divisions that followed lessons learned in early combat in North Africa. Lt. Gen. Leslie McNair, commander, Army Ground Forces, and Maj. Gen. (later Gen.) Jacob Devers, then chief of the Armored Force, created an incredibly flexible organization, styled the "Type U.S. Armored Division, Sept. 1943." The earlier division concept of 1942 had established two combat commands, lettered A and B (CCA & CCB), which allowed commanders to improvise task organizations to meet likely situations. The problem with the 1942 design was that "it was too tank heavy and lacked infantry and mechanized artillery."[26]

Later studies led the Army to create a well-balanced all-arms division, and added a third brigade-size headquarters, Combat Command Reserve (CCR).[27] Based on General McNair's goal, new divisions like the 4th AD were lean and simple, offensive in orientation, with attachments developed as necessary. Under the doctrine that had developed from the Louisiana Maneuvers and training throughout the growing Army, the corps was to be a tactical headquarters to handle a mix of infantry and armor divisions. It was the field army that allocated divisions to the corps, with combat service and service support assets when needed. Once combat began, units found it necessary to keep attached units at the division level. While other divisions kept attachments and task forces constant, the 4th Armored continued to change its mix of separate arms such as tanks, infantry, engineers, and artillery units throughout the 1944–45 campaign.[28]

When 4th AD arrived in Europe, it had nine battalions: three armor, three infantry, and three artillery, along with attached engineer, antitank, and tank destroyer units. It had a total of 11,000 officers and men. As the division broke out of Normandy in August 1944, it found that its training had given it the ability to create ad hoc units to overcome German resistance and to adapt to the extensive road network. These factors increased the speed of its advance. The 4th AD advanced on parallel routes in order to reduce the number of vehicles on a single route, thus preventing traffic jams, and hitting the Germans from many directions. It was an agility that the division had maintained in training that "kept the advance moving."[29]

The division's fighting from July 1944 to October 1944 epitomized decentralized combat while fighting toward a common goal. After their breakout from Normandy, 4th AD had to advance westward into Brittany to capture the peninsula's ports, as planned prior to D-day. Wood saw the situation had dictated new plans, as did Patton, and they recommended moving east after breaking out of Normandy and encircling German forces attempting to counterattack into the flank of the 3rd Army. Planners at Lt. Gen. Omar Bradley's 12th Army Group and at Eisenhower's Supreme Allied Forces headquarters saw no change in the situation. Orders came down from higher up: "Execute as planned!"[30]

The 4th AD assisted follow-on infantry forces in clearing Germans from the Channel ports in western France, but at the price of losing precious time in cutting off and destroying German forces that were fleeing east to the German border. During this delay in August and early September—and also because fuel priorities were going to the British attempting to break out in the northern part of the beachhead— German forces had a chance to consolidate and reinforce, offering new resistance to the 4th AD. In a reversal of what had occurred during the previous five years of the war—where well-led, cohesive German units outfought Allied units—the 4th AD fought hastily thrown together German units, over-controlled by a centralized headquarters (Hitler). In this scenario, the U.S. forces were better led, trained, more cohesive, and had higher morale due to the teamwork developed over the previous three years and the months of recent fighting in France. Despite the 4th AD's advantages, the Germans could still fight and intended to counterattack the stalled 3rd Army forces, including 4th AD, in the province of Lorraine in eastern France.

From the time the division rumbled through German lines at 945 on 29 July in the breakout from Normandy, it continually improvised with a different solution for every problem it encountered. On 30 July, after refueling their vehicles, the 4th AD was instructed by Patton to seize all four bridges over the Selune River at the town of Avranches.[31] It is important to note that Wood sent the orders to conduct this critical mission over radio. CCB would attack the town from the north, and CCA would seize the bridges. CCA formed its task forces, also by radio orders, and CCA's commander, Col. Bruce Clarke, had four separate task forces moving within an hour. Two of the bridges fell during the first assault, while the remaining two had to be seized after a prolonged battle with German SS troopers. This first encounter demonstrated how valuable the 4th AD's strenuous training had been at moving decisively, exploiting the enemy's confusion, and saving lives.[32]

The move westward into Brittany to clear German holdouts in the Channel ports diverted U.S. armor from pursuing the main German force that was retreating eastward. Wood had the foresight to point parts of the division east in anticipation of orders that would allow him to continue the pursuit. When he received approval from his corps commander Maj. Gen. Manton S. Eddy to move, the division quickly caught retreating German columns.

Lt. Col. Creighton Abrams, commander of 1–33 Armor. Abrams was the top armor leader for two generals, George S. Patton Jr. and J. S. Wood.

Library of Congress

As the 4th AD began its march toward Germany, it demonstrated more flexibility, ingenuity, and mobile firepower. The division's combat commands and task forces frequently changed configuration, based on changing tactical conditions. Wood made many of these adjustments by verbal FRAGO. He would observe the situation from the air in his small Piper Cub airplane, then land alongside a column using either a road or a field. Wood would pull the map out of his shirt, spread it, and point: "There's your boundaries, the units left, right and following us and the first, second and third objectives—let's get at it right now!" After brief details of enemy information, air and artillery support, Wood flew to the other combat commands, artillery headquarters, and to his division headquarters to brief his staff and put his concise attack order on a map and a few message-blanks. By the time the Army corps order arrived at Wood's headquarters, at least one—and sometimes all the 4th AD objectives—had been taken and Wood's combat commands were mopping up.[33]

The benefit of bottom-up decision-making and cohesion paid handsome dividends in the pursuit across France. With tanks usually in the lead, Wood's columns moved along secondary roads catching fleeing enemy units on the main road, bypassing roadblocks, and moving on. Logistical units—including maintenance teams, medics, and supplies—were mixed in with the division combat columns. It was not uncommon for logistical units to engage German units missed or left behind by the advancing combat units. During their three years of training, Wood had also ensured that the first responsibility of his logistical units was the ability to defend themselves against attack. Artillery also moved with the lead columns and was expected to keep up. Wood avoided the habit that most other division and corps commanders had developed during World War I—slowing their advance in order to wait for their artillery. In the 4th AD, whenever the lead elements needed fire support, the artillerymen would pull off the road and "hip-shoot" the fire mission.[34] Forward observers were in front in tanks or overhead in airplanes (Piper Cubs) calling for suppressive fires, pinning German units down, and hence assisting with rapid maneuver.[35]

The 4th AD had also worked out incredible cooperation with the Army Air Corps, especially the P-47 fighter-bombers of the XIX Tactical Air Command (TAC) attached to the 3rd Army. The airplanes, acting as light cavalry did in the past, screened ahead to attack targets marked by air controllers riding with the tanks or by artillery observers in their light aircraft. The commanders of Wood's task forces would use the "flying artillery" of the XIX TAC to fill the gaps when artillery was not available for immediate suppression.

The ground and air units also had developed teamwork and standard operating procedures that kept friendly fire or fratricide incidents to a minimum. The success of the fighter-bomber to the combined arms teams of the 4th AD was an obvious payoff after long months of practice. Training had led to confidence and mutual understanding by imaginative and highly competent leaders at all echelons, working with the driving spirit of their commanding general.

Despite the division's glaring success, Eisenhower decided to make them the secondary effort. By mid-September, Eisenhower's broad front policy—which diverted scarce resources to the British army's advance into Belgium and Holland—had given German forces the opportunity to regroup. Patton had also ordered attacks across the entire front of the 3rd Army throughout September, which also took away limited resources and slowed the 4th AD's rapid advance.

Dwindling resources was not the only cause of the division's stall. Its immediate headquarters, the XII Corps, had become concerned about its flanks, which helped bring the advance to a standstill. The XII Corps Commander, Major General Eddy, felt he needed to eliminate German forces bypassed by the 4th AD, so he ordered his infantry to stop supporting the division and concentrate on destroying pockets of resistance. In early September, despite being within reach of the German border, these factors, plus growing German resistance, brought the 4th AD to a standstill.[36]

By September 1944, the Germans were eager to return to the offense. The German forces arrayed against the 4th AD possessed few advantages. The Normandy breakout had cost the them some of their best units, and other strong units were sent north to fight the British and U.S. First Army. The German advantages were their superior equipment, such as the Panther and Tiger tanks, their knowledge of the terrain, and their posture on the defense. On the other hand, they were handicapped by poorly trained soldiers, units thrown together just prior to battle, and officers new to their units.[37] Although combat experienced and well educated in the art of war, turbulence handicapped the officer corps in Fifth Panzer Army and Army Group G. "One significant problem with German command and control was the constant rotation of leadership at higher levels."[38]

Despite a shortage of gasoline, Wood's division continued to defeat and repel fresh German forces and their counterattacks in mid-September. Ordered to encircle the town of Nancy and seize the high ground to the east of Arracourt, Wood was forced to divide the division into two thrusts, north and south of Nancy. During these operations, the division, particularly Clarke's CCA, provides examples of agility, initiative, and depth. CCA conducted a river crossing, a forward passage of lines, a counterattack, then an exploitation and pursuit against reinforced German units defending in channelized terrain. These operations came to a climax when the division reunited at Arracourt and fought a mobile defense against better equipped and more numerous German troops.[39]

Insights into the Future

Oddly, there was a reversal of accepted historical roles during this period. While Wood and his subordinates sped up their actions, moving quickly on verbal mission orders, the German commanders operated under an extremely centralized system. The German military culture in 1944 turned into one where, "Generally, commanders lacked flexibility to make changes and were subject to court martial if they did so without first checking with Berlin. Orders were spelled out in great detail and subordinates had to follow them to the letter."

Hitler and his headquarters in Berlin and the *Oberkommando Wehrmacht* (OKW) attempted to control the actions of units down to and even below division level, employing the most modern communications devices to keep in constant contact with the front, army groups, and army commanders. While Hitler attempted to manage two major warfighting fronts, his commanders wasted precious time waiting for permission to act. Hitler's fanaticism stifled all initiative.

The climate of fear filtered down to regimental and even battal-ion commanders. Orders once easily transmitted verbally became detailed written transmission of actions. Subordinates were then expected to follow these orders to the letter. Gone were the days of Auftragstaktik, or mission orders; commanders now copied the orders of higher headquarters, making no adjustments to them. Only a few commanders—such as Erwin Rommel, Hermann Balck, and Eric Manstein—still possessed the moral courage and character to argue with Hitler over bad decisions.[40]

Another problem with the German shift toward centralized com-mand and control was the constant rotation of commanders, not due to death in combat but the assumptions of new duties. Changes occurred at the theater, army group, army corps, and division level. Command-ers also assumed new formations just prior to executing difficult mis-sions.[41] For example, commanders of the two newly formed Panzer brigades, the 111th and 113th, had to expose themselves in combat vehicles with attacking units to motivate and ensure their orders were carried by less seasoned subordinates. As a result, both commanders were killed around Arracourt as the battle was being fought to a deci-sion. Their places were filled by commanders also new to the position and situation.[42]

As the battles around Arracourt came to an end, the 4th Armored Division had destroyed 241 German tanks and inflicted high casual-ties. After the victory at Nancy and Arracourt, the division, combat commands, and task force commanders looked east toward Germany and proposed the seizure of Saarbrücken. They continued to focus on how to defeat and destroy the enemy. The Germans had feared this, since no reserves were present to shore up the front. This exploitation was halted only by bad weather and the caution of senior U.S. com-manders at levels above the 4th AD.[43]

What We Can Learn from the 4th Armored Division?

What can the U.S. Army learn today from these events as it recov-ers from the seemingly endless insurgency campaigns in Iraq and Afghanistan? In the 1980s, the Army was recovering from Viet-nam and senior officers took lessons from the actions of the 4th AD and used them as examples in the development of the Army's new AirLand Battle doctrine. A great effort had been made in the Army's education system to ensure all officers knew and understood the Army's first maneuver doctrine, outlined in the 1982 and 1986 versions of FM 100-5, *Operations*.[44]

Lieutenants, in their first exposure to formal Army education at their officer basic course, were inculcated with the tenets of AirLand Battle doctrine—agility, initiative, depth, and synchronization. The problem was that the education and training methodologies did not evolve with the doctrine in these manuals. Additionally, the personnel system, while making small tweaks to how officers were managed—such as lengthening battalion and brigade command times to two years—still retained the legacy structure of a personnel system stuck in the Industrial Age. Later, these officers would serve as battalion executives, operations officers, and company commanders leading units in the Gulf War I, adhering to the friendly graphics vice what the actual enemy is doing, to firepower as opposed to maneuver, to rigid control as opposed to mission command. While the doctrine emphasized agility and initiative, it was countered by the term "synchronization," which emphasizes top-down control; this was a reflection of the culture of the time.

There is no excuse for the Army to adhere to this cultural bias today. We understand how we learn as people, and it is dramatically different than how we train and educate. In order to practice what Wood and his division accomplished the Army needs to flatten itself in more than name.

The operations of 4th AD exemplified how officers should practice these tenets. The division's relentless pursuit of an offensive upheld *agility*, both physically and mentally. It takes physical stamina for officers and men to stay focused and to sustain tempo for days. They must be mentally agile to evaluate the battle and to exploit enemy gaps as they discover them.

The division demonstrated *initiative* throughout its training and in combat, from Wood down to the lowest ranking soldier. Wood's ability to control a division with only short verbal orders consisting of a few lines, or what the Army calls FRAGOs, is an extraordinary accomplishment that should be emulated by today's Army, even with its computer-generated orders.

In applying *depth*, the 4th AD engaged in nonlinear warfare, attacking enemy weaknesses miles behind German lines. These fights, while mentally and physically stressful, placed demoralizing pressure on the enemy.[45]

Were the 4th AD's operational techniques enabled by factors we can recreate today?

- Logistics were forced forward, traveling with combat formations. Also, units lived off German supplies left by fleeing troops. Unit commanders did not fear for the security of their logistical units because they knew how to fight—they were soldiers first and technicians second.
- The division maintained small staffs. Competence and experience eliminated the need for most paperwork.
- Command, control, communications, and intelligence were not deterministic. There was no separate chart or process to ensure they occurred. Constant practice ensured unity of effort.
- The division never massed its combat power up front. Using aircraft and autonomous reconnaissance units, it was able to maintain uncommitted units as a large tactical reserve. In effect, it was a "reconnaissance pull," allowing Wood and the CCA and CCB commanders to shift to routes of least resistance in order to maintain initiative and momentum.[46]
- The incorporation of assisting Army Air Corps fighter-bombers were used as "flying artillery." The planes attacked German tactical reserves and enhanced the movement of the ground element. The 4th AD was a maneuver-oriented division. It did its utmost to avoid useless casualties in frontal assaults. It sought to collapse the enemy from within, by attacking his headquarters and support assets.[47]

    Future units might find themselves fighting the same way—widely dispersed, coming together to fight or raid enemy weaknesses, and then dispersing to avoid strikes by nuclear or chemical weapons. They must be agile, with commanders possessing the initiative, to destroy high value enemy targets pinpointed by intelligence gathering systems and relayed by digital technology, or moving quickly to exploit enemy weaknesses. In these rapidly changing environments and threats, commanders will also have to make rapid decisions. Units will have to be trained in encountering different enemies in the spectrum of conflict from low intensity in urban environments to high intensity in desert terrain employing different tactics, and countering them with a combination of drills and tactics that will rapidly destroy or neutralize an enemy's units or his will to fight. In the future, time will not allow the U.S. Army three years to prepare.

In order to embrace the mission command doctrine, the U.S. Army must grasp, accept, and possess a culture of Auftragstaktik on the foundation of an improved personnel system, creating leaders who can command units of excellence that are to go into combat on a moment's notice.

16

Conclusion: It Is Not Easy, but the Payoff Will Be Great!

The principle thing now is to increase the responsibilities of the individual man, particularly his independence of action, and thereby to increase the efficiency of the entire army. . . . The limitations imposed by exterior circumstances causes us to give the mind more freedom of activity, with the profitable result of increasing the ability of the individual.[1]

—HANS VON SEECKT, Chief German General Staff

This book offers the *why* and the *how* of Auftragstaktik for developing leaders and personnel. These techniques and principles provide the baseline for developing the kind of adaptability that will enable a culture of Auftragstaktik. Like an effective OODA loop, this culture will remain in constant motion—recurring, evolving, and improving.

While I am a big fan of computer simulations, they are not addressed in this book because they cannot be effectively used until leaders and teachers master the facilitation and teaching basics outlined herein. Computer simulations in the form of war games or battlefield simulations—flight simulators, tank simulators, or online war-games (not first-person shooter games), for example—are outstanding tools, but they are useless if teachers do not know or understand how to integrate them into a training program to develop adaptability.

The Problem Defined

J. F. C. Fuller's *Foundations of the Science of War* states: "The confusion between the meanings of science and art in the head of the average soldier is most pronounced."[2] Soldiers do not understand that "a science teaches us to know, an art to do."[3] If you replace "the average soldier" with TRADOC you get to the essence of the problem. TRADOC specializes in scientific management of "knowledge." Its personnel do not specialize in teaching the art of war fighting.

Unfortunately, this problem is now DOD-wide. All training and education is tracked via the Joint Professional Military Education (JPME) certification system. It appears that one of the underlying assumptions for the adoption of a systems approach to training and education was that the more a service member "knows," the more he or she can "do." The truth is, as Heraclitus observed in 500 BC, in war, "out of every one hundred men, ten shouldn't even be there, eighty are just targets, nine are the real fighters, and we are lucky to have them, for they make the battle. Ah, but the one, one is a warrior, and he will bring the others back."[4] This is true whether they just graduated from the War College or are fighting for ISIL with no formal education.[5]

To complicate matters, there is now a perception that everyone who deployed in support of the Iraq War operations accomplished their mission and everyone who deployed is a hero. This perception disproves my hypothesis and causes everyone to scratch their head when a true teacher is "abrasive." In their minds the scientific approach to training and education in the military has a proven track record. Even the Department of Education (DOE) uses it with their "common core" doctrine. What could possibly be wrong with it?

To make matters even worse, TRADOC is now tasked to basically "stuff ten pounds of shit into a five-pound bag without spilling a drop." My fellow mavericks and I conducted an unofficial analysis in 2014 of every Annual and Ancillary Training/Education required by the Army alone at the time. We found that in order to "know" everything required by order or directive, we would have to train/teach 32 hours a day—365 days a year. *Hmmm.* How is that even possible when there are only 24 hours in a day? It is not. The truth is that no one had ever looked at the requirements holistically. They just kept piling them on, making commanders responsible for what their units do (or fail to do). This chasm between perception and reality continues to grow every time there is a rape allegation, a DUI, a suicide, etc.[6]

As long as the "requirements" continue to increase to mitigate the "risk," TRADOC cannot change—in fact, it will only get worse. It is not personal, it is systemic. TRADOC's entire infrastructure is based on the scientific management of "knowledge," which breaks doctrine down into testable, quantifiable parts. From my reading, this began when Gen. William Depuy took over TRADOC in the 1970s. Every subject is assigned to a curriculum developer (civilian, usually a retired senior NCO or officer) who arranges these parts into terminal (i.e., "testable") learning objectives (TLO) and enabling learning objectives (ELO). Every hour of instruction is accounted for in the Program of Instruction with a constant eye toward the efficient transfer of terminal learning objectives (retention be damned). That is why bold and great teachers are constantly told to "stick to the POI" whenever they attempt to improve retention and understanding among our subordinates outside of the formal lesson cards.[7]

In spite of the high quality of their teaching about the art of war based on sound history and personal experience (just as the Germans have done), Col. John Boyd, Col. Mike Wyly, and the teachers at ARC and DMI are likely viewed with a jaundiced eye by the scientific managers who judge their methodology to be "inefficient" and hard to quantify and test. These doctrinal managers also probably view these "unorthodox" methods as a threat to their livelihood (since master instructors do not need curriculum developers). Until both DOD and DOE dismantle their scientific management models, all reform efforts will continue to exist on the fringes. Why? Because every time a senior leader sees something like the innovative Adaptive Soldier Leader Training and Education workshop and asks "is there anything we need to do to update our POI to reflect what they just taught?" The answer they receive from their curriculum developer is, "No, our POI is signed and certified. We cover everything required by doctrine, including the subjects just covered by Mr. Vandergriff."[8]

Neither party realizes that they are talking about two different things (art vs. science).[9]

What Has to Be Done?

The strategic approach and tactical techniques inherent in the adaptation of Auftragstaktik will force and require major changes in the way the U.S. Army educates, employs, structures, and trains its future forces and leaders. Broadening professional education would be a good start—from initial-entry training to the top War College level—to deal with the wide spectrum of issues that commanders will confront in the complex war fighting environments of the future. Fortunately, as provided in this text, there are recent examples of how to do it. What the ARC does for the tactical level can easily translate into operational and strategic-level courses. TRADOC just has to be willing to commit the time and resources to finding the right teachers, as well as working with the personnel system to get out of its Industrial Age methods of selecting and managing those people who show the ability to teach and not just instruct.[10]

These organizations must also understand that even in competent conventional warfare, the Army builds trust on high levels of professionalism and unit cohesion. As one captain put it, leaders must be prepared to "group together from a new perspective a number of measures that have been used before but were viewed separately."[11]

Superior education and training will be critically important to the institutionalization of Auftragstaktik in the Army. Not only will the Army need to produce adaptive leaders, but the institutions tasked to develop leaders will need to become adaptive as well—to evolve as the future operating environment evolves. Flattening means empowering, but only after subordinates are well prepared through strenuous development approaches.

The OBT&E (ASLT&E) training doctrine using the ACM methodology will provide principles that allow implementation of ideas from the top-down as well as bottom-up. It is so central to the future of the Army that it applies to squad leaders as well as to the joint-force commander. The leaders of the Army of the future should have to make a truly gross error to create a negative blotch on their careers. Evaluations and performance reviews cannot continue to haunt adaptive leaders throughout their careers if they have only made an honest mistake.

Moving the Army agencies toward a learning-based organizational structure, where its institutions as well as its leaders are adaptive, will bring the collective creativity of their personnel to bear in solving problems at the tactical, operational, and strategic levels of war and and police actions.

The culture will become one that rewards leaders and personnel, regardless of rank, who act and penalizes those who fail to act. Today's culture needs to evolve so that the greater burden rests on superior officers, who have to nurture—teach, trust, support, and correct—the student who now enters the force with the ability to adapt.

Future leaders will also have the responsibility to self-police their own ranks, particularly early on, if they become teachers within an ACM. This makes evaluating, "racking and stacking" of graduates easier. It will also help determine early on who will have the character traits to become an adaptive leader. The criteria should include observations of the student leaders in several scenarios.

Before selecting or promoting subordinates, a teacher should always ask, "Would you want this person to serve in your unit?" Throughout an ACM-based course the teacher will instill in students the importance of accurate reporting and taking action when the situation demands it. The Army's culture of the future will not tolerate inaction. Indecisiveness or the inability to make a decision will become the culture's cardinal sin.

Adaptability will become a product of the future organization that practices Auftragstaktik; it will depend on a relatively simple change in teaching technique in order to deal with the increasing complexities of war. Comprehending and mastering the concept of adaptability will come through rigorous education and tough training early on—quality, not quantity—to produce adaptive leaders.

Leaders' ability to adapt will guide decisions on how to accomplish their missions while also helping them recognize and compensate for differences in the temperament and ability of other organization's officers, NCOs, and civilian staff through unit training and professional development. Adaptability will provide a stable support structure to infuse and sustain Army leaders' initiative in future operating environments.

Today's Army leadership must understand that by simply using the word "adaptability" in PowerPoint presentations and saying they are going to implement it, or repackaging curricula and personnel policies to include rhetoric about adaptability, while leaving the substance unchanged, will not adequately prepare leaders to be adaptive. The entire Army must be prepared to support, nurture, and reinforce this important trait.

This book presented a conflict between rhetoric and reality: the desire to evolve the culture of the Army, so it can deal with the increasingly complex problem-solving of the future of conflict in a resource-constrained environment. The reality is that it is going to be hard to achieve this by changing cultures founded and stuck in the Industrial Age, while enhanced with the latest communication technology. This tension will result in a short-term crisis where these organizations may find its most promising junior leaders voting with their feet and leaving. Why? Because it is all too likely that these future leaders will discover that the leadership of these organizations is ignoring them due to their low rank and grade, despite their abilities to think and act at higher levels of responsibility.

If this "trust problem" is fixed, the Army will find that it has also solved the larger problem. These organizations will wind up retaining the "right" folks—those with a "calling to the service" who can prepare and lead them in the twenty-first century. Establishing OBT&E to enable success in Auftragstaktik and allowing it to continue to evolve into the future is the first step in changing current culture to truly prepare these organizations to deal with the complex battlefield of the twenty-first century.

Many Army organizations are saying the right things, and they are beginning to execute ideas evolving from this rhetoric. Cultural change is generational and occurs with the understanding that critical thinking is a learned behavior that is underpinned by education. Their educational systems, moreover, can be our most effective lever of cultural change. Many of our most important cultural shifts trace their origins to the schoolroom. A thorough review of the institutional educational system is required to assess its effectiveness at engendering critical thinking.

Notes

Preface

1. James G. Pierce, *Is the Organizational Culture of the U.S. Army Congruent with the Professional Development of its Senior Level Officer Corps?* (Carlisle, Pa.: U.S. Army War College, 2010), iii.

Chapter 1. John Boyd, the OODA Loop, and Auftragstaktik

1. Discussions with Franklin C. Spinney.
2. Based on discussions with Dr. Chet Richards, 10 May 2010.
3. Dr. Chet Richards, "Conflict in the Years Ahead" (Atlanta, Ga.: J. Addams and Partners, August 2006), slide 47.
4. Fred Leland, "Developing 'Fingertip Feel': Shaping and Reshaping Dynamic Encounters and Gaining the Advantage," August 2010, http://lesc.net/system/files/Developing+Fingertip+Feel+finaldraft.pdf.
5. Richards, "Conflict," slide 46.
6. Gary Klein, *Sources of Power* (Boston: MIT Press; reprint, Anniversary ed., 2017), 104–10.
7. Discussions with Dr. Chet Richards, 8 October 2008.
8. Richard E. Simpkin, *Race to the Swift: Thoughts on Twenty-First Century Warfare* (London: Brassey's Defense Publishers, 1985), 18.
9. Chet Richards, "John Boyd, *Conceptual Spiral*, and the Meaning of Life" (Hilton Head, S.C.: J. Addams & Partners, 24 October 2012), 3, http://fasttransients.files.wordpress.com/2010/03/boyd_cs_meaning_of_life6.pdf.
10. Thanks to Dr. Chet Richards for this essay on Fingerspitzengefuhl from his blog http://slightlyeastofnew.com/, 18 July 2014. Also see http://zenpundit.com/?p=3516.
11. Based on discussions with Dr. Chet Richards, 25 March 2008.
12. Dr. Chet Richards, "Fingerspitzengefuhl," 14 July 2014.
13. Boyd, "Patterns," slide 76.
14. Richards, "Fingerspitzengefuhl."
15. Richards, "Fingerspitzengefuhl."
16. This thought comes from numerous discussions with Dr. Chet Richards over the years.
17. The idea of Einheit was promulgated by Heinz Guderian to explain the concept of mobile, combined arms doctrine during the interwar period of 1933–39. Einheit fostered the integration (unity) of infantry and armored units at the tactical level: company/battalion.
18. Based on discussions with Dr. Chet Richards.
19. Based on discussions with Franklin C. Spinney, Pierre Sprey, and Chet Richards.
20. Spinney, Sprey, and Richards discussions.
21. Boyd, "Patterns," slide 73.
22. Guderian's own accounts of the crossing and the race toward the English Channel in Heinz Guderian, *Erinnerungen eines soldaten* (Neckargemünd, Germany: Kurt Vowinkel Verlag, 1960), 79–126.

23. H.Dv. 300/1, *Truppenführung*, 123.

24. Boyd "Patterns," slide 74. Günther Blumentritt (10 February 1892–12 October 1967) served as a division and corps commander in World War II.

25. Boyd "Patterns," slide 74

26. Boyd, "Patterns."

27. Boyd, "Patterns," slide 75.

28. William S. Lind, *Maneuver Warfare Handbook* (Boulder, Colo.: Westview Press, 1985), 22–30.

29. Boyd, "Patterns."

30. Boyd, "Patterns."

31. Ola, Kjoerstad, "German Officer Education in the Interwar Years" (Glasgow: University of Glasgow, 2010), 2–5.

32. Antoine-Henri, Baron de Jomini, *The Art of War*, trans. Capt. G. H. Mendell and Lt. W. P. Craighill (New York: Dover Publications, 2007), 294.

33. Boyd, "Patterns," slide 75.

34. H. Dv. 300/1 *Truppenführung*, 123.

35. H. Dv. 300/1 *Truppenführung*, 145.

36. H. Dv. 300/1 *Truppenführung*, 119. Also see Kjoerstad, "German Officer Education," 28–31.

37. Boyd, "Patterns," slide 76.

38. Boyd, "Patterns."

39. Boyd, "Patterns," slide 79.

40. Boyd, "Patterns."

41. Boyd, "Patterns."

42. Boyd, "Patterns"; discussions with Dr. Chet Richards, 21 May 2010.

43. Richards, "Conflict," slide 51.

44. Richards, "Conflict," slide 56.

Chapter 2. The German Way of Command

1. Adolf von Schell, *Battle Leadership* (Quantico, Va.: Marine Corps Association, 1988), 17.

2. Ola Kjoerstad, "German Officer Education in the Interwar Years" (Glasgow: University of Glasgow, 2010), 2–5.

3. Bruce Condell and David T. Zabecki, eds., *On the German Art of War, Truppenführung* (Boulder, Colo.: Lynne Rienner Publishers, 2001), ix.

4. Several books on the subject as well as even U.S. doctrine allude to this fact, but very few seem to grasp the significance of it, because so few practice it in times of "peace."

5. John T. Nelson II, "Auftragstaktik: A Case for Decentralized Battle," *Parameters* (Carlisle, Pa.: U.S. War College, September 1987), 21.

6. Daniel J. Hughes, "Abuses of German Military History," *Military Review* (December 86): 67–68.

7. Hughes, "Abuses," 67.

8. Hughes, "Abuses," 10.

9. Discussions with Pierre Sprey and Franklin C. Spinney, 4 December 2007.

10. Bruce I. Gudmundsson, *Stormtroop Tactics: Innovation in the German Army 1914–1918* (Westport, Conn.: Praeger, 1995), 18.

11. Richard E. Simpkin, "Command from the Bottom," *Infantry* 75, no. 2 (March–April 1985): 34.

12. Ola Kjoerstad, "German Officer Education" 42–50.

13. H. Dv. 487 *Führung und Gefecht der verbundenen Waffen (F.u.G.)*, Neudruck der Ausgabe 1921–1924 in 3 teilen (Osnabrück: Biblio Verlag, 1994).

14. Condell and Zabecki, eds., *German Art of War*, 3.
15. H.Dv. 300/1 *Truppenführung*, 3.
16. Quote is from Ola Kjoerstad, "German Officer Education," 67. Also see Oberleutnant Hauck, "Wissen und Können," *MW*, no. 38 (1927): col. 1395.
17. Ola Kjoerstad, "German Officer Education," 64–69.
18. Major General von Haeften, "Heerführung im Weltkriege" *MW*, no. 18 (1920): col. 389.
19. Kessel, *Moltke*, 100–103.
20. Department of the Army, Field Manual 7–0, *Training for Full-Spectrum Operations*, Draft, June 2007.
21. Charles E. White, *The Enlightened Soldier: Scharnhorst and the Militärische Gesellschaft in Berlin 1801–1805* (Westport, Conn.: Praeger, 1989), 45–54.
22. Bruce I. Gudmundsson, "The Evolution of Mission Command," *Tactical Notebook*, Summer 1995, 52–57.
23. William S. Lind, *Maneuver Warfare Handbook* (Boulder, Colo.: Westview Press, 1985), 87.
24. Franz Uhle-Wettler, "*Auftragstaktik*: Mission Orders and the German Experience," in *Maneuver Warfare: An Anthology*, ed. Richard Hooker, (Novato, Calif.: Presidio Press, 1993), 237.
25. Captain J. R. Lumley, "On the Training of Prussian Officers, Their Promotion, and How Their Capabilities Are Tested," *Journal of the Royal United Services Institute for Defence Studies* 25, no. 4 (London: W. Mitchell and Son, 1882), 745–64.
26. The author is indebted to the insights of Dr. Bruce I. Gudmundsson and William S. Lind for providing examples of the German application of mission command in peacetime. See also Robert T. Foley, "Institutionalized Innovation: The German and the Changing Nature of War, 1871–1914," *Royal United Services Institute* 147, no. 2 (April 2002): 84–90.
27. Jörg Muth, *Command Culture: Officer Education in the U.S. Army and the German Armed Forces, 1901–1940, and the Consequences for World War II* (Denton: University of North Texas Press, 2011), 205.
28. Richard F. Timmons, "Lessons from the Past for NATO," *Parameters* XIV, no. 3: 7. (October 1984).
29. I am indebted to Dr. Jörg Muth, author of *Command Culture* for the multiple discussions we have had over email regarding this subject.
30. Muth, *Command Culture*, 205.
31. Fred Anderson, *Crucible of War: The Seven Years' War and the Fate of Empire in British North America, 1754–1766* (New York: Vintage Books, 2001), 22–25.
32. Jay Luvaas, *Frederick the Great on the Art of War* (New York: Free Press, 1966), 34–36.
33. Christopher Duffy, *Frederick the Great: A Military Life* (New York: Routledge & Keegan Paul, 1985), 112.
34. Email from Dr. Jörg Muth to author 21 March 2012.
35. Robert M. Citino, *The German Way of War: From the Thirty Years' War to the Third Reich*, (Lawrence: University Press of Kansas, 2005), 34–70.
36. H. Delbruck, *Geschichteder Kriegskunst*, vol. IV (Berlin, Germany 1900–1936), 363, 426; also see J. Colin, *Education Militaire de Napoleon* (Paris, 1900).
37. H. W. Koch, *A History of Prussia* (New York: Barnes & Noble Books, 1986), 146.
38. Christopher Clark, *Iron Kingdom: The Rise and Downfall of Prussia, 1600–1947* (Cambridge, Mass.: Belknap Press of Harvard University Press, 2009), 307.
39. Obitz Eckardt, *Gerhard von Scharnhorst. Vom Wesen und Wirken der preußischen Heeresreform, Ein Tagungsband* (Bremen: Temmen, 1998), 45–46.

40. See Charles E. White, *The Enlightened Soldier: Scharnhorst and the Militärische Gesellschaft in Berlin 1801–1805* (Westport, Conn.: Praeger, 1989) for a great description of the beginning of the cultural transformation of the Prussian (then German) army from centralized to decentralized control.

41. Eberhard Kessel, *Moltke* (Stuttgart: K. F. Koehler, 1957), 9–19.

42. Trevor Dupuy, *A Genius for War: The German Army and General Staff, 1807–1945*, (Annandale, Va.: Dupuy Institute, 1991), 62.

43. Kessel, *Moltke*, 210–24.

44. Helmuth von Moltke, *Geschichte des deutsch-französischen Krieges von 1870–71, vol. 3, Gesammelte Schriften und Denkwürdigkeiten des General-Feldmarschalls Grafen Helmuth von Moltke* (Berlin, Germany: E. S. Mittler & Sohn, 1891–93), 8.

45. Moltke, *Geschichte*, 9–10.

46. Email from Dr. Jörg Muth to author, 21 March 2012. Also see Samuel P. Hays, "Introduction," in *Building the Organizational Society*, ed. Jerry Israel (New York: Free Press, 1971), 3.

47. Muth, *Command Culture*, 108.

48. Karl Demeter, *The German Officer-Corps in Society and State 1650–1945*, trans. Angus Malcom (London: Wiedensfield and Nicolson, 1965), and F. L. Carstens, *The Reichswehr and Politics 1918–1933* (Berkeley: University of California Press, 1973).

49. Demeter, *German Officer-Corps*, 68.

50. Gudmundsson refers to several sources on the German Jäger tradition. The best primary source according to Gudmundsson is: Johan Ewald, *Abhandlung über den Kleinen Krieg* (Kassel, Germany: Johann Jacob Cramer, 1785). This book is also available in English: Johan Ewald, *A Treatise on Partisan Warfare*, trans. Robert A. Selig and David Curtis Skaggs (Westport, Conn.: Greenwood Press, 1991). Gudmundsson also quotes Balck from Wilhelm Balck, "Die Entwicklung der taktischen Anschauungen in der englischen Armee nach dem Burenkrieg," *Vierteljahresheft für Truppenführung und Heereskunde,* March 1906, 450–51; Balck compares British light infantry tactics to those of the Prussian Jäger.

51. Jörg Muth to author, 21 March 2012; the significance of Dr. Muth's brilliant work is his comparison of non-hazing in German military schools and the reliance on hazing in the United States Military Academy before World War II as seen as a tool of leader development. Dr. Muth's argument is that such use of hazing demoralized and undermined the professionalism and trust necessary to conduct Auftragstaktik.

52. Muth to author, 21 March 2012.

53. Condell and Zabecki, eds., *German Art of War,* 21

54. Muth, *Command Culture*, 86–114, 149–80. In several chapters Muth describes in detail, supported by primary sources, how the Germans ran all their military schools up through the Kriegsakademie. Also see Demeter, *German Officer-Corps*, 8.

55. William Mulligan also emphasizes the importance of trust in William Mulligan, *The Creation of the Modern German Army* (Oxford, UK: Bregham Books, 2005).

56. It originated with the *Akademie für junge Offiziere der Infanterie und Kavallerie* (Academy for young officers of the infantry and cavalry) in 1801, later becoming known as the Allgemeine Kriegsschule (General War Academy). It was officially reestablished as one of three officer colleges by Gerhard von Scharnhorst in Berlin on 15 October 1810. It was housed in a building on Unter den Linden (1845/25) designed by Karl Friedrich Schinkel.

57. David N. Spires, *Image and Reality: The Making of the German Officer, 1921–1933* (Westport, Conn.: Greenwood Press, 1984), 125.

58. Walter Goerlitz *History of the German General Staff, 1657–1945,* trans. Brian Battershaw (New York: Praeger, 1954).
59. Condell and Zabecki, eds., *Truppenführung,* ix. Also discussions with Dr. James S. Corum, 2–3 October 2011, Baltic Staff College, Targa, Estonia.
60. Dr. Phillip Kyber, "Translation of Taped Conversation with General Hermann Balck," (Arlington, Va: Department of Defense, 1985), 25–26.
61. BDM Corporation, "Balck and von Mellenthin on Tactics" (Arlington, Va, 1980), 22.
62. "Balck and von Mellenthin on Tactics," 25.
63. James Deer, *Die Träger des Ritterkreuzes des Eisernen Kreuzes 1939–1945: Die Inhaber der höchsten Auszeichnung des Zweiten Weltkrieges aller Wehrmachtteile* [*The Bearers of the Knight's Cross of the Iron Cross 1939–1945: The Owners of the Highest Award of the Second World War of All Wehrmacht Branches*]. [*Friedberg, Germany: Podzun-Pallas, 1986*]. The 1a is the senior, or first, general staff officer (*Erster Generalstabsoffizier*).
64. "Conversation with Balck," 26.
65. Simpkin, *Race to the Swift,* 261.
66. Simpkin, *Race to the Swift,* 239.
67. Gaedcke, 37–38.
68. Simpkin, *Race to the Swift,* 234–35.
69. Field Marshal Erich von Manstein, *Lost Victories,* ed. and trans. Anthony G. Powell, with a forward by Capt. B. H. Liddell Hart and intro. by Martin Blumenson (Chicago, Ill.: H. Regency Co., 1958; repr., Novato, Calif.: Presidio Press, 1982), 191–92.
70. Simpkin, "Command from the Bottom," 34–37.
71. Hauptmann Gallwitz, "Der Unterführer"(Berlin, Germany: GE MW, 1930), no 13, col. 480.
72. Helmut Karl Bernhard von Moltke, "Aus den Verordnungen fur die hoheren Truppen-fuhrer vom 24 Juni 1869," in *Moltkes Militarische Werke, Zweiter Theil, Die Tatigkeit als Chef des Generalstabs im Frieden,* Preubischer Generalstab (Berlin, Germany: Ernst Siegfried Mittler und Sohn, 1900), 178.
73. Uhle-Wettler, "*Auftragstaktik,*" 242.

Chapter 3. Barriers to Mission Command

1. Jack C. Lane, *Armed Progressive: General Leonard Wood* (San Rafael, Calif.: Presidio Press, 1978), 150.
2. Emory Upton, *The Armies of Asia and Europe* (Washington, DC: Government Printing Office, 1878). 219.
3. Richard C. Brown, "General Emory Upton: The Army's Mahan," *Military Affairs* 17, no. 3 (Fall 1953): 16.
4. Emory Upton, *The Military Policy of the United States* (Washington, DC: Government Printing Office, 1904), 1–101. The manuscript remained unpublished until Secretary of War Elihu Root made it public in 1904 during his last year in office. Its contents then were familiar to reformers, and most of the ideas appeared in Peter S. Michie, *The Life and Letters of Emory Upton* (New York: D. J. Appleton, 1885). Also see Andrew J. Bacevich, "Progressivism, Professionalism, and Reform," *Parameters* 5, no. 1 (March 1975): 4.
5. Frederick W. Taylor, *Scientific Management: Comprising Management, the Principles of Scientific Management and Testimony before the Special House Committee* (New York: Harper and Row, 1964), 4–6.
6. Alfred Chandler, *The Visible Hand: The Managerial Revolution in American Business* (Cambridge, Mass.: Harvard University Press, 1957), 45–56.

7. Russell F. Weigley, "The Elihu Root Reforms and the Progressive Era," in *Command and Commanders in Modern Warfare*, ed. William Geffen, (Colorado Springs: U.S. Air Force Academy 1969), 24; Frederick Winslow Taylor, *Principles of Scientific Management* (New York: Harper Brothers, 1911), 10–16.

8. James H. Hayes, *The Evolution of Military Officer Personnel Management Policies: A Preliminary Study with Parallels from Industry* (San Monica, Calif.: Rand, 1978), 80.

9. Peter Karsten, "Armed Progressives: The Military Reorganizes for the American Century," in *Building the Organizational Society*, ed. Jerry Israel (New York: Free Press, 1972), 197–98. The term "line officer" cannot be related in terms of age to today's twenty-two- to twenty-four-year-old lieutenants, and twenty-five-year-old captains. On the eve of the Spanish-American War, the youngest captain in the army was older than most of the captains in the German army. Nevertheless, "junior officers" are second and first lieutenants and captains, whereas "middle" or "field grade" refers to majors, lieutenant colonels, and colonels.

10. Department of the Army, *The Personnel Replacement System, the United States Army* (Washington, DC: Government Printing Office, February 1954), 122–24. Even as early as the Civil War, soldiers realized that the policy of not rotating units out of the line to assimilate replacements was a wasteful one. In December 1864, Maj. Gen. Benjamin Butler recommended the use of a regimental replacement depot system. Later, when Brig. Gen. Emory Upton pushed for a professional army, he also advocated a European system of unit rotations and recruiting from geographical locations.

11. Weigley, "Elihu Root Reforms," 11. Paul Hammond, *Organizing for Defense* (Princeton, N.J.: Princeton University Press, 1961), 23.

12. Morris Janowitz and Roger W. Little, *Sociology and the Military Establishment* (Beverly Hills, Calif.: Sage, 1974), 98.

13. Marvin A. Kreidberg and Merton G. Henry, *History of Military Mobilization in the United States Army, 1775–1959* (Washington, DC: Department of the Army, June 1955), 706. The officer strength is based on one officer per sixteen enlisted personnel. The ratio is the average of the ratio in the years just before and just after the Civil War.

14. Kreidberg and Henry, *Military Mobilization*, 10–13; Dept. of the Army, *Personnel Replacement System*, 190.

15. Maj. Gen. Robert Alexander, *Memories of the World War 1917–1919* (New York: Macmillan, 1931), 21–24. See also Dept. of the Army, *Personnel Replacement System*, 199–228.

16. Dept. of the Army, *Personnel Replacement System*, 188.

17. Maj. Gen. John J. Pershing to the Adjutant General, U. S Army, 9 September 1917, in *The United States Army in World War I 1917–1919, vol. 2* (Washington, DC: Government Printing Office, 1948), 39. See also Lane, *Armed Progressive*, 173–75. Lane presents Chief of Staff Leonard Wood's argument against the Uptonian view that civilians would require years of training in a unit to become effective professionals; Allan Millett, *The General: Robert L. Bullard and Officership in the United States Army, 1881–1925* (Contributions in Military Studies, no. 10) (New York: Praeger, 1975), 315–17. Pershing "had to have general officers who were military looking (in the parade ground sense)."

18. Kreidberg and Henry, *Military Mobilization*, 548–52.

19. Maj. Gen. Robert Alexander, *Memories of the World War 1917–1919* (New York: Macmillan, 1931), 21–24. See also Dept. of the Army, *Personnel Replacement System*, 199–228.

20. Kreidberg and Henry, *Military Mobilization*, 548–52.

21. E[ben] Swift, *Field Orders, Messages, and Reports* (Washington, DC: Government Printing Office), Document UB283.A45.

22. J. von Verdy du Vernois, "Military Wargaming," *Journal of the Royal United Service Institution* (London: Royal United Services Institute for Defence and Security Studies, 1877), 50.

23. Gen. Verdy du Vernois, *A Simplified War Game*, trans. Eben Swift (St. Louis: Hudson-Kimberly, 1897), 1–5. Timothy K. Nenninger, *The Leavenworth Schools and the Old Army Education, Professionalism and the Officer Corp of the United States 1881–1918* (Westport, Conn.: Greenwood Press, 1978), 9. The continued attempt at copying the Germans did not end with Elihu Root in 1903. William DuPuy's work in the 1970s launched another "German renaissance." For all its faults, it was a sincere attempt at meaningful reform that was inspired by DuPuy's admiration for the Germans he fought in 1944–45.

24. Maj. Eben Swift introduced the MDMP in the 1890s. Major Swift translated a French interpretation of a German method used in tactical decision games. The French mistakenly systemized a tutorial device, and Swift broke the process into even more procedures. He created the famous five-paragraph field order. This formalism feeds inward focus because effort is now directed toward how the order is written rather than why it is written. Swift did not understand that the German method was simply an educations tool to introduce students to the concept of harmonization and never left the introductory level. The flaw with the MDMP is that it forces staffs to focus on "checking the blocks" of the matrix instead of focusing on the enemy, mission, and commander's intent. In fact, the enemy only occupies a small portion of the MDMP matrix.

25. John W. Masland and Laurence I. Radway, *Soldiers and Scholars: Military Education and National Policy* (Princeton, N.J.: Princeton University Press, 1957), 81–82.

26. Weigley, "Elihu Root Reforms," 24; Taylor, *Principles of Scientific Management*, 10–16.

27. Walter Willis, *Arms and Men: A Study in American Military History* (New Brunswick, N.J.: Rutgers University Press, 1986), 158–62. See also John M. Gates, "The Alleged Isolation of U.S. Army Officers in the Late 19th Century," *Parameters* 10, no. 3 (Autumn 1980): 14.

28. Interviews with Capt. Robert Bateman, 13 August 1998, and Bruce I. Gudmundsson, 21 August 2000. One of the best arguments for French influence exists in the publication of the French manual, *A Manual for Commanders of Large Units* (1930). This manual filled the gap between the 1923 *Field Service Regulations* and later tactical manuals published in 1942; it was a translation of the French manual of the same name. However, it was never accepted as official doctrine retained as a "narrative" publication until the *Field Service Regulations* was updated on the eve of World War II.

29. Robert Doughty, *Seeds of Disaster* (New York: Archon Books, 1986), 2–9. One need only compare the 1930 edition of *A Manual for Commanders of Large Units* to U.S field manuals written in 1942 to see the close resemblance.

30. U.S. War Department, Office of the Chief of Staff, *A Manual for Commanders of Large Units (Provisional), vol. 1, Operations* (Washington, DC: Government Printing Office, 1930).

31. Thanks to Dr. Bruce I. Gudmundsson for these thoughts.

32. V. Ney, *Evolution of the U.S. Army Division, 1939–1968* (Fort Belvoir, Va.: Combat Operations Research Group, January 1969), 41, 90, 112; Walter R. Wheeler, *The Infantry Battalion in War* (Washington, DC: Infantry Journal, 1936), 5.

33. John R. Maass, "Benning Revolution," in *A History of Innovation: U.S. Army Adaptation in War and Peace* ed. Jon T. Hoffman (Washington, DC: Center of Military History, 2009), 28–33. Also see Daniel Bolger, "Zero Defects: Command Climate in First U.S. Army, 1944–1945," *Military Review* 73, no. 4 (1993): 66–67. Marshall would always have a bitter view of the education officers received at Leavenworth.

34. Forrest Pogue, *Education of a General, 1880–1939* (New York: King Press, 1963), 252, 347.

35. Van Creveld, *Fighting Power* (New York: Praeger, 1983), 23–45.

36. For examples of the authoritarian leadership style see David R. Campbell, *Fighting Encircled: A Study in Leadership* (Washington, DC: U.S. Army Center of Military History, 1987), 9–10, 21; Richard Mallonee II, *Naked Flagpole* (San Jose, Calif.: Presidio Press, 1980), 16–29; Samuel A. Stouffer et al., *The American Soldier: Combat and Its Aftermath* (Princeton, N.J.: Princeton University Press, 1949), 2:49–51, 97, 112–21.

37. Daniel Bolger, "Zero Defects," *Military Review* (Fort Leavenworth, Kans.: March 1986), 65–66.

38. This occurred in World War II with a large amount of outright reliefs. Today, it occurs with a subtle remark or the wrong word and even a lack of a recommendation on an Officer Evaluation Report. This is made worse when a senior (the evaluator or senior rater) does not confront the officer that the harm was done. The senior thus avoids confrontation and relies on the "system" to take care of officers later in their careers when they are not promoted or selected for a school or command.

39. Campbell, *Fighting Encircled*, 21–24.

40. Maj. John C. Sparrow, *History of Personnel Demobilization of the U.S. Army* (Washington, DC: Government Printing Office, 1958), 166.

Chapter 4. Institutionalizing the Process

1. This chapter is based on discussions with hundreds of personnel from July 2005 to September 2014. I try to highlight the key people whom I have also named in the acknowledgments as being the foundation to this part of the book.

2. Chad Serena, *A Revolution in Military Adaptation: The U.S. Army in the Iraq War* (Washington, DC: Georgetown University Press, 2010), 2–6, 161. Also see Eliot Cohen and John Gooch, *Military Misfortunes: The Anatomy of Failure in War* (New York: Random House, 1990), 5–28.

3. Brig. Gen. David Fastabend and Robert Simpson, "Adapt or Die: The Imperative for a Culture of Innovation in the United States Army," *Army* (February 2004): 3–5.

4. The author is indebted to the work of members of the Asymmetric Warfare Group (AWG) and Kevin McEnery, who wrote an unpublished paper entitled "Changing Army Culture," which is the background to the influence of General DePuy on today's Army training and culture. McEnery was gracious in assisting me with this section of the book.

5. William Donnelly, *Transforming an Army at War: Designing the Modular Force, 1991–2005* (Washington, DC: U.S. Army Center for Military History, 2007), iii. This seems to be an opinion expressed by Donnelly; no analytical support for this statement is provided.

6. Lt. Col. Kevin McEnery, "Changing Army Culture," unpublished paper (Fort Meade, Md.: Asymmetric Warfare Group, 2007), 3, 21; Nicholas R. Marsella, "Effective Joint Training: Meeting the Challenges," *Parameters* (November–December 2004), http://www.army.mil/professionalwriting/volumes/volume3/february_2005/1_05_3.html. TRADOC Regulation 10–5, *U.S. Army Training and Doctrine Command Organization*

and Functions, 22 December 2005. TRADOC Regulation 350–70, *Training Development*, 9 March 1999, www.tradoc.army.mil/TPUBS/regs/r350-70/350_70_vi_2.htm.

7. This comes with discussions with forty-seven junior- and middle-grade officers from June 2005 to December 2007 who talk about more centralization of training management, as well as the pressure on field grades to do everything right when they are in their critical branch qualifying or key development (KD) jobs as majors.

8. Mark Sherry, *The Army Command Post and Defense Reshaping, 1987–1997* (Fort Monroe, Va.: US Army Training and Doctrine Command, 1991), 119; . Douglas Macgregor, *Breaking the Phalanx: A New Design for Landpower in the 21st Century* (Westport, Conn.: Praeger 1997), 31.

9. Input of Lt. Col. John Sayen, USMC (Ret.), 7 January 2007. Sayen is an expert on force structure and organization, as well as equipment.

10. Gen. William S. Wallace, "Victory Starts Here! Changing TRADOC to Meet the Needs of the Army," *Military Review* (May–June 2006) 69.

11. McEnery, "Changing Army Culture," 6. Also see Walt Ulmer and Mike Malone, *Study of Professionalism* (Carlisle, Penn.: U.S. Army War College, 1970), 33–40. The author also benefited from numerous discussions with Lt. Gen. Walt Ulmer, USA (Ret.).

12. Col. Richard M. Swain, "Selected Papers of William E. DePuy" (Fort Leavenworth, Kans.: Combat Studies Institute, January 1985).

13. Maj. Paul Herbert, "Deciding What Has to Be Done: General DePuy and the Creation of FM 100-5, Operations," in *The Leavenworth Papers* (Fort Leavenworth, Kans.: Command and General Staff College, July 1988).

14. Fastabend and Simpson, "Adapt or Die," 5.

15. Col. George Reed, "Systems Thinking and Senior Level Leadership," unpublished paper (Carlisle, Penn.: Army War College, August 2004).

16. Lt. Col. Paul L. Savage and Maj. Richard A. Gabriel, "Turning Away From Managerialism: The Environment of Military Leadership," *Military Review* (July 1980): 57.

17. McEnery, "Changing Army Culture," 6. Also see David McCormick, *The Downsized Warrior: America's Army in Transition* (New York: New York University Press, 1998).

18. John C. Tillson, Merle L. Roberson, and Stanley A. Horowitz, *Alternative Approaches to Organizing, Training and Assessing Army and Marine Corps Units* (Alexandria, Va.: Institute for Defense Analysis, November 1992), 23. A "band of excellence" resembles a roller coaster of training ups and downs with the band representing the mean average of the surges of training that occur with constant inflow and outflow of personnel.

19. Gen. Paul F. Gorman, *The Secret of Future Victories* (Fort Leavenworth, Kans.: Combat Studies Institute, 18 June 1979), 56–57.

20. Robert A. Doughty, *The Evolution of U.S. Army Tactical Doctrine, 1946–1976* (Leavenworth Papers no. 1) (Fort Leavenworth, Kans.: Combat Studies Institute, August 1979).

21. Paul H. Herbert, *Deciding What Has to Be Done: General William E. DePuy and the 1976 Edition of 100-5* (Leavenworth Papers no. 16) (Fort Leavenworth, Kans.: US Command and General Staff College, July 1988), 4.

22. Savage and Gabrial, "Turning Away," 58.

23. Herbert, "Deciding What Has to Be Done," 44–45.

24. Barry Posen, *The Sources of Military Doctrine: France, Britain, and Germany Between the World Wars* (Ithaca, N.Y.: Cornell University Press, 1984).

25. Robert W. Komer, "Strategy and Military Reform," in *Defense Reform Debate*, ed. Asa A. Clark IV (Baltimore: Johns Hopkins University Press, 1984), 14 (fn 1).

26. Robert A. Doughty reached this conclusion in his study of U.S. Army doctrine since World War II. See Doughty, "Evolution," 49.

27. James Kitfield, "Army Chief Struggles to Transform Service during War," *National Journal* (29 October 2004), http://www.govexec.com/federal–news/2004/10/army–chief–struggles–to–transform–service–during–war/17929/.

28. McCormick, "Changing Army Culture," 120–56; Dave McCormick talks about the selections for early retirement boards used to help accomplish the Army's drawdown.

29. James G. Pierce, *Is the Organizational Culture of the U.S. Army Congruent with the Professional Development of its Senior Level Officer Corps?* (Carlisle, Penn.: U.S. Army War College, 2010), iii.

30. Herbert, "Deciding What Has to Be Done," 23.

31. McEnery, "Changing Army Culture," 6; Dept. of the Army, *Army Capstone Concept*, iii–11. For the past several decades, the Army's doctrine consistently referenced the vital nature and essential element of "adaptability" both organizationally and operationally. A review of historical documents and Army field service manuals—FM 100-5 *Operations* and FM 3-0 *Operations*, as well as FM 22-100 *Military Leadership* and FM 6-22 *Army Leadership*—for the past fifty years demonstrates the imperative that doctrine, strategy, operations, tactics, organizations, and leaders must be flexible and adaptable in the face of fluid, changing environments, missions, requirements, and adversaries, as circumstances may require.

32. Gen. Peter Schoomaker, "The Future of the United States Army." Remarks given at the American Enterprise Symposium, "The Future of the United States Army," 11 April 2005.

33. Asymmetric Warfare Group, "Outcome Based Training and Education: Fostering Adaptability in Full-Spectrum Operations," briefing, December 2008, slide 7.

34. From discussions with CSM William "Morgan" Darwin, December 2007 through March 2009.

35. Interview with Col. Casey Haskins, 23 June 2008.

36. Haskins interview, 23 June 2008.

37. Col. Casey Haskins, "Commander's Mid-tour Assessment, 198th Infantry Brigade," unpublished memorandum (Fort Benning, Ga.: U.S. Army Infantry Center, 13 August 2007).

38. Col. Mike Galloucis, "Changing the Army Culture," unpublished memorandum, Army CSA Staff group (Washington, DC: Dept. of Army, 13 February 2005).

39. William M. Darwin, "Adaptability Learning Symposium," Asymmetric Warfare Group (Fort Meade, Va.: AWG, 11 December 2007), slide 3.

Chapter 5. The Result

1. Major Daniel P. Snow, "United States Army Officer Personnel Reforms and the Decline of Rank Flexibility, 1890s–1920s," *School of Advanced Military Science (SAMS)* (Fort Leavenworth, Kans.: SAMS, May 2015), 52.

2. Discussions with William S. Lind, May 2008. Also based on my lecture to the USMC Expeditionary Warfare School, September 2007.

3. Dr. Robert Bjork, "How We Learn Versus How We Think We Learn: Implications for the Organization of Army Training," unpublished presentation, Science of Learning Workshop (Fort Monroe, Va.: U.S. Army Training and Doctrine Command, 1 August 2006).

4. Timothy Karcher, *Understanding the "Victory Disease" from the Little Bighorn to Mogadishu and Beyond* (Fort Leavenworth, Kans.: Combat Studies Institute Press, 2004). 5–7.

5. Haskins, "Commander's Mid-tour Assessment," 5.

6. "Active Defense" is the U.S. Army doctrine outlined in the 1976 edition of 100-5, *Operations*. The doctrine focused on weapons systems and attrition while employing an "elastic defense."

7. McEnery, "Changing Army Culture," 8. Also see, Les Brownlee and General Peter Schoomaker, "Serving a Nation at War: Toward a Campaign Quality Army with Joint and Expeditionary Qualities," *Parameters* (2004): 19.

8. Robert Davis, *The Challenge of Adaptation: The U.S. Army in the Aftermath of Conflict, 1953–2000* (Fort Leavenworth, Kans.: Combat Studies Institute Press, 2008), 84.

9. Haskins, "Commander's Mid-tour Assessment," 5.

10. McEnery, "Changing Army Culture," 7. Also see both the officer and NCO Army Training and Leader Development Panels' reports: www.army.mil/features/ATLD/ATLD.htm.

11. For the theoretical development of these ideas, see John D. Steinbruner, *The Cybernetic Theory of Decision: New Dimensions of Political Analysis* (Princeton, N.J.: Princeton University Press, 1974) and Peter F. Drucker, *Innovation and Entrepreneurship: Practice and Principles* (New York: Harper and Row, 1985), especially chapter 14.

12. Muth, *Command Culture*, is the best book comparing two dialectic education systems from 1900 to 1940: those of the Germans and United States. Unfortunately, after talking to a number of people that have attended many courses and schools, remains of the archaic system remain.

13. Kenneth Allard, *Command, Control and the Common Defense* (New Haven, Conn.: Yale University Press, 1991), 44–56.

14. John L. Romjue, "From Active Defense to AirLand Battle: The Development of Army Doctrine from 1973–1982," *TRADOC Historical Monograph Series* (Fort Monroe, Va.: U.S. Army Training and Doctrine Command, June 1984): 14; General William R. Richardson, FM 100-5: "The AirLand Battle in 1986," *Military Review* 66, no. 3 (March 1986): 6.

15. Paul H. Herbert, "Deciding What Has to Be Done: General William E. DePuy and the 1976 Edition of FM 100-5," *Leavenworth Papers 16* (July 1988): 3.

16. Herbert, "Deciding What Has to Be Done," 22.

17. General Paul F. Gorman, *The Secret of Future Victories* (Fort Leavenworth, Kans.: Combat Studies Institute, 18 June 1979), 56–57.

18. P. J. Dermer, "CGSC: Learning Institution or Inhibitor?" unpublished paper (Fort Leavenworth, Kans. 1996), 2.

19. Based on numerous discussions with field grade officers, and former battalion and brigade commanders from 2005 to July 2014.

20. Briefing by Brig. Gen. Terry Ferrell, 12 May 2011, http://v-e-n-u-e.com/In-the-Box-A-Tour-Through-the-Simulated-Battlefields-of-the-U-S-Army.

21. Macgregor, *Breaking the Phalanx*, 161–63. For good discussions on the issue, see Capt. Robert Bateman, "Training for Maneuver," *Armor*, January–February 1997. Bateman advocates a free-play force-on-force environment with few parameters as a better way of determining who the best commanders are. He opined that the Army should switch the CTCs to this model in order to regain proficiency in maneuver warfare.

22. Discussions with Col. Douglas Macgregor, USA (Ret.), 13 December 2011. Macgregor stated, "The division's size seems at variance with warfare's trends . . . a large warfighting formation like a division could significantly constrain contingency planning and response options. What the Army needs is a warfighting organization with a form that parallels the shift of warfighting functions and activities to progressively

lower levels. One way to modify the division organization is to disestablish divisions as standing organizations. . . . Brigade task forces would continue to wear division patches and would maintain their traditional links to parent divisions. Structuring these brigades to operate more or less independently to ensure their deployability. . . . Assign brigades those elements which are routinely cross–attached for deployment to combat or training to ensure their smooth cooperation in war."

23. Lt. Col. Andrew R. Dziengeleski, "Improving the ARFORGEN Model: An Army National Guard Perspective," *School of Advanced Military Studies (SAMS)* dissertation (Fort Leavenworth, Kans.: Combined Arms Center, May 2010). Also see Stuart Johnson, John Peters, Karin Kitchens, Aaron Martin, and Jordan Fischbach, *A Review of the Army's Modular Force Structure* (Santa Monica, Calif.: RAND National Defense Research Institute, 2012), 10.

24. Lt. Col. Scott M. Halter, "What Is an Army but the Soldiers? A Critical Performance Assessment of the U.S. Army's Human Capital Management System," *Military Review* (Jan.–Feb. 2012): 16–23.

25. Muth, *Command Culture*, 209.

26. Comment from an anonymous command sergeant major to author, June 2010.

27. Report of the Defense Science Board Task Force on *Understanding Human Dynamics*, Office of the Under Secretary of Defense for Acquisition, Technology and Logistics, March 2009, http://www.acq.osd.mil/dsb/reports/ADA495025.pdf.

28. Halter, "What Is an Army but the Soldiers?" 4–7.

29. Brig. Gen. Mark C. Arnold, "Don't Promote Mediocrity," *Armed Forces Journal* (May 2012), http://www.armedforcesjournal.com/2012/05/10122486.

30. Ronald Barr, "High Command in the United States: The Emergence of a Modern System 1898–1920," in *Leadership and Command: The Anglo-American Experience Since 1861*, ed. G. D. Sheffield (London: Brassey's Defence Publishers, 2002), 57.

31. Arnold, "Don't Promote Mediocrity," 2–3.

32. David E. Johnson, *Commanding War: The Western Origins of American Military Hierarchy* (Santa Monica, Calif.: RAND, 2004), 157–58. The author has had numerous discussions from 2010 through 2012 with Dr. Johnson on these subjects.

33. Maturin M. Ballou, *Treasury of Thought* (Boston: Houghton Mifflin Company, 1899), 407.

34. Eitan Shamir, *Transforming Command: The Pursuit of Mission Command in the U.S., British and Israeli Armies* (Stanford, Calif.: Stanford University Press, 2011), 62.

35. James G. Pierce, *Is the Organizational Culture of the U.S. Army Congruent with the Professional Development of its Senior Level Officer Corps?* (Carlisle, Penn.: U.S. Army War College, 2010), iii. Dr. Pierce postulated that "the ability of a professional organization to develop future leaders in a manner that perpetuates readiness to cope with future environmental and internal uncertainty depends on organizational culture." This hypothesis was based on the assumption that organizational culture enables organizational adaptation; organizational culture perpetuates adaptability and promotes relevance and continued existence. Pierce's conclusion is alarming. He finds that Army leadership "*may be inadequately prepared to lead the profession toward future success* (emphasis added)."

Chapter 6. What Is OBT&E (ASLT&E)?

1. From discussions with CSM William "Morgan" Darwin, USA (Ret.), December 2007 through March 2009.

2. The subject of TRADOC changing the name from OBT&E to ASLT&E, while forcing many of the practitioners and original thinkers on OBT&E away from consulting

on it, is the subject of another book and beyond the scope of this book. The author as of August 2014 has been asked back to the *Maneuver Center of Excellence* at Fort Benning to teach his workshop that is outlined in this and follow-on chapters, as well as by the commanding general of Cadet Command (as well as hundreds of cadre members) to provide input to evolving the new POI of Cadet Command. In February and March 2014, the Army chief of staff's Strategic Studies Groups (SSG) approached the author about how to measure and evaluate adaptability. The real issue with OBT&E and Auftragstatik is that as they are truly practiced, they would threaten the current structure of TRADOC.

3. Command Sergeant Major Darwin provided this definition of OBT&E. Also based on multiple discussions with Col. Casey Haskins from 2007–13.

4. Discussions with Dr. Steven Stewart, 23 March 2005.

5. Army Field Manual 7–0, *Training for Full-Spectrum Operations* (Fort Leavenworth, Kans.: Combined Arms Center, 12 December 2008), 3–7.

6. See the work of John Taylor Gatto, and Kline, *Why America's Children Cannot Think* (2002).

7. This is based on interviews and discussions with hundreds of soldiers, leaders, and civilians involved with TRADOC schools. Despite the advocacy for adaptability development, the structure that General DePuy put in place in order to facilitate the control he wanted in order to evolve Army training in the 1970s remains in place. All these agencies and individuals have vetoes or a say in what happens within an organizations or a unit's training.

8. Donald E. Vandergriff, "Review of Army Training," unpublished paper, September 2006, 4–5.

9. The Asymmetric Warfare Group, located at Fort Meade, Maryland, was originally founded in 2005 as the Improvised Explosive Device Task Force; it became the AWG in 2006. It takes the latest lessons learned in active theaters of operations and helps commanders and staffs translate these lessons into tactics, techniques, and procedures (TTPs). It now falls under TRADOC and runs the Adaptive Training Program at Fort A. P. Hill, Virginia, that teaches watered-down versions of OBT&E to volunteers from units and courses from throughout the Army.

10. Based on author's numerous discussions with CSM Morgan Darwin, November–December 2007.

11. Asymmetric Warfare Group, "Outcome Based Training and Education: Fostering Adaptability in Full-Spectrum Operations," briefing, December 2008, slide 7.

12. AWG interview with SFC Steve Case, 19 March 2007.

13. A. H. Maslow, "A Theory of Human Motivation," *Psychological Review* 50, no. 4 (1943): 370–96, http://psychclassics.yorku.ca/Maslow/motivation.htm.

14. AWG interview with instructor SFC Steve Case, 19 March 2007.

15. CATC cadre instructions to student, 12 October 2007, Fort Jackson, South Carolina.

16. Author's discussion with Command Sergeant Major Darwin, 18 November 2008.

17. Discussion with Darwin, 18 November 2008.

18. Discussion with Darwin, 18 November 2008.

19. Discussion with Darwin, 18 November 2008.

20. From email exchange with Maj. Chris Kennedy, 7 November 2008.

21. From email exchange with CSM Patrick Laidlaw, 30 October 2008.

22. Dr. Gary Klein, *Sources of Power: How People Make Decisions* (Cambridge, Mass.: MIT Press, 1999).

23. Dr. Robert Bjork, "How We Learn Versus How We Think We Learn: Implications for the Organization of Army Training," unpublished briefing presented at Science of Learning Workshop, UCLA, Los Angeles, Calif. (1 August 2006). Dr. Bjork is considered a leading authority on the science of learning.

24. Bjork, "How We Learn," 5.

25. Bjork, "How We Learn," 6.

26. Email exchange with Maj. Chad Foster, 25 October 2008.

27. U.S. Army Training and Doctrine Command, "TRADOC Area of Interest 2: Leader Development and Professional Military Education" (Fort Monroe, Va.: U.S. Army Training and Doctrine Command, February 2006), 1.

28. The Basic Officer Leadership Course (BOLC) II, which was instituted in June 2006 as a sort of basic training for lieutenants before they were shipped off to their officer basic courses, was cancelled in October 2009. The shortages of captains and majors that kept units from manning their officer billets at 100 percent forced the Army to reconsider how it was moving lieutenants through the pipeline.

29. Email exchange with Maj. Chad Foster, 21 October 2008.

30. Author discussions with CSA Gen. George Casey, 5 September 2008. Immediately after this meeting and his reading of chapter 3 of this author's book, *Manning the Legion*, the CSA sent out the copy to all two-star commanders in the Army, including those who commanded all the training centers.

31. U.S. Army Accessions Command memorandum, subject: "Basic Officer Leaders Course (BOLC) Policy and Guidance," Fort Monroe, Va. (24 April 2008), 4.

32. From email exchange with CSM Zoltan James, commandant, NCO Academy, Fort Benning, Ga., 31 October 2008.

33. Email exchange with CSM Zoltan James, 31 October 2008.

34. At the heart of the reforms led by Gerhard Scharnhorst shortly after the destruction of the Prussian army at Jena in 1806 were ways to develop officers who could make rapid decisions in the chaos of the battlefield. Prussia's military education of its officer cadets was based on an education approach developed by a Swiss educator, Johann Heinrich Pestalozzi. In the late 1700s, Pestalozzi developed his theory that students would learn faster on their own if allowed to "experience the thing before they tried to give it a name." More specifically, the Prussians used Pestalozzi's methods to educate leaders on how to identify the core of a problem and then deal with the centerpiece of the problem without "wasting time working their way to finding a solution." North Carolina State University, Department of Agricultural and Extension Education, College of Agriculture and Life Sciences, http://www.cals.ncsu.edu/agexed/aee501/pestalozzi.html.

35. Email exchange with Capt. Thomas Pike, 2 June 2008.

36. Email exchange with Capt. Thomas Pike, 2 June 2008.

37. Email exchange with Capt. Casey Giese, 14 May 2008.

38. Email exchange with Capt. Alec Barker, 23 April 2008.

39. From discussion with Lt. Col. Paul Wilcox, 16 September 2007. Maj. (now Lt. Col.) Paul Wilcox ran his BOLC II company on OBT&E principles and was very successful. He took over 1st Squadron, 11th ACR at Fort Irwin on 1 July 2014.

40. Donald E. Vandergriff, "Swift to Swiss: Tactical Decision Games and Their Place in Military Education," *Performance Improvement Journal* (Rockville, Md.: ISPI, February 2006).
41. Email exchange with Lt. Col. Chad Foster, 25 November 2008. Foster provided this anonymous cadet's remarks from a survey taken about the MS 300 course.
42. Email exchange with SFC Robert Elzy, 12 March 2008.
43. Email exchange with Lt. Col. Chad Foster, 25 October 2008.
44. Email exchange with Capt. Andrew Watson, Infantry BOLC III instructor, Fort Benning, Ga., 25 October 2008. Author is also indebted to Col. Duke Davis, former commander of 194th Infantry Brigade, Fort Benning, Georgia, as well as commander of 2nd Battalion, 11th Infantry Regiment (Infantry Basic Officer Leaders Course).
45. Email exchange with Command Sergeant Major Zoltan James, 31 October 2008.
46. Major General Custer publicly stated this at the April 2009 Culture Conference hosted by the Military Intelligence Center of Excellence.
47. Capt. Alec Barker, "Review of Raising the Bar," unpublished book review (Reston, Va., April 2008).
48. CSA Marching Orders Cadet Command guidance for 2013, Maj. Gen. Jefforey Smith, http://www.ausa.org/publications/ausanews/specialreports/13/11/Pages/FutureAr myleadersmustbeadaptive,versatile,culturallyastute.aspx.
49. CSA Marching Orders.
50. Colonel Haskins did recognize the value of CATC after being introduced to the concept, and quickly used CATC as an asset to assist changes he was already implementing.
51. U.S. Army, "US Army Leader Development Strategy (ALDS)" (Fort Leavenworth, Kans.: Army Center of Leadership, 2013).
52. Fastabend and Simpson, "Adapt or Die," 5.
53. Discussions with Lt. Col. Chad Foster, 25 April 2009.

Chapter 7. Who Teaches (Facilitates)?
1. US Army, Field Manual 3-34, *Engineer Operations* (Fort Leonard Wood, Mo.: U.S. Army Engineer School, 2009), 6–87.
2. Muth, *Command Culture*, 67-69. Muth takes great pains to explain the effort the Germans put into placing the best teachers in front of their cadets as well as the wide latitude they are given regarding how to teach their subjects. This can also be found in numerous articles written by German officers in the interwar period, for example, Oberleutnant Hauck, "Wissen und Können," *MW 1927*, no. 38, col. 1395.
3. Generaloberst von Seeckt, "Über Heer und Krieg der Zukunft," *MW 1928*, no. 38, col. 1459.
4. Bernard Brodie, in Clausewitz, *On War*, 787.
5. Ike Skelton, "JPME: Are We There Yet?" *Military Review* (May 1992): 2.
6. Author interview with Capt. Paul Wilcox, June 2005. Wilcox got his wish. He commanded a tank and headquarters and headquarters company in the 4th Infantry Division in Iraq and at Fort Hood, then became a platoon TAC at the Army's new Basic Officer Leader Course (BOLC) II at Fort Benning, Georgia, where he assumed command of one of the BOLC II training companies as his third command. Then after time as a battalion and brigade operations officer, he went on to Command and Staff College as a tactics instructor, then back to command 1st Squadron, 11th ACR.
7. Six cohorts (years) of cadets from Georgetown University reflect on how well they were prepared to make decisions in combat, in contrast to their peers from other

ROTC programs, as well as USMA and OCS. The author currently stays in touch with most of them, even those who got out of the Army. They all relate to how ACM made them better leaders and decision-makers.

8. Brig. Gen. Huba Wass de Czege, *Army Staff College Level Training Study* (Carlisle, Penn.: U.S. Army War College, 1983). This was also a label placed on the graduates of the Army's elite School of Advanced Military Studies designed by Wass de Czege in 1981–82 and put in action in 1983.

9. Douglas Macgregor, *Transformation Under Fire: Revolutionizing How America Fights* (Westport, Conn.: Praeger Publishers, 2004), 211–20. Also see Cohen and Gooch, *Military Misfortunes*, 5–28.

10. Based on discussions with Dr. Steven Stewart.

11. Jon Moilanen, "Leader Competency and Army Readiness," *Military Review* 82 (July–August 2002): 62.

12. Moilanen, "Leader Competency," 78.

13. Zaghloul Morsey, ed., *Thinkers on Education* (New York: UNESCO International Bureau of Education, 1997), 21–45.

14. Discussions with Col. Robert Frusha, commander of the Eastern ROTC Region, 17 July 2004. Frusha made many positive changes to the ROTC leader's training course, a program that was once considered a gentleman's course or summer camp. The leader's training course is held between sophomore and junior years of ROTC, and also allows many programs to laterally transfer cadets into their programs without the cadet having to progress through the Military Science I and Military Science II courses.

15. This was also referred to as "deliberate practice" in K. Ross and J. W. Lussier, "Adaptive Thinking Seminar" (Arlington, Va.: Army Research Institute, 2000).

16. J. A. LePine, J. A. Colquitt, and Amir Erez, "Adaptability to Changing Task Contexts: Effects of General Cognitive Ability, Conscientiousness, and Openness to Experience," *Personnel Psychology* (2000): 563–93.

17. Dr. Bruce I. Gudmundsson has done extensive work in the use of case method and is successfully implementing it to enhance Marine Corps leader development, accessed 12 June 2014, http://casemethodusmc.blogspot.com/.

18. The author participated with the Marine Corps Training and Education Command in the winter, spring, and summer of 2012 to create *Instructional Tactics and Assessment Techniques Pocket Guide* (Orlando, Fla.: MESH Solutions, 2012). This is a giant leap forward for any service or organization willing to devote the time and resources to how teaching is both an art and science, and that they must be properly and thoroughly prepared.

19. Gary Klein, "The Recognition-Primed Decision (RPD) Model: Looking Back, Looking Forward," in *Naturalistic Decision Making*, ed. C. Zsambok and G. Klein (Mahwah, N.J.: Erlbaum, 1997), 285–92.

Chapter 8. Creating Outcomes and Measures

1. This idea of OBT&E is the result of several years of practice, analysis, and synthesis of many dedicated Army professionals within the Asymmetric Warfare Group (AWG). The contributions of officers, NCOs (active and retired), scientists, laymen, soldiers, and civilians—all interested in the betterment of our Army without regard for personal recognition or aggrandizement—are the hallmark of our nation.

2. Chad Foster, "The Case for Outcomes-Based Training and Education," *Armor* (November–December 2009): 20.

3. The author is indebted to Col. Casey Haskins for his mentorship from 2007 to 2012 and for teaching me how training and education should be conducted.

4. Discussions with CSM Morgan Darwin, 7 November 2009.

5. Don Cicotte, "Total Impact: Leaders Gather for Outcome Based Training Workshop," U.S. Army, accessed 25 June 2009, http://www.army.mil/-news/2009/03/18/18399-total-impact-leaders-gather-for-outcome-based-training-workshop/; Foster, "The Case"; Casey Haskins, "Outcomes-Based Training and Education," unpublished paper (West Point, NY: Department of Military Instruction, March 2009); W. R. McDaniel, *Outcome-Based Training and Education (OBTE) Integration Workshop—Final Report* (Laurel, Md.: National Security Analysis Department, Johns Hopkins University, 2009), accessed 30 July 2009, https://portal.awg.army.mil/portal/server.pt/search?in_hi_opt_comm_community=446&in_se_sel_1=everything&q=outcome-based+training+and+education; Mary E. Ferguson, "Outcome-Based Training and Education," *NCO Journal* 17, no. 3 (Summer 2008): 19–23, accessed 25 June 2009, https://www.army.mil/article/8691/commandants_gather_discuss_whats_necessary_for_ncoes_transformation; Donald E. Vandergriff, *Raising the Bar: Creating and Nurturing Adaptability to Deal with the Changing Face of War* (Washington, DC: Center for Defense Information, 2006); Donald E. Vandergriff, "From Swift to Swiss," *Performance Improvement* 45, no. 2 (2006): 31–39, accessed 21 June 2009, http://www3.interscience.wiley.com/journal/112752446/issue; Leonard Wong, *Developing Adaptive Leaders: The Crucible Experience of Operation Iraqi Freedom* (Carlisle, Penn.: Strategic Studies Institute, 2004), 29, accessed 30 July 2009, http://www.strategicstudiesinstitute.army.mil/pubs/people.cfm?authorID=1.

6. James J. Smith, "Outcomes Based Education vs. Outcomes Based Training and Education. Is there a Difference," masters thesis (West Point, N.Y.: USMA Center for Teaching Excellence, June 2010), 13.

7. Robert Shaw, "Outcome Based Training and Education (OBT&E)," *Asymmetric Warfare Group Newsletter* 1, no. 1 (2009), accessed 25 June 2009, http://army.daiis.mi.army.smil.mil/org/aawo/awg/default.aspx.

8. William Wallace, FM 3-0, *Operations*, ed. William Wallace, supersedes FM 3-0, 14 June 2001 edition (Ft. Leavenworth, Kans.: U.S. Army Training and Doctrine Command, February 2008), 3–1, accessed May 2008, www.us.army.mil.

9. Bruno V. Manno, *Outcome-Based Education: Miracle Cure Or Plague?* (Washington, DC: Thomas Fordham Institute, 1994), 6, accessed 25 June, 2009, http://www.edexcellence.net/detail/news.cfm?news_id=215&id=.

10. Col. Sam Adkins, "Assessment of OBT&E," white paper (Arlington, Va.: G3 Leader and Soldier Development, June 2010); quote is from Lt. Gen. Dan Bolger, Army G3 in his assessment of OBT&E.

11. Discussions with Col. Casey Haskins, 21 June 2009.

12. Col. Casey Haskins and Donald E. Vandergriff, "What is OBT&E," white paper presented to TRADOC commander, Gen. Martin Dempsey, May 2010.

13. This came from an offsite discussion with the leaders of the Special Forces Q-Course on developing outcomes and measures for the Q-course, Key West, Florida, March 2012.

14. From offsite at Special Forces Dive School, Key West, Florida, dealing with Outcomes Based Training and Education with Special Forces cadre of the Special Forces Qualification Course March 2012.

15. Wallace, FM 3-0, *Operations*, 3–1.

16. David Gardner, *A Nation at Risk* (Washington, DC: U.S. Department of Education, 1983), accessed 21 July 2009, http://www.ed.gov/pubs/NatAtRisk/index.html.

17. Haskins, "Outcomes-Based Training"; McDaniel, *Outcome-Based Training*.

18. Haskins, "Outcomes-Based Training"; McDaniel, *Outcome-Based Training*.

19. Ferguson, "Outcome-Based Training," 19–23.

20. Don Cicotte, "Leaders Gather for Outcomes Based Training Workshop" (Fort Meade, Md.: Asymmetric Warfare Group, 18 March 2009), http://www.army.mil/news/2009/03/18/18399-total-impact-leaders-gather-for-outcome-based-training-workshop/.

21. McDaniel, *Outcome-Based Training*, 1.

22. Foster, "The Case," 3.

23. Vandergriff, "From Swift to Swiss," 31–32.

24. Haskins, "Outcomes-Based Training," 3.

25. Haskins, "Outcomes-Based Training," 1.

26. Haskins, "Outcomes-Based Training," 2.

27. Smith, "Outcomes Based Education," 14.

28. Vandergriff, *Raising the Bar*, 33–34

29. Maj. Chad Foster, "Adaptive Course Model as part of OBT&E," presentation to OBT&E Integration Workshop, Johns Hopkins University Applied Physics Lab, March 2009. These were the outcomes from the MS300 course at USMA.

30. Foster, "Adaptive Course Model."

31. Maj. James Smith interview conducted on 28 July 2009 with Dr. Bruce Keith, Academic Affairs Division director and lead proponent for developing West Point's academic outcomes. The author is indebted to Major Smith for sharing his work with him for this book.

32. Vandergriff, *Raising the Bar*, 33–34.

33. Foster, "The Case," 3.

34. This was a constant emphasis by Colonel Haskins and was practiced by him at both Fort Benning (when he commanded the OSUT Brigade) as well as while he was DMI at the USMA. This is in line with what the Germans expected from their commanders, but they did not have to deal with several agencies, such as Range Control or the quality assurance offices the U.S. Army created in the 1970s because it did not trust its commanders to be in charge of their training.

35. This was derived from a Special Forces offsite held at Key West, Florida, March 2012 with cadre from the Special Forces Q-Course.

36. This example is derived from the "Deciding Under Pressure and Fast" workshop taught more than a hundred times since 2007. Recently taught May–August 2014 to all cadre at the 316th Cavalry Brigade, Armor School, Maneuver Center of Excellence, Fort Benning, Georgia.

37. Special Forces Leaders OBT&E offsite, Key West, Florida, 12 April 2012.

38. Special Forces offsite, Key West, Florida, March 2012.

39. These were the MOEs that the SF leaders developed to support the outcome dealing with physical fitness. The author does not know if these were later adopted by the Special Warfare Training Group (SWTG) at Fort Bragg. SWTG oversees the 1st–5th battalions; these units run various courses for Special Forces soldier development.

40. The first point Colonel Haskins brought up in his talks was, "What is the first thing students do when they get to a course?" After receiving various answers, he replied, "They want to know how to pass, and what is the test, so we develop them for the test without giving them the answers." Additionally, under ACM there are no true/false or multiple-choice questions. All tests are problem-solving exams based on what the student has learned up to that point. I spoke with a major on 18 July 2014 who graduated the CGSC course in 2013 at Fort Lee, Virginia. He stated that their evaluation consisted of "true and false" and "multiple choice" tests.

41. This comes as a big shock to many instructors, who are now allowed to adjust their lesson plans based on their personal experiences and knowledge in order to get their students or personnel to the outcome. Most instructors who become teachers adapt well, and take more ownership in the course. One teacher at the new Army Reconnaissance Course (ARC) in the summer of 2009, a sergeant first class, told me he loved coming to work every day because he was part of the course and was trusted to teach the students to the outcome in the way he knew best.

42. Foster, "The Case."

43. William G. Spady, "Re-Forming the Reforms: How Total Leaders Face Education's Biggest Challenge," government of South Australia, accessed 10 July 2014, http://www.learningtolearn.sa.edu.au/Colleagues/pages/default/spady/?reFlag=1.

44. Another concept given great emphasis by Col. Casey Haskins to his instructors.

45. Charlotte Thomson Iserbyt, *The Deliberate Dumbing Down of America: A Chronological Paper Trail* (Ravenna, Ohio: Conscience Press, 1999), xxvi, http://www.deliberatedumbing down.com/MomsPDFs/DDDoA.sml.pdf.

46. As commander of the 198th Infantry Brigade and as director of DMI at USMA, Colonel Haskins constantly took on these institutions (such as the Range Control agency at each post) for interfering with his training.

Chapter 9. Tactical Decision Games or Exercises

1. National Interagency Fire Center and the Marine Corps University, *Design and Delivery of Tactical Decision Games and Sand Table Exercises,* (Quantico, VA: Marine Corps University, 2003). Many of the ideas used here was taken from the above handbook, Assessed January 2005 at https://www.fireleadership.gov/toolbox/documents/TDGS_STEX_Workbook.pdf.

2. John Schmitt, *Mastering Tactics: A Tactical Decision Game Workbook* (Quantico, Va.: Marine Corps Association, 1994), 1–4.

3. William S. Lind, *The Maneuver Warfare Handbook* (Boulder, Colo.: Westview Press, 1985), 56–78.

4. Lt. Gen. P. K. van Riper, *Combat Decision-making Presentation*, Amphibious Warfare School, Quantico, Va., October 1998.

5. C. White, *The Enlightened Soldier: Gerhard Scharnhorst and the Militarische Gesellschaft* (New York: Praeger, 1998), 122–24.

6. W. H. Kilpatrick, *Introduction to Heinrich Pestalozzi: The Education of Man—Aphorisms* (New York: Philosophical Library, 1951), 11–13.

7. Bruce I. Gudmundsson personal email to author, 16 December 2004.

8. H. G. von Molke, "Moltke on the Art of War," in *Moltke on the Art of War: Selected Writings*, ed. D. J. Hughes, trans. D. J. Hughes and H. Bell (Novato, Calif.: Presidio Press, 1993), 47.

9. White, *Enlightened Soldier*, 170.

10. White, *Enlightened Soldier*, 171.

11. Survey of Georgetown Army ROTC cadets, 2000–2004 by the author.

12. Also see the game "Follow Me," the simulation used at DMI to present TDEs in electronic format, so the cadet can go back and review what they did or did not do, http://www.decisive-point.com/military/followme.html. Thanks to Vincent "T. J." Taijeron and Maj. Steve Banks for their input on this subject and their efforts to transform TDEs from the classroom to simulation. They ran the Simulations Center at the USMA in support of DMI from 2008–11.

13. Maj. Mark Sonstein, "Outcomes Based Training and Education for Today's Tactical Decision Makers, an Examination of My Teaching Techniques," *Master Teacher Program* (West Point, N.Y.: Teaching Center of Excellence, 2010). Thanks to Major Sonstein for his input to this book and providing his work for his master's program.

14. Sonstein, "Outcomes," 4.

15. Wayne Cherry and Joseph McLamb, "Fighting a Hundred Battles," *Armor* (May–June 2001): 43–45.

16. Maj. John F. Schmitt, "How We Decide," in *Designing TDGs: A Tactical Decision Games Workbook* (Quantico, Va.: Marine Corps University, 1998).

17. The author is indebted to Maj. John F. Schmitt for his input on how to build a leader development program to develop adaptability; he provided his lessons learned from when he ran the naval ROTC Marine detachment at Northwestern University 1996–98.

18. Discussion with Col. Casey Haskins, 4 August 2008, regarding the class introduction for new DMI instructors and introduction to Adaptive Course Model or ACM led by the author.

19. Sonstein, "Outcomes," 1–2.

20. Notes gathered from discussions with Maj. John Schmitt and Bruce I. Gudmundsson, numerous dates from May 2008 to present.

21. The *Marine Corps Gazette* has a repository of TDGs that can be accessed at *Marine Corps Gazette*, Tactical Decison Games, accessed 23 July 2014, https://www.mca-marines.org/gazette/tactical-decision-games. Also see http://www.usma.edu/dmi/sitepages/military%20science.aspx#.

Chapter 10. War-Gaming

1. Max Boot, *War Made New: Technology, Warfare, and the Course of History, 1500 to Today* (New York: Gotham Books, 2006).

2. *The von Reisswitz, Kriegsspiel: The Prussian Army Wargame*, accessed 11 June 2014, http://grogheads.com/whatever/history/3898.

3. Konrad Lischka, "Wie preußische Militärs den Rollenspiel-Ahnen erfanden," *Der Spiegel* (22 June 2009), accessed 10 February 2014, http://www.spiegel.de/netzwelt/spielzeug/kriegsspiel-wie-preussische-militaers-den-rollenspiel-ahnen-erfanden-a-625745.html.

4. Lind, *Maneuver Warfare Handbook*, 43–70. The author is indebted to Col. Mike Wyly, USMC (Ret.) and William S. Lind for their insights on war-gaming.

5. Historical Division, *Wargames* (Heidelberg, Germany: Headquarters, U.S. Army Europe, 1952). German General Rudolf M. Hoffman, along with three other German generals—Halder, Fangohr, and List—reconstructed how the Wehrmacht taught tactics before and during World War II for U.S. Army interviewers.

Chapter 11. Free-Play Force-on-Force Exercises

1. U.S. Army, Army Regulation 350-2, Opposing Force (OPFOR) Program (Washington, DC: Dept. of the Army, April 2004), 1.
2. AR 350-2, 1.
3. Based on numerous discussions with Col. Greg Fontent, USA (Ret.), whom I consider one of the experts at red teaming; see also "Red Teaming and Alternative Analysis," *Red Team Journal*, http://redteamjournal.com/about/red-teaming-and-alternative-analysis/.
4. In July 2008, Colonel Haskins asked me to spend a week walking around and observing the training taking place at Camp Buckner and interview cadets to glean their prospective on the training under OBT&E. The feedback was dramatic and very positive compared to what cadets told me they had participated in prior to the summer of 2008.
5. AR 350-2, 5.
6. Accessed on 26 July 2014, at http://simunition.com/en/.
7. See "Baltimore Police Sergeants Training Using Adaptive Leadership Methodology with Don Vandergriff's AAR"; for the full AAR, http://lesc.net/blog/baltimore-police-sergeants-training-using-adaptive-leadership-methodology-don-vanderg riffrsquos.
8. A "canned STX lane" or situational training exercise is a common training exercise in units, courses, and ROTC units. It involves a squad or platoon being given a task, such as: "Assault a bunker." The participants are given a rectangular training lane in which to conduct this operation against a scripted OPFOR. The OPFOR is told to perform in a specific way, allowing the BLUFOR or attacking forces to win. A cadet is successful at this operation if he or she can demonstrate the entire checklist that the cadre carry to grade the event. The OPFOR is not allowed to win.

Chapter 12. Combat Physical Fitness

1. Donald E. Vandergriff, "Raising the Bar: Creating Leaders to deal with the Changing Face of War," 9th edition, unpublished study (Washington, DC: Georgetown University Army ROTC, 3 June 2005), http://www.dnipogo.org/vandergriff/rotc/rotc.htm. This was the second time in my Army career I had been assigned a task based on my academic emphasis on adaptability and Auftragstaktik to study something beyond my assigned duties at Georgetown ROTC. The first time was the summer of 2004 when Col. Robert Frusha asked me to study how to improve ROTC Basic Summer Camp in the summer of 2004. Also from 2009–11, I conducted reviews of the physical fitness program for Baltimore City Police Commissioner Frederick Bealfeld and also found their physical readiness program very lacking in preparation for what their officers needed for the street. Adaptability physical readiness was part of the four-week sergeants leaders course conducted from August 2010 to March 2011, with police sergeants continually telling me, "I need to start working out again like this, so I am more prepared."
2. Maj. Andrew Perry, Morgan State University, Survey conducted for "Raising the Bar," 22 March 2005.
3. USAPS website, "The Right Dose of Running," http://www.benning.army.mil/usapfs/TrainingSupport/trainingsupportindex.htm.
4. Michael Lewis, "Army's New Road Map for Physical Fitness" (Fort Monroe, Va.: Training and Doctrine Command, March 2010), http://www.army.mil/article/44456/PRT__The_Army__039_s_new_road_map_for_physical_readiness/.
5. "Army Readiness Study Will Shape Fitness Future," *Athletic Business*, March 2013, http://www.athleticbusiness.com/military/army-readiness-study-will-shape-fitness-future.html.

6. Maj. Mark P. Hertling, "Physical Training for the Modern Battlefield: Are We Tough Enough?" *School of Advanced Military Studies Monograph* (Ft. Leavenworth, Kans.: U.S. Army Command and General Staff College, 1987), 23.

7. FM 21-20, *Physical Fitness Training* (Ft. Jackson, S.C., 2007).

8. Maj. Mark R. Forman, "Too Fat to Fight—Too Weak to Win, Soldier Fitness in the Future?" *School of Advanced Military Studies Monograph* (Fort Leavenworth, Kans.: U.S. Army Command and General Staff College, 1997), 47.

9. Forman, "Too Fat to Fight," 47.

10. Forman, "Too Fat to Fight," 47.

11. Having reviewed the POIs of several armor courses at the Maneuver Center of Excellence during the summer of 2014, I noted that several have implemented two advances. Both are excellent evolutions and comply with the recommendations in this chapter. First, they do not hold Diagnostic APFT tests (taken when the student arrives at a course to determine their fitness level; this test should be signed off by the commander or previous course director before a student ever arrives at a course). Instead, they tell students that they know the standard and are held accountable for their performance at the final APFT. Second, they have replaced the traditional physical fitness sessions of stretch, push-ups, sit-ups, and run with combat PT events.

12. Hertling, "Physical Training," 25.

13. Lt. Pat Fagan, Survey conducted for "Raising the Bar," 25 January 2005. Fagan is currently a practicing lawyer in the city of Atlanta and we remain in contact.

14. FM 21-20, *Physical Fitness Training*, 3–1.

Chapter 13. Evaluations

1. Col. Casey Haskins used this phrase a lot when lecturing about how to use OBT&E.

2. Based on numerous discussions and his lectures of Col. Casey Haskins.

3. Discussions with Col. Casey Haskins, 12 July 2008.

4. Walter Ulmer, "Creating and Assessing Productive Organizational Climates," *Army War College Course Handout* (Carlisle, Penn.: U.S. Army War College, 2002) 1. The author has also had several discussions with Lieutenant General Ulmer over the last twelve years about these issues.

5. Walter Ulmer, "Creating and Assessing Productive Organizational Climates," 1–3.

6. Maj. Frank Brewster, "Using Tactical Decision Exercises to Study Tactics," *Military Review* (November–December 2002): 3.

7. Sonstein, "Outcomes," 4.

8. Sonstein, "Outcomes," 5.

9. Sonstein, "Outcomes," 11.

Chapter 14. Army Reconnaissance Course (ARC)

1. The author is indebted to the cadre of the U.S. Army Reconnaissance Course, particularly Capt. (now Maj.) Levi Thompson, the course director, and MSgt. (promotable) Jacob Stockdill, senior instructor, for their input and insights to this chapter from June–August 2014. The author is also indebted to countless current and past cadre for their professionalism and dedication in making ARC one of the best courses in the U.S. Army.

2. The author worked with Kevin McEnery, Maj. (now Lt. Col.) Bradley Nelson, and Capt. Robert C. Perry, along with the Asymmetric Warfare Group to develop the Army Reconnaissance Course using OBT&E and ALM Principles.

3. Robert S. Cameron, "To Fight or Not to Fight? Organizational and Doctrinal Trends in Mounted Maneuver Reconnaissance from the Interwar Years to Operation Iraqi Freedom," manuscript (U.S. Army Armor Center, 2009), 43–44.
4. The author is indebted to Capt. Nick Simpson, ARC course director, 2011–12, for his input to this chapter.
5. TRADOC Pamphlet 525-8-2, *The U.S. Army Learning Concept for Training and Education* (Ft. Monroe, Va., 14 September 2010).
6. Perry and McEnery, "Army Reconnaissance Course," 19.
7. FBCB2 is a Linux-based (older versions are Solaris based) communication platform designed for commanders to track friendly and hostile forces on the battlefield. It increases a vehicle commander's situational awareness of the battlefield by gathering information near real-time based on vehicle locations being updated on the battlefield. This information is viewed graphically and exchanged via both free and fixed text message formats (as opposed to verbal collection of reports).
8. From student surveys and from the ARC blog site.
9. From student surveys and from the ARC blog site.

Chapter 15. J. S. Wood, the 4th Armored Division, and Mission Command

1. General Bautz served as Gen. Creighton Abrams' S3 (operations officer) and XO in the 37th Armored Regiment (later redesignated the 37th Tank Battalion), 4th Armored Division, during the training of the division from 1942 through 1944, and in its critical campaigns in France and Germany, 1944–45. Shortly after relieving Bastogne, General Bautz was moved up to be S3 for Combat Command A (brigade), 4th Armored Division.
2. U.S. War Department, FM 17-100, *Armored Command Field Manual, The Armored Division* (Washington, DC: Government Printing Office, 1944), 2–4. This manual was written based on the experiments and training conducted by the 4th Armored Division from 1942 through 1943.
3. Discussions with Brig. Gen. Mike Lynch, USA (Ret.), 24 May 1998; John Wood and Heinz Guderian suffered the same fate. Both were relieved for having out-thought their seniors, thus gaining credit that deflated their superiors' egos.
4. Lewis Sorley, *Thunderbolt—From the Battle of the Bulge to Vietnam and Beyond: General Creighton Abrams and the Army of His Times* (New York: Simon & Schuster, 1992), 46.
5. William S. Lind, "The Theory and Practice of Maneuver Warfare," in *Maneuver Warfare: An Anthology*, ed. Maj. Richard D. Hooker (Novato, Calif.: Presidio Press, 1993), 7. This is a compressed APEX (i.e., the steps involving analysis, planning, and execution). This reflects the true meaning of maneuver warfare based on the ability to exploit favorable operational and tactical options as they arise, while overcoming unfavorable situations and circumstances that could cause failure.
6. Maj. Dean A. Nowowiejski, "Achieving Digital Destruction: Challenges for the M1A2 Task Force," in *Armor*, January–February 1995, 21. Situational awareness is the thorough knowledge of both friendly and enemy elements. In a technological sense, this is translated to a small screen in the M1A2 for commanders to view their place in the larger formation and unit. This will hopefully decrease fratricide (friendly fire) incidents.
7. Brig. Gen. Albin F. Irzyk, "The Name Enough Division," *Armor*, July–August 1987, 8–12; General Irzyk served as S3, XO, and commander of 8th Tank Battalion during the 4th Armored Division's fighting in Europe.

8. Discussions with Major General Bautz, 12 August 1997.

9. Author interviews with Army officers March–August 1997. Officers' complaints centered on the turnover of personnel as soon as a unit returned from productive and infrequent CTC rotations.

10. At the time, there was no rigid management of officers. Successful career patterns varied, but those of successful peacetime officers at the time relied more on political connections or working in positions that were under the view of senior officers than on competence in the field. George C. Marshall, Dwight D. Eisenhower, and George S. Patton Jr. all thought they had come to the end of their careers by their mid-thirties due to dead-end assignments.

11. Hanson W. Baldwin, *Tiger Jack* (Fort Collins, Colo.: Old Army Press, 1979), 104–6; "The prophets of the future form of war were without honor in their own country."

12. Hanson W. Baldwin, "'P' Wood of the 4th Armored," *Army* (January 1968), 50–51.

13. Russell F. Weigley, *History of the United States Army* (Bloomington: Indiana University Press, 1984), 598–600.

14. Sorley, *Thunderbolt*, 36–37; these were not Wood's own words; rather, they are Dr. Sorley's interpretation of several prominent officers' insights into Wood's methods. General Bautz reinforced these approaches during a discussion with the author about General Wood's leadership style.

15. Baldwin, *Tiger Jack*, 113.

16. Sorley, *Thunderbolt*, 50; Baldwin, *Tiger Jack*, 113.

17. Sorley, *Thunderbolt*, 36–37. This was based on Adna Chaffee's concept of armor.

18. Baldwin, *Tiger Jack*, 52.

19. Balwin, *Tiger Jack*, 144–47.

20. Paul Mallon, "Leadership of Army Will Be Cleaned Up: Fighting Field Officers of Old School Being Replaced," *Memphis Commercial Appeal*, 2 June 1941.

21. Eugene H. Sloan, *With the Second Army: Somewhere in Tennessee* (Murfreesboro, Tenn.: Middle Tennessee State College, 1956), 3.

22. Woody McMillin, *In the Presence of Soldiers: The 2nd Army Maneuvers and Other World War II Activity in Tennessee* (Nashville, Tenn.: Horton Heights Press, 2010), 36–37.

23. Discussions with Major General Bautz, 27 July 1997; also see Baldwin, *Tiger Jack*, 124–27.

24. John T. Hoffman, ed., *History of Innovation: U.S. Army Adaptation in War and Peace* (Washington, DC: Center of Military History, U.S. Army, 2009), 57.

25. George Butler, *The Military March of Time in Tennessee* (Nashville, Tenn.: Office of the Adjutant General, 1944), 24.

26. Dod Eugene Houston, *Hell on Wheels: The 2d Armored Division* (San Rafael, Calif.: Presidio Press, 1975), 31.

27. Christopher R. Gabel, *The U.S. Army GHQ Maneuvers of 1941* (Washington, DC: Center of Military History, U.S. Army, 1992), 8.

28. Jonathan M. House, *Toward Combined Arms Warfare: A Survey of 20th-Century Tactics, Doctrine, and Organization* (Fort Leavenworth, Kans.: U.S. Army Command and General Staff College, Combat Studies Institute, August 1984), 108.

29. Christopher R. Gabel, *The Lorraine Campaign: An Overview, September–October, 1944* (Fort Leavenworth, Kans.: U.S. Army Command and General Staff College, Combat Studies Institute, February 1985), 14.

30. After-action reports of the 4th Armored Division, 29 July–30 September 1944, provided by Major General Bautz in November 1995.

31. Major General Bautz made an appearance on the television show, *Modern War*, hosted by William Lind on 17 January 1997; he discussed the actions of 4th Armored Division and maneuver warfare. Afterward, a group of U.S. Marine Corps lieutenants asked General Bautz how long it took his battalion (Task Force 1–37 Armor, or Task Force Abrams) to move from an assembly area to conduct an attack. General Bautz remarked that it took thirty minutes to conduct a hasty attack from the time they received the order to "getting on the road." The lieutenants replied they were being taught to plan a platoon deliberate attack in six hours.

32. Col. Bruce Clark would later become Gen. Bruce Clark, hero of the defense of St. Vith during the Battle of the Bulge in December 1944. In the early 1960s, he was supreme commander of NATO.

33. Baldwin, *Tiger Jack*, 41–42.

34. "Hip-shoot" means firing artillery missions off a compass bearing using quick mathematical calculations to determine range and azimuth. Given more time (thirty to forty-five minutes) a battery could "survey" and stake out its new firing position, enabling it to use more precise calculations to deliver more accurate fire missions.

35. Major Richard H. Barnes, "ARRACOURT–SEPTEMBER 1944," Armor, (Fort Knox, KY: US Army Magazine, May 2001), p. 25-27.

36. After-Action Reports of the 4th Armored Division, 29 July–30 September 1944, provided by Major General Bautz to the author, November 1995.

37. Christopher Gabel, *The 4th Armored Division in the Encirclement of Nancy* (Fort Leavenworth, Kans.: Combat Studies Institute, 1986), 33.

38. Barnes, *Arracourt–September 1944*, 35–36.

39. Commanders and Staff of Combat Command A, 4th Armored Division, U.S. Army, *The Establishment and Defense of the Nancy Bridgehead* (Fort Leavenworth, Kans.: Military History–Battle Analysis, Combat Studies Institute, 1994), 3–5

40. Barnes, *Arracourt–September 1944*, 35.

41. For examples of this evolution, from decentralized to centralized command and control, see Mellenthin, *Panzer Battles*, 312–18. Also see Manstein, *Lost Victories*, 538–43.

42. Barnes, *Arracourt–September 1944*, 36–37.

43. Donald E. Vandergriff, "The Exploitation from the Dieulouard Bridgehead: An Example of Maneuver Warfare that Applies Today," *Armor,* September–October 1995, 6–9.

44. Discussions with Gen. Donn Starry, USA (Ret.), 7 November 1997. General Starry was commander of Training and Doctrine Command, 1979–82. General Starry was involved in the creation of the AirLand Battle doctrine, as well as writing more than fifty articles for various military journals on leadership, cohesion, and doctrine. General Starry also commanded the 11th Armored Cavalry Regiment in Vietnam, the U.S. Army Armor Center, U.S. Army V Corps, and U.S. Readiness Command.

45. Gabel, *Encirclement of Nancy*, 23–24; the actions of the division offer a good comparison with the AirLand Battle doctrine.

46. "Reconnaissance pull" describes the action of reconnaissance units that find gaps in enemy defenses, or surfaces, and "pull" follow-on units through toward enemy weaknesses.

47. Baldwin, *Tiger Jack*, 26.

Chapter 16. Conclusion

1. Robert Citino, *Path to Blitzkrieg: Doctrine and Training in the German Army, 1920–39* (Boulder, Colo.: Lynne Rienner Publishers, 1999), 57.

2. J. F. C. Fuller, *Foundations of the Science of War*, 20 (fn 7), accessed 12 October 2015, https://www.pearsonhighered.com/assets/hip/us/hip_us_pearsonhighered/samplechapter/013265797X.pdf.
3. Archbishop Thompson, *Laws of Thought*, 10, https://www.gutenberg.org/files/15114/15114-pdf.pdf.
4. *Ancient History Encyclopedia*, "Heraclitus of Ephesos," 14 July 2010, http://www.ancient.eu/Heraclitus_of_Ephesos/.
5. Department of the Army Pamphlet (DA PAM) 600-3, *Commissioned Officer Professional Development and Career Management* (Washington, DC: Headquarters, Dept. of the Army, February 2010), 11.
6. The author is indebted to Maj. P. J. Tremblay, USMC, for his input and edits for this chapter.
7. For an explanation of the conflicting research and theses adopted by different researchers and historians regarding this era, see Edward Coffman, "The Long Shadow of the Soldier and the State," *Journal of Military History* 55, no. 1 (January 1991): 69–82; Carol A. Reardon, "The Study of Military History and the Growth of Professionalism in the US Army Before World War I" (PhD diss., University of Kentucky, 1987), 4–5; and Peter J. Schifferle "Anticipating Armageddon: The Leavenworth Schools and US Army Military Effectiveness, 1919–1945" (PhD diss., University of Kansas, 2002), 8–26. For a description of the disciplinary shift toward the study of "war and society," attempting to place military institutions and events into ever-broadening contexts, see Eliot A. Cohen and John Gooch, *Military Misfortunes: The Anatomy of Failure in War* (New York: Free Press, 1990), 39. Of all the researched works, Vandergriff's comes closest to the focus of this analysis. See chapter 2, "The Minuteman, Emory Upton, and Elihu Root," in Donald E. Vandergriff, *The Path to Victory: America's Army and the Revolution in Human Affairs* (Novato, Calif.: Presidio Press, 2002).
8. For example, Coffman and Millis have entire chapters entitled "Managerial Revolution," while Janowitz claims the original purpose of military social research was to describe the transformational developments of the first half of the twentieth century that led to the modern military establishment and its struggle between heroic leaders and military managers.
9. Maj. Daniel P. Snow, "United States Army Officer Personnel Reforms and the Decline of Rank Flexibility, 1890s–1920s," *School of Advanced Military Science (SAMS)* (Fort Leavenworth, Kans.: SAMS, May 2015), 52.
10. James G. Pierce, *Is the Organizational Culture of the US Army Congruent with the Professional Development of Its Senior Level Officer Corps?* (Carlisle, Penn.: Strategic Studies Institute, September 2010), 7. Artifacts are easily observable; however, they only provide a superficial glimpse of an organization's culture because the true significance or meaning that lies behind their use can be difficult to decipher and interpret.
11. Discussions with Capt. James Snow, 12 December 2013.

Selected Bibliography

Adams, Thomas K. "Military Doctrine and the Organization Culture of the United States Army." PhD dissertation, Syracuse University, 1990.

Ancker, Clinton J., III "The Evolution of Mission Command in U.S. Army Doctrine, 1905 to the Present." *Military Review* 93, no. 2 (February 2013): 39–42.

Armstrong, Neil G. "A Balanced Approach: Thought for the Adoption of Mission Command by the Joint Force." Monograph, Naval War College, 2013.

Army Doctrinal Reference Publication 6–0, *Mission Command*. Washington, DC: Government Printing Office, 2012.

Army Doctrine Reference Publication 6–22, *Leadership*. Washington, DC: Government Printing Office, 2012.

Balck, Wilhelm. *Entwicklung der Taktik im Weltkriege*. Berlin, Germany: Verlag von R. Eisenschmidt, 1922.

Barno, David. "The Army's Next Enemy? Peace." *Washington Post*, 12 July 2014.

Bayerisches Kriegsministerium. *Exerzier-Reglement für die Infanterie*. Munich, Germany, 1906.

Bond, Brian. *The Pursuit of Victory: From Napoleon to Saddam Hussein*. New York: Oxford University Press, 1996.

Boyd, J. 1987. "A discourse on Winning and Losing." www.http://dnipogo.org/john-r-boyd/.

Builder, Carl H. *The Masks of War: American Military Styles in Strategy and Analysis*. Baltimore: Johns Hopkins University Press, 1989.

Buley, Benjamin. *The New American Way of War: Military Culture and the Political Utility of Force*. New York: Routledge, 2008.

Burgess, Cortis B., et al. "Mission Command White Paper." Research paper. TRADOC Commander's Colloquium: Fort Leavenworth, 30 March 2015.

Burley, Shaun A. "Contrasting Styles of Command: French and German Approaches during the 1940 Campaign." *Defence Studies* 5, no. 1 (Spring 2005): 138–50.

Cameron, Kim S., and Robert E. Quinn. *Diagnosing and Changing Organizational Culture Based on the Competing Values Framework*. San Francisco: Jossey-Bass, 2011.

Citino, Robert M. *The German Way of War: From the Thirty Years' War to the Third Reich*. Lawrence: University Press of Kansas, 2005.

———. *The Path to Blitzkrieg: Doctrine and Training in the German Army, 1920–1939*. Boulder, Colo.: Lynne Rienner Publishers, 1999.

Clausewitz, Carl von. *On War*. Edited and translated by Michael Howard and Peter Paret. Princeton, N.J.: Princeton University Press, 1976.

Clemens, Michael. "Mission Command and Mentorship." *Cavalry & Armor Journal* 5, no. 1 (January 2014): 5–6.

Clemente, Steven E. *For King and Kaiser! The Making of the Prussian Army Officer, 1860–1914*. New York: Greenwood Press, 1992.

Condell, Bruce, and David T. Zabecki, eds. *On the German Art of War, Truppenführung*. Boulder, Colo.: Lynne Rienner Publishers, 2001.

Cone, Robert W., Richard Creed Jr., and Adrian D. Bogart III. "Strategic Leadership for Strategic Landpower." *Military Review* 94, no. 4 (July 2014): 22–27.

Conley, Kathleen. "Operationalizing Mission Command: Leveraging Theory to Achieve Capability." *Joint Force Quarterly*, no. 68 (2013): 23–28.

Connell, Mike. "Custer and the Man Who Saved Him." *Times Herald.* Accessed 10 June 2015. http://archive.thetimesherald.com/article/20111009/OPINION02/110090313 / Custer-man-who-saved-him.

Corum, James S. *The Roots of Blitzkrieg: Hans von Seeckt and German Military Reform.* Lawrence: University Press of Kansas, 1992.

Covey, Stephen M. R., and Rebecca R. Merrill. *The Speed of Trust: The One Thing that Changes Everything.* New York: Free Press, 2006.

Cowley, Robert, and Geoffrey Parker, eds. *The Reader's Companion to Military History.* New York: Houghton Mifflin Company, 1996.

Craig, Gordon A. *The Politics of the Prussian Army: 1640–1945.* New York: Oxford University Press, 1955.

Creveld, M. van. *Command in War.* Cambridge, Mass.: Harvard University Press, 1985.

Crissman, Douglas C. "Improving the Leader Development Experience in Army Units." *Military Review* 93, no. 3 (May 2013): 6–15.

Cuddy, Amy J. C., Peter Glick, and Anna Beninger. "The Dynamics of Warmth and Competence Judgements, and Their Outcomes in Organizations." Accessed 23 March 2016. http://www.people.hbs.edu/acuddy/in%20press,%20cuddy,%20glick,%20&%20 beninger,%20ROB.pdf.

Daniels, Chip, and Mark Poole. "Harnessing Initiative and Innovation." *Military Review* 92, no. 5 (September 2012): 18–21.

Davis, R. R. "Helmuth von Moltke and the Prussian-German Development of a Decentralized Style of Command: Metz and Sedan 1870." *Defence Studies* 5, no. 1 (Spring 2005): 32–40.

Dempsey, Martin. Chairman of the Joint Chiefs of Staff Mission Command White Paper. 3 April 2012. Accessed 21 August, 2014. http://www.dtic.mil/doctrine/concepts/white_papers/cjcs_wp_mission command.pdf.

Dennis, Matt, and Tom Guthrie. "Training for Mission Command in FSO: The 4E Framework." *Infantry* 100, no. 2 (April 2011): 39–41.

Department of the Army. Chief of Staff of the Army Leader Development Task Force Final Report. Washington, DC, 2013.

———. 2015 Army Posture Statement. Washington, DC, 2015.

Deutsch, Harold C. *Hitler and His Generals: The Hidden Crisis, January–June 1938.* Ann Arbor, Mich.: Edwards Brothers, 1974.

Diefenbach, Karl. "Staatsbürger in Uniform, Ausgangspunkt und Ziel der Inneren Führung." In *Reader Sicherheitspolitik, Die Bundeswehr vor neuen Herausforderungen*, Erg.-Lfg. 1, no. 98 (1 January 1998): 17–32.

DiMarco, Louis A. *War Horse, A History of the Military Horse and Rider.* Yardley, Penn.: Westholme, 2008.

Dorn, Edwin, and Howard D. Graves. *American Military Culture in the Twenty-First Century.* CSIS Report. Washington, DC: CSIS Press, 2000.

Drotningsvik, Øyvind og Odd Sveinung Hareide. "Personellsituasjonen i MTB-våpenet." Masters thesis. University of Stavanger, 2012.

Dubik, James M. "Mission Command and Army Training Doctrine." *Army* 62, no. 9 (2011): 22–26.

Dubravac, Shawn. *Digital Destiny: How the New Age of Data Will Transform the Way We Work, Live, and Communicate.* Washington, DC: Regnery, 2015.

Dunnivan, Karen O. "Military Culture: A Paradigm Shift?" Monograph. Air War College, 1997.

Echevarria, Antulio J. *After Clausewitz: German Military Thinkers Before the Great War*. Lawrence: University Press of Kansas, 2000.

Einbeck, Eberhard. *Das Exempel Graf Sponeck, Ein Beitrag zum Thema Hitler und seine Generale*. Bremen, Germany: Carl Schünemann Verlag, 1970.

Eitan, Shamir. *Transforming Command: The Pursuit of Mission Command in the U.S., British and Israeli Armies*. Stanford, Calif.: Stanford University Press, 2011.

Erichsen, A. *Oppdragsbasert ledelse (OBL) i norsk sjømilitær kontekst* [Mission-based leadership in a Norwegian naval context]. København: Institutt for ledelse og organisasjon. Forsvarsakademiet i København, 2014.

Espevik, R. *Magellan Forever*. Bergen: Royal Norwegian Naval Academy, Department for Sea Power and Leadership Development, 2009.

Finkel, Meir. *On Flexibility, Recovery from Technological and Doctrinal Surprise on the Battlefield*. Stanford, Calif.: Stanford University Press, 2011.

Freytag-Loringhoven, Hugo Friedrich Philipp Johann. *Das Exerzier-Reglement für die Infanterie vom 29. Mai 1906 Kriegsgeschichtlich Erläutert*. Berlin, Germany: Ernst Siegfried Mittler und Sohn, 1906.

German Federal Minister of Defense. *Joint Service Regulation ZDv 10/1, Innere Führung (Leadership Development and Civic Education)*. Bonn, Germany, 2008.

German Oberste Heeresleitung, "Die Abwehr im Stellungskriege." In *Urkunden der Obersten Heeresleitung über ihre Tätigkeit 1916/1918*, edited by Erich Ludendorff. Berlin, Germany: E. S. Mittler und Sohn, 1921.

German Truppenamt. *D. V. Pl. Nr. 487. Führung und Gefecht der verbundenen Waffen (F. u. G.)*. Charlottenburg, Germany: Verlag Offene Worte, 1921.

———. *H. Dv. 300/1, Truppenführung (T.F.)*. Berlin, Germany: E. G. Mittler und Sohn, 1933.

Glantz, David M., and Jonathan M. House. *When Titans Clashed, How the Red Army Stopped Hitler*. Lawrence: University Press of Kansas, 1995.

Gremmo, Marie-Jose, and Philip Riley. "Autonomy, Self-Direction and Self-Access in Language Teaching and Learning: The History of an Idea." *System* 23, no. 2, 1995.

Hattie, John. *Visible Learning. A Synthesis of over 800 Meta-Analyses Relating to Achievement*. Oxford, UK: Routledge, 2009.

Herwig, Holger H. *The Marne, 1914: The Opening of World War I and the Battle That Changed the World*. New York: Random House, 2009.

Holec, Henri. *Autonomy and Foreign Language Learning*. Oxford, UK: Pergamon Press, 1981.

Holec, Henri, et al. "Conclusions on the 2004 Brunette Seminar on Learner Autonomy Report." *Independence* 38 (Summer 2006): 121–26.

Hürter, Johannes. *Hitlers Heerführer: Die Deutschen Oberbefehlshaber im Krieg gegen die Sowjetunion, 1941/42*. Munich: Oldenbourg Wissenschaftsverlag, 2007.

Huttonen, I. *Towards Learner Autonomy in Foreign Language Learning in Senior Secondary School*. Oulu, Finland: University of Oulu, 1986.

Knox, MacGregor, "Mass Politics and Nationalism as Military Revolution: The French Revolution and After." In *The Dynamics of Military Revolution 1300–2050*, edited by MacGregor Knox and Murray Williamson. New York: Cambridge University Press, 2001.

Krieg, Thilo. *Constantin von Alvensleben. Ein militärisches Lebensbild*. Berlin, Germany: Ernst Siegfried Mittler und Sohn, 1903.

Libero, Loretana de. "Tradition und Traditionsverständnis der Deutschen Luftwaffe." In *Tradition und Traditionsverständnis der Deutschen Luftwaffe, Geschichte, Gegenwart, Perspektiven*, edited by Heiner Möllers. Potsdam, Germany: Militärgeschichtliches Forschungsamt, 2012.

Lupfer, Timothy T. *The Dynamics of Doctrine: The Changes in German Tactical Doctrine during the First World War.* Fort Leavenworth, Kans.: Combat Studies Institute, 1981.

Manstein, Erich von. *Lost Victories.* Chicago: Henry Regnery, 1958.

———. *Verlorene Siege.* Bonn, Germany: Athenäum Verlag, 1955.

Melvin, Mungo. *Manstein, Hitler's Greatest General.* New York: Thomas Dunne Books, 2010.

Mintzberg, H. *The Structuring of Organizations: A Synthesis of the Research.* Englewood Cliffs, N.J.: Prentice-Hall, 1979.

Moltke, Helmut Karl Bernhard von. "Aus den Verordnungen für die höheren Truppenführer vom 24. Juni 1869." In *Moltkes Militärische Werke, Zweiter Theil, Die Tätigkeit als Chef des Generalstabs im Frieden,* edited by Preußischer Generalstab. Berlin, Germany: Ernst Siegfried Mittler und Sohn, 1900.

———. "Kurze Darstellung der Ereignisse vom 15. Juli bis 17. August 1870." In *Moltkes Militärische Werke, Band III, Kriegsgeschichtliche Arbeiten, Zweiter Theil,* edited by Preußischer Generalstab. Berlin, Germany: Ernst Siegfried Mittler und Sohn, 1899.

———. "Kurze Uebersicht des Feldzuges 1864 gegen Dänemark." In *Moltkes Militärische Werke, Band III, Kriegsgeschichtliche Arbeiten, Zweiter Theil,* edited by Preußischer Generalstab. Berlin, Germany: Ernst Siegfried Mittler und Sohn, 1899.

———. *On the Art of War, Selected Writings,* edited by Daniel J. Hughes, translated by Daniel J. Hughes and Harry Bell. New York: Random House, 1993.

Murray, Nicholas A. "Capturing Eben-Emael: The Key to the Low Countries." In *16 Cases of Mission Command,* edited by Donald P. Wright. Fort Leavenworth, Kans.: Combat Studies Institute Press, 2013.

Murray, Williamson A. "The West at War 1914–18." In *The Cambridge Illustrated History of Warfare, The Triumph of the West,* edited by Geoffrey Parker. New York: Cambridge University Press, 1995.

Murray, Williamson A., and Allan R. Millet. *Military Innovation in the Interwar Period.* New York: Cambridge University Press, 1996.

Muth, Jörg. *Command Culture: Officer Education in the US Army and the German Armed Forces, 1901–1940, and the Consequences for World War II.* Denton: University of North Texas Press, 2011.

———. *The Language of Mission Command and the Necessity of an Historical Approach.* https://thestrategybridge.org/the-bridge/2016/6/4/the-language-of-mission-command-and-the-necessity-of-an-historical-approach.

Nissestad, Odd Arne. "Leadership Development: An Empirical Study of Effectiveness of the Leadership Program at the Royal Norwegian Naval Academy and Its Impact on Preparing Officers to Execute Leadership in Today's Conflict and the Conflicts in the Years Ahead." PhD thesis, Norwegian School of Economics, Bergen, 2007.

Norwegian Armed Forces. *Defence Doctrine for Maritime Operations.* Bergen, 2015.

Norwegian Armed Forces. *Forsvarets pedagogiske grunnsyn* [The governing pedagogical principles of the defence forces]. Bergen, 2007.

Norwegian Armed Forces. *Forsvarssjefens grunnsyn på ledelse i Forsvaret* [Chief of Defence fundamental view on leadership in the military]. Bergen, 2012.

Norwegian Armed Forces. *Joint Operational Doctrine.* 2nd ed. Bergen, 2007.

Norwegian Armed Forces. *Joint Operational Doctrine.* 3rd ed. Bergen, 2014.

Oetting, Dirk W. *Auftragstaktik: Geschichte und Gegenwart einer Führungskonzeption.* Frankfurt am Main, Bonn: Report Verlag, 1993.

Paret, Peter. "Napoleon and the Revolution in War." In *Makers of Modern Strategy from Machiavelli to the Nuclear Age,* edited by Peter Paret. Princeton, N.J.: Princeton University Press, 1986.

Parker, Geoffrey, ed. *Cambridge Illustrated History of Warfare*. New York: Cambridge University Press, 1995.

Preußisches Kriegsministerium. *D.V.E. Nr. 130 Exerzier-Reglement für die Infanterie*. Berlin, Ernst Siegfried Mittler und Sohn, 1906.

———. *Exerzir-Reglement für die Infanterie* (signed 1888). Berlin, Ernst Siegfried Mittler und Sohn, 1889.

———. *Exerzir-Regelement für die Infanteri der Königlich Preußischen Armee*. Berlin, Germany: Georg Decker Königl. Geh. Oberhofbuchdrucker, 1812.

———. *Exerzir-Reglement für die Infanterie der Königlich Preußischen Armee*. Rev. 25 May 1867. Berlin, Germany: Decker Königl. Geh. Oberhofbuchdrucker, 1847.

———. *Extracts from Moltke's Military Correspondence Pertaining of the War of 1870–71*. Edited by Historical Section of the Prussian General Staff. Berlin, 1896. Translated by Harry Bell. Fort Leavenworth, Kans.: CGSC Library, 1910.

Raya, Manuel Jiménez, Terry Lamb, and Flávia Vieira. *Pedagogy for Autonomy in Language Education in Europe: Towards a Framework for Learner and Teacher Development*. Dublin: Authentik Language Learning Resources, 2007.

Reinders, Hayo, and Terry Lamb, eds. *Supporting Independent Language Learning: Issues and Interventions*. Bayreuth Contributions to Glottodidactics, vol. 10. Frankfurt am Main: Peter Lang, 2006.

Remarque, Erich Maria. *Im Westen nichts Neues*. Cologne, Germany: Kiepenheuer & Witsch, 1959.

Richards, Chet. *Certain to Win. The Strategy of John Boyd Applied to Business*. Philadelphia: Xlibris, 2004.

Ridgway, Matthew B. *Soldier: The Memoirs of Matthew B. Ridgway*. New York: Harper & Brothers, 1956.

Rommel, Erwin. *Infantry Attacks*. Minneapolis, Minn.: Zenith Press, 2009.

Røte, F. *Analyse av læringsrommet for opplæring av vaktsjefer i Fregattvåpenet. Forsvarsakademiet. Fakultet for Strategi og Militære Operationer*. VUT-II/STK, 2009–2010.

Royal Norwegian Naval Academy. *Man the Braces! Leadership Training Philosophy of the Royal Norwegian Naval Academy*. HOS Grafisk: Bergen, 2009.

Schmitt, John F., and Gary Klein, "Fighting in the Fog: Dealing with Battlefield Uncertainty." *Marine Corps Gazette* 80, no. 8 (August 1996). https://www.mca-marines.org/gazette/1996/08/fighting-fog-dealing-battlefied-uncertainty.

Schneiderhan, Wolfgang. "Innere Führung ein hoher Anspruch an die Praxis, Rede an der Führungsakademie der Bundeswehr." 20 June 2003. In *Gesellschaft, Militär, Krieg und Frieden im Denken von Wolf Graf von Baudissin*, edited by Martin Kutz. Baden-Baden, Germany: Nomos Verlagsgesellschaft, 2004.

Shamir, E. *Transforming Command: The Pursuit of Mission Command in the U.S., British and Israeli Armies*. Stanford, Calif.: Stanford University Press, 2011.

Soldatengesetz in der Fassung der Bekanntmachung vom 30. Mai 2005. (BGBl. I S. 1482), das durch Artikel 6 des Gesetzes vom 11. Juni 2013 (BGBl. I S. 1514) geändert worden ist.

Spradbrow, E. *Overcoming the Dark Side: Consequences of Destructive Leadership*. Oslo: Norwegian Defense University College, 2016.

Sweetman, John. *Tannenberg, 1914*. London: Cassel, 2002.

Trebbi, Turid. "Freedom—A Prerequisite for Learner Autonomy? Classroom Innovation and Language Teacher Education." In *Learner and Teacher Autonomy: Concepts, Realities and Response*, 33–46. Amsterdam: John Benjamins, 2008.

Trebbi, Turid, Arntzen Synnøve, Barbara Danielsen, and Anne Linda Løhre. "Learner Autonomy in the Norwegian Foreign Classroom: Teacher Initiatives Towards an Alternative Way of Learning." In *Pedagogy for Autonomy in Language Education in Europe: Towards a Framework for Learner and Teacher Development.* Dublin: Authentik Language Learning Resources, 2007.

U.S. Department of the Army. Army Doctrine Reference Publication 1–02, *Terms and Military Symbols, C2.* Washington, DC: Government Printing Office, November 2012.

———. Army Doctrine Reference Publication 6–0, *Mission Command.* Washington, DC: Government Printing Office, September 2012.

———. Field Manual 6–0, *Mission Command.* Washington, DC: Government Printing Office, September 2011.

Van Creveld, Martin. *The Art of War: War and Military Thought.* New York: Harper Collins, 2000.

———. *Command in War.* Cambridge, Mass.: Harvard University Press, 1985.

———. *Fighting Power: German and US Army Performance 1939–1945.* Westport, Conn.: Greenwood Press, 1982.

Vandergriff, Donald E. "Misinterpretation and Confusion: What is Mission Command and Can the U.S. Army Make It Work?" In *Land Warfare Papers*, no. 94. Arlington, Va.: Institute of Land Warfare (AUSA), 2013.

———. *Path to Victory: America's Army and the Revolution in Human Affairs.* Novato, Calif.: Presidio Press, 2002.

———. *Raising the Bar: Creating and Nurturing Adaptability to Deal with the Changing Face of War.* Washington, DC: Center for Defense Information, 2006.

———. *Swift to Swiss.* Annapolis, Md.: Performance Improvement, 2006.

Wawro, Geoffrey. *The Franco-Prussian War: The German Conquest of France in 1870–1871.* New York: Cambridge University Press, 2003.

Whetten, David A., and Mike Woods. *Effective Empowerment and Delegation.* New York: Pearson Education, 1996.

Widder, Werner. "Auftragstaktik and Innere Fuhrung: Trademarks of German Leadership." *Military Review*, October 2002. http://www.ramblemuse.com/rmtp/wp-content/uploads/2010/06/Widder_2002_Auftragstaktik_ MilRevr.pdf.

Wilson, James Q. *Bureaucracy.* New York: Basic Books, 1989.

Winslow, Donna. US Army Research Institute Note 2001–04, *Army Culture.* Alexandria, Va.: US Army Research Institute for the Behavioral and Social Sciences, 2000.

Wittmann, Jochen. *Auftragstaktik: Just a Command Technique or the Core Pillar of Mastering the Military Operational Art?* Berlin, Germany: Carola Hartmann Miles–Verlag, 2012.

Wright, Donald P., ed. *16 Cases of Mission Command.* Fort Leavenworth, Kans.: Combat Studies Institute Press, 2013.

Wrzesniewski, Amy, et al. "Multiple Types of Motives Don't Multiply the Motivation of West Point Cadets." *Proceedings of the National Academy of Sciences of the United States of America* 111 no. 30 (2014): 90–95.

Yardley, Ivan, and Andrew Kakabadse. "Understanding Mission Command: A Model for Developing Competitive Advantage in a Business Context." *Strategic Change* 16, no. 1 (2007): 69–78.

Zabecki, David T. "Defense in-Depth." In *The Encyclopedia of World War I: A Political, Social, and Military History*, edited by Spencer C. Tucker. Santa Barbara, Calif.: ABC-CLIO, 2005.

Index

NOTE: Page numbers in *italics* indicate photographs or graphics.

AARs (after-action reviews): in ACM courses, 109, 113–14, 148; pattern analysis in TDEs, 161–62; TA certification and, 104–5; for TDE attack/withdraw scenario, 165–66; TDE design and, 153; in war games, 183–85. *See also* TRADOC

Abrams, Creighton, 246, *251*

accountability, CATC problem-solving and, 85–86

active defense, 68, 71, 275n6

active listening, 119

"Adapt or Die: The Imperative for a Culture of Innovation in the United States Army," 55

adaptability: of ACM teachers, 114–15; Army's doctrine on, 264, 274n31; Auftragstaktik and, 263; DePuy's structure for Army training, 277n7; OBT&E and, 99–100; physical fitness and, 199–200, 212–13

Adaptability Handbook, 157

Adaptive Course Model (ACM), 86–95; attendee preparation for, 104; benefits of, 147–48, 279–80n7; briefing and instructions for, 118–19; combat PT, 201; curriculum and leader evaluation system, 95; curriculum for, 145; description of, 87; evaluations, 216–19; facilitating TDE delivery, 116–17; facilitation techniques, 119–20; facilitator responsibilities, 117–18; on growing the decision-maker, 81; leader development and, 120–21; OBT&E and, 79; outcomes for, 123; questions encouraged during, 147; scenario and case study education, 110–14; teachers of adaptability (TA) in, 102–3; teaching Auftragstaktik using, 3; teaching methods for, 106–10; teaching principles in, 114–16; testimonials on effectiveness

of, 88–95, 100; visiting teaching fellowships for, 106; youth football team and, 125–26

advanced individual training (AIT), 151

after-action reviews. *See* AARs

agility: 4th AD exemplifying, 256; physical fitness and, 199

AirLand Battle doctrine, 11, 68, 256, 289n46

Air-Sea Battle, 76

ALDS (Army Leadership Development Strategy), 97, 98

American officers, European and Prussian visit (nineteenth century), 29–30

analogies, dangers of reasoning by, 76

applicatory method, Swift's, U.S. military education and, 48

Armor (USMA) magazine, 157

Armored Division, 4th: lessons from, 52–53, 255–58; McNair on armored divisions and, 249–50; Woods and, 246–47, 248–49; in World War II, 241–44, 250–54, *255*, 287nn5–6

Army, U.S.: education system since 1980s, 67–68, 70–71; French approach to war and, 47–52; future training by, 262–64; teachers' role in, 102. *See also* Command and General Staff College; personnel system; TRADOC

Army Basic Instructor Course, 96

Army Instructor Training Course (AITC), 103–6

Army Learning Model (ALM, 2015), 25, 96, 97, 98

Army magazine, "Adapt or Die: The Imperative for a Culture of Innovation in the United States Army," 55

Army Physical Fitness Test (APFT), 196

Army Reconnaissance Course (ARC): accountability and adaptability, 229–31;

evaluations, 235–39; at Fort Benning, *225*; Goldeneye and Blackjack,
234–35; OBT&E institutionalized at,
239–40; Operation Bushmaster, 231–34;
overview, 224–29; translating for operational and strategic training, 262
Army Training and Leader Development
Panels, 63
ASLT&E (Adaptive Soldier Leader Training and Education), 79, 81, 126, 131,
138–40, 262, 283n46. *See also* OBT&E
Assembly (USMA) magazine, 157
Asymmetric Warfare Group (AWG),
82–86, 90, 277n9, 280n1
athletic test: Kriegsakademie admission
and, 33. *See also* physical fitness
attacking force, Western or Industrial Age
principle on force ratio for, 19
Auftragstaktik: centralized governance vs.,
1–2; evaluations, 216; focus of U.S. operations order on, 19–22; military effectiveness and, 24–25; as mission tactics,
Schell on, 18; Moltke and formulation
of, 29; *Patterns of Conflict* on, 11; peacetime leader development under, 34–35;
single personalities and, 22; teachers' role
in, 102; TRADOC and, 276–77n2; U.S.
Army's mission command doctrine and,
257, 262–64. *See also* EDFAS; Kriegsakademie; Kriegsschule
Austria, Prussian victory over, 28
authoritarian leadership, in U.S. Army, 53,
272n38
avoiding-a-solution approach, TDE design
and, 153

Balck, Hermann: Guderian's troops and,
14; Hitler and, 255; on individuality
of German fighting man, 20; intuitive
feel for flow of the battle and, 8; Mellenthin and, 39; on officer component,
37; speed of maneuver warfare and,
16; on written orders, 36
Baltimore Police Department, Sergeants
Leaders Course for, 189, 285n1
(ch 12)

Barker, Alec, 92
Basic Officer Leader Course (BOLC), 90,
278n28
Bautz, Edward, 241, 243, 287n1 (ch 15)
Bismarck, Otto von, 170
Bjork, Robert, 87, 88, 92
Blackjack, Operation, 228, 234–35
BLUFOR (blue forces), in free-play force-
on-force exercises, 189, 191–92
Blumentritt, Gunther, 11, 16
Board for Dynamic Training, 57
Boot, Max, 170
Boyd, John R.: Balck and Mellenthin
discussions with, 20; decision-making
theory of, 5; on implicit vs. explicit
communication, 15–16; OODA Loop
of, 6; *Patterns of Conflict*, 10–11; on
superior–subordinate contract, 12–13;
teaching philosophy, 261
Bradley, Omar, 68, 250
Brewster, Frank, 219
British army, combined arms in World War
I and, 45
bureaucracy, German, American officers
on military efficiency and, 29–30
Bushmaster, Operation, 227, 231–34
Butler, Benjamin, 270n10

Case, Steve, 83–84
Casey, George, 90, 278n30
Cavalry Journal (USMA) magazine, 157
centralized governance, Auftragstaktik vs.,
1–2
character, Germans on, 33, 34, 39–40
checklists: ARC and, 240; Army training and evaluation program as, 71;
OBT&E and, 131–32; OPFOR
actions and, 69; synchronization and
synchronization matrix as, 68
Cheney, Dick, 11
chief of staff, German, 38–39
Clarke, Bruce C., 246, 251, 254, 289n32
Clausewitz, Carl von, 28–29
climbing, combat PT and, 209–10
coaching, 107
Cobra, Operation, 249

cognitive development (CD), 142–43
Combat Applications Training Course (CATC), 79, 81, 82–86, 123, 279n50
Combat Olympics, 211–12
command and control systems, Fingerspitzengefühl and, 10
Command and General Staff College (CGSC), 48, 50, 52, 68, 241
Command Culture (Muth), 24, 275n12
command experience, TDEs and, 150
Command Post Exercises, war-gaming and, 174
commanders: best, NTC operations and, 73, 275n21; division, selection of, 46–47; leader development and, 35
commander's intent, Auftragstaktik emphasis on, 19–20
commissioning, German military education and, 32
common outlook (Schwerpunkt), 11–12
communication, Auftragstaktik and, 16
competency-based education, 80–81, 85–86, 88, 136
computer simulations, 258
Concept of the Operation (paragraphs 3a, U.S. operations order), 19–20
Continental Army Command, 1973 reorganization of, 57
contract: as freedom to choose, Auftragstaktik and, 16; between superior and subordinate, 12–13
Coordinating Instructions (paragraph 3b, U.S. operations order), 19–20
core competencies, TDE design and, 155
correspondence, written, German military education on, 23
Corum, James, 19
Crimean War (1854–56), 28
critical thinking, 48, 98, 264
culture: for fighting outnumbered, TRADOC on, 58–59; fourth-generation warfare, 59–60, 61; organizational behavior vs. organizational values and, 57; Pierce on leader development and, 276n35, 290n10; U.S. Army definition of, 55
Custer, John M., III, 95

Darwin, Morgan, 123
decision–hypothesis link, explicit control and, 17
decision-making: ACM and development of, 86–95; leader qualities for, 25–35; OODA Loop and, 5, 6–8; Prussian teaching of, 144–45; scenarios for learning, 112; training trips for, 174; war-gaming and, 172
decisions as instructions rule, enforcing, for TDE, 117, 118
defense district examination (Wehrkreis-Prüfung), 33
Defense Officer Personnel Management Act (DOPMA), 75, 77
Dempsey, Martin E., 78, 122
Denmark, Prussian victory over, 28
depot battalions, unit rotation system and, 43
DePuy, William: active defense concept, 71; copying the Germans, 271n23; on exhibiting initiative to prevail in combat, 59; flexibility and initiative and philosophy of, 61–62; personal leadership philosophy, 58; scientific management philosophy and, 261; structure for Army training and, 277n7
Descartes, René, 48–49
Desert Storm, 54–55, 59–60, 61
detail, level of, TDE design and, 152
developmental training, OBT&E as, 123
Devers, Jacob, 249
dilemmas, creating, TDE design and, 153
Discourse on Winning and Losing (Boyd), 8
discussions, in ACM courses, 115
division staffs, German, 36–38
doctrine: adaptability, 264, 274n31; AirLand Battle, 11, 68, 256, 289n46; Army's mission command, Auftragstaktik and, 257, 262–64; debate during 1980s on, 62; force development model and, 60–61; Pershing's, on open warfare, 45; TCS (training), 56, 57, 62, 81. *See also* TRADOC
double loop system, Leader Evaluation System as, 216–17

draftee soldiers, DePuy's personal leadership philosophy and, 58
drawdown of 1990s, 59, 61, 62–63, 274n28
du Vernois, Verdy, 47, 171
dumb questions, in ACM courses, 109
Dunford, Joseph, 77

Eddy, Manton S., 251, 253
EDFAS (Einheit, Behändigkeit, Fingerspitzengefühl, Auftragstaktik, and Schwerpunkt), 8. *See also specific elements of*
education, training compared with, 143
Einheit (trust or unity), 10, 265n17
Eisenhower, Dwight D., 250, 288n10
Elzy, Robert, 93
enabling learning objectives (ELO), 261
enthusiasm, of ACM teachers, 114
Erziehung (refinement education and childhood training), 39–40
"Essence of Winning and Losing, The" (Boyd), 8
estimates: training trips for, 174; wargaming and, 172
Ethical Egoism, 42–43
evaluations: ACM curriculum and leader, 95, 216–19; ARC, 235–39; benefits of, 222–23; checklists and, 71; how-to for, 220–22; overview, 214–16; for Prussian TDEs, 145; TDEs, 167–68. *See also* AARs
examinations: defense district (Wehrkreis-Prüfung), 33; German military education and, 23
experiential learning or training, 278n34; in ACM courses, 110; TDEs and, 150. *See also* Auftragstaktik
explicit control, rare use of, 17

facilitators. *See* instructors
Fahnenjunker, leader selection and, 30
Fastabend, David A., 98
FBCB2 (Force XXI Battle Command Brigade and Below) tracker, 233, 287n7 (ch 14)
feedback loop: scenarios and, 112; TA certification and, 105–6. *See also* AARs

Field Manual 7-0, *Training*, 22, 80, 97
Field Manual 17-100, *Armored Command Field Manual, The Armored Division*, 241, 287n2
Field Manual 100-5, *Operations*, 256
Field Manual/ADP 6-22, *Army Leadership*, 97
fighting outnumbered, 57, 58–59
Fingerspitzengefühl, description of, 8–10
fire-and-movement tactics, during World War II, U.S. Army and, 50
five-paragraph operations orders, 48, 241
foot marches, combat PT and, 209
force development model, Army doctrine for, 60–61
force ratio, German attacking force in World War II and, 19
force-on-force method, with TDE scenarios, 116–17
Forces Command, reorganization of Continental Army Command and, 57
foreign language study, German military education and, 33
Fort Benning: ACM at, 89, 90; Army Reconnaissance Course at, *225*; CATC at, 82; Haskins on training at (2007), 64–65; Maneuver Center for Excellence, 277n2, 286n11; map exercise at, *146*; Marshall as commandant of Infantry School at, 50; OBT&E and, 79, 96
Fort Irwin, California, 62, 71–74, 186
Fort Leavenworth, 48, 54, 187, 272n33. *See also* Command and General Staff College
Fort Polk, Louisiana, 62, 186
Foster, Chad, 88–89, 93–94, 100, 122, 142
Foundations of the Science of War (Fuller), 260
fourth-generation warfare (4GW) culture, 59–60, 61
France: army's combined arms in World War I, 45; military decision-making process of, 47–52, 271n28
Franco-Prussian War (1870–71), 28, 171
Freakley, Benjamin C., 90

Frederick the Great, 15, 26–27, *27*, 29
Frederick Wilhelm I, 26
free-play force-on-force exercises: after-action reviews of, 23; conducting, 189–94; German performance evaluation and, 24; Kriegsakademie curriculum and, 34; OPFOR in, 186–89; Rommel and, 194–95; U.S. Army's use of, 186
French Revolution, 28
friction: German command and control system and, 15–16; introducing, to teach adaptability and mission command, 162; in Kriegsspiel, dice as, 171; simulating, TDEs and, 151; TDEs causing, 154–55; teams and diminishing, 10; war-gaming and, 172
Frusha, Robert, 196
Führerausfall (leader fatality), Kriegsakademie war games and, 34
Führung und Gefecht der Verbundenen Waffen (1921 flight manual), 21
Fuller, J. F. C., 244, 245–46, 260

Gaedcke, Ludwig Heinrich, 37–38
Gavin, James, 53
General Staff, German, 34, 36–37
Georgetown University, 86, 279–80n7
German Army: as most decentralized in Europe, 20; professional bonding in mission trust of, 11–12
German Empire, Prussian victories and, 28
German military education system: Auftragstaktik and, 22–23; chief of staff role, 38–39; daily command briefing, 37–38; Erziehung and, 39–40; instructor selection for, 101; intangible solution to training and, 5; Kriegsakademie teachers, 33–34; leader development and, 30–33, 268n31; officer to enlisted force ratio and, 36–37; peacetime leader development and, 34–35; process for developing orders, 36; TDEs used in, 144–45; teaching tools of, 70

German way of command: Auftragstaktik and, 19–22; in context and environment, 22–25; early World War II victories and, 19; Hitler and, 254–55; Schell on mission tactics, 18
Germany: officer aspirants and public education in, 30; Unification wars, Auftragstaktik during, 35; U.S. Army Combat Training Center in, 62
Giese, Casey, 92
Goldeneye, Operation, 227, 234–35
Gorman, Paul F., 71
granularity of information, TDE design and, 152
Great General Staff, German, 34
Greenwood, John, 169
guardsmen, mobilized, obsolete training for, 65–66
Guderian, Heinz: on Einheit, 265n17; on Fingerspitzengefühl, 8; relieved for out-thinking seniors, 287n3; on Schwerpunkt, 11, 265n22; at Sedan, France (1940), *9*, 14; speed of maneuver warfare and, 16; Wood's use of theories of, 245–46
Gudmundsson, Bruce I., 20, 280n16
guiding actions, evaluations of, 217

Haskins, Casey: CATC and, 279n50; evaluations at West Point and, 220; free-play force-on-force exercises, 188; on outcomes development, 133–36, 282n39; on training at Fort Benning (2007), 64–65
Hauptkadettenanstalt (main cadet institution), 30
Hellwig, Ludwig, 170
Heraclitus, 260
High-Tech Light Division (HTLD), 62, 274n26
hip-shooting artillery, 282, 289n34
historical battles, TDE design and, 155
Hitler, Adolf, 254–55
Hodges, Courtney H., 53
Hörsaalleiter (teachers), at Kriegsakademie, 33–34

hot-seat thinking, TDEs and, 150, 160
house of cards technique, for TDE attack/
    withdraw scenario, 165
"How We Learn Versus How We Think We
    Learn: Implications for the Organiza-
    tion of Army Training" (Bjork), 87
Hurtgen Forest, Hodges' attack into
    (1944), 53

implicit communication, Boyd on Auftrag-
    staktik and, 15–16
implicit guidance and control, explicit
    control and, 17
in ACM courses, focus on, 119, 120
independence, of German officers, 20–21
individual replacement system (IRS),
    43–44, 73–74, 270nn9–10
Industrial Age barriers: assembly line of
    soldiers and, 43–47; centrally con-
    trolled, attritional doctrine as, 52–53;
    Ethical Egoism and, 42–43; military
    decision-making process, 47–52; mis-
    sion control mindset and, 81; Root
    and, 41–42; Taylor and Taylorism
    and, 42. See also Root, Elihu; Taylor,
    Fredrick
Infantry Journal, 52
information, limiting, TDE design and,
    153
Information Age, Army leader behavior
    and, 59
initiative: definition difficulties, 59; 4th AD
    exemplifying, 256
injuries, running-related, 198
Instructions for the Representation of Tactical
    Maneuvers under the Guise of a Wargame,
    170
instructors. See teachers; teachers of adapt-
    ability
intangible problem-solving: Army Recon-
    naissance Course and, 225; as difficult
    to measure but observable, 123, 126;
    Germans on education and training
    and, 5; youth football training and,
    125–26
interactive training, TDEs and, 150
interest, generating, TDE design and, 151

intuition: TDE introduction to, 160. See
    also Fingerspitzengefühl
Irzyk, Albin F., 243

James, Zoltan, 90, 91, 95
Jena and Auerstaedt, Battle of (1806), 27
Joint Professional Military Education
    (JPME) certification system, 260
Jomini, Antoine-Henri baron de, 51

Kadettenschulen (cadet schools), Program
    of Instruction for, 30–32
Kennedy, Chris, 87
Klein, Gary, 7, 87, 186, 214
Knobelsdorff, Otto von, 37
knowledge development (KD), training
    and education for, 143
Kriegsakademie, 23, 32, 33
Kriegsschule (war schools), 31, 32, 268n56
Kriegsspiel (war game), 170–71, 171, 172,
    182
Kriegsspiel rules, teaching map exercise
    using, 146

Laidlaw, Patrick, 87
leader assessment, Auftragstaktik develop-
    ment and, 25–35
leader development: in ACM courses,
    108, 120–21; analytical, for U.S. Army,
    49–50; Auftragstaktik and, 3–4; com-
    manders and, 35; Frederick the Great
    and, 27; German Army, 11–12, 20–21,
    23; German military education and,
    30–33; hazing and, 30, 31, 268n51;
    OBT&E environment and, 81–82; in
    peacetime, 34–35; personnel reform
    and, 2–3; physical fitness and, 196–97,
    198, 199, 200; Pierce on organiza-
    tional culture and, 276n35; Prussian
    Act of 1809 on, 28; teaching tools for,
    32–33; U.S. Army during 1980s, 62;
    U.S. Army's Industrial Age approach to,
    41–42; U.S. misinterpretation of French
    misunderstanding of German teaching
    methods for, 47–48. See also TRADOC
Leader Evaluation System (LES), 216–19
Lear, Ben, 248–49

learning organization, TDEs and, 151
Leeson, Bill, 171
lessons learned, for TDE, summarizing, 117, 118
Leuthen, Battle of (1757), *27*
light infantry divisions, adaptive concepts for, 62
limits on time. *See* time limits
linear top-down firepower-heavy culture, DePuy and, 58, 59

Macgregor, Douglas, 72, 196
management science, McNamara and, 75–76
managing the TDE, in ACM courses, 116
Maneuver Warfare Handbook, 162, 181, 184
Manstein, Erich von, 38–39, 255
Manteuffel, Hasso-Eccard von, 38
Manual for Commanders of Large Units (1930), 51, 271nn28–29
Manual of 1888 (German command system), 29
map exercises, 48, 174
Marine Corps Gazette, TDEs of, 157, 284n21
Marine Corps, U.S., *Patterns of Conflict* (Boyd's PowerPoint presentation) for, 11
Marshall, George C., 50, 51–52, 53, 288n10
Maslow's hierarchy of needs, 84
matrix: as Army teaching tool, 70. *See also* synchronization and synchronization matrix
McEnery, Kevin, 224, 230
McKinley, William, 41
McNair, Leslie, 248, 249
McNamara, Robert, 75–76
measures of effectiveness (MOE): ARC, 236–39; examples of, 134–36; outcomes training and, 129, 133–34; physical fitness, for Q-course, 137–38, 282n39, 283nn40–41; for TDE ambushing scenario, 157–58; for TDE attack/withdraw scenario, 162
Mellenthin, Friedrich von, 20, 36, 39

mental agility, of ACM teachers, 114–15
mentorship, 112, 114, 115, 148, 222–23
Meuse-Argonne campaign, 45
military decision-making process (MDMP), 47, 271n24
military genius, as superfluous, military professionalism and, 54
Military Intelligence Basic Officer Leader Course (MIBOLC), 91
military occupational specialty (MOS), 44, 101–2
military social research, 290n7
Milley, Mark, 77
mission command (mission concept): Boyd on, 10–13; effective business practices compared with, 76; Schwerpunkt and, 13–15; skills development for, 1. *See also* Industrial Age barriers
mission essential task list development, readiness assessment and, 61
mistakes, during training, learning and, 140
Mitchell, William "Billy," 45–46
mobility, physical fitness and, 199
modifying terrain perspective TDEs, 156
Moilanen, Jon, 107
Mollwitz, battle of (1741), 26
Moltke, Helmuth von, 28, *28*, 145, 170
Multiple Integrated Laser Engagement System (MILES), 71, 188
multiple interpretations and solutions, TDE design and, 152–53
Muth, Jörg, 24, 30, 41, 74, 279n2

Napoleon, personnel policies of, 76
Napoleonic Wars (1792–1815), 28
Neipperg (Austrian commander), 26
Noncommissioned Officer Academy (NCOA), 90, 91
noncommissioned officer evaluation report (NCOER), intangible attributes in, 126
noncommissioned officers (NCOs), 101–2, 227
non-state groups, terrorism and, 60
Oberkommando Wehrmacht (OKW), 254–55

objective: for TDE ambushing scenario, 157–58; for TDE attack/withdraw scenario, 162

Obstacle, Up and Over, combat PT and, 206–7

obstacle courses, combat PT and, 209

OBT&E (Outcomes-Based Training and Education), 225; ACM, 86–95, 262; adoption of, 78–100; applying mission command concepts in, 126; ARC and, 227, 239–40; Auftragstaktik taught using, 3; CATC, 82–86; continuing evolution and, 98–100; cultural learning evolution with, 95–98; definition of, 123; development of, 280n1; as developmental training, 79; effective teaching in ACM as part of, 114–16; evaluations, 221–22; implementing, 138–40, 283n46; Operation Bushmaster, 232–34; planning training outcomes for, 131; supporting Army Learning Model 2015, 25; TRADOC and, 276–77n2; warning orders and, 124. *See also* Adaptive Course Model; ASLT&E; Combat Applications Training Course; outcomes

Odierno, Raymond T., 97

off-duty conduct, German leader development and, 23

officer corps: Pershing compensating for lack of, 45. *See also* commanders

officer evaluation report (OER), intangible attributes in, 126

officer to enlisted force ratio, 32, 35, 37–38

officers: in ARC, 227; as instructors, 101–2

On the German Art of War, Truppenführung (Condell and Zabecki), 19

On War (Clausewitz), 28–29

one-move TDEs, 151

OODA (Observation, Orientation, Decision, and Action) loop: Boyd on, 5; description of, 6–8; of the enemy, Boyd on upsetting, 10–11; Fingerspitzengefühl and, 9; Germans' use of, 16; graphic depicting, 6; speed and accuracy in, 17

open warfare, discarded for combined arms in World War I, 45

operating environment simulation difficulties, TDEs and, 151

operations research systems analysts (ORSAs), initiative definition and, 59

OPFOR (opposing forces): in free-play force-on-force exercises, 186–89, 192–93, 285n8; National Training Center use of, 72–73, 275n21; relying on checklists vs. actions of, 69

orders: battlefield, Mellenthin on, 36; five-paragraph operations, scientific management philosophy and, 48; five-paragraph operations, Wood on, 241; issuing, war-gaming and, 172, 174; operations, U.S. sections in, Auftragstaktik and, 19–20; operations, vague U.S., in ACM courses, 109; verbal vs. written, Auftragstaktik and, 36; written, 4th Armored Division and, 241–44; written, Woods on, 246–47

organizational culture, 276n35, 290n10

outcomes: creation of, 136–37; intangible attributes in, 123, 126; measures of effectiveness and, 133–36, 282n34; physical fitness, for Q-course, 137–38, 281n13; planning training using, 130–31; principles of, 126–28; teaching how-to of, 128–29; for training and education design, 129–30; training and education with focus on, 131–33; training or learning objectives compared with, 122. *See also* OBT&E

packing list problem, 230, 233

Panzer Corps, XIX, 14, 194–95. *See also* Guderian, Heinz

pattern analysis, TDEs and, 161

Patterns of Conflict (Boyd's PowerPoint presentation), 10–11

Patton, George S., Jr., 245, 250, 288n10

peacetime: Auftragstaktik practice during, 19, 266n4; German leader development and, 34–35

performance, minimum acceptable level
of, outcome goals and, 129–30
Perkins, David, 74
Perry, Robert C., 224, 230
Pershing, John J., 45, 46–47, 270n17
personal experience, TDE design and, 155
personnel reform, leader development
and, 2–3
personnel system: centralized, asymmetric
wars and, 2; command selection and,
72–73, 275–76n22; European depot
manning-type, 43; German decentralized, 23; German staff officers
and, 37–38; individual replacement
system and, 43–44, 73–74, 270nn9–10;
Napoleon's, 76; OBT&E and, 25, 97;
out-of-date assumptions of, 74–75;
Snow on, 67; Taylor and Root, 41–43;
unit-based replacement system and,
44; U.S. Army, 25. See also German
military education system; training
Pestalozzi, Johann Heinrich, 143, 278n34
physical fitness (physical training or PT):
adaptability and, 212–13; ARC and,
229–30; climbing, 209–10; combat, ACM, 201; combat, analysis
of, 196–98; combat, assessment of,
199–200; combat, TDEs, 201–8; Combat Olympics, 211–12; foot marches,
209; obstacle course, 209; Q-course,
137–38, 282n39, 283nn40–41; team
sports, 211
Pike, Thomas, 91, 92
pre-mortems, in ACM courses, 114
preparation for TDE, 117
presentation of scenarios, 117, 118
pretraining, TDEs as, 144–45
problem-solving skills teaching methodology, 48, 82–86
professional soldiers, mission-focused
training and, 62
proficiency, ACM and, 114
Programs of Instruction (POI): ACM for,
88, 90, 92; order and control and,
80–81; terminal learning objectives
and, 261; of the Voranstalt and Haupt-

kadettenschule, 30. See also Adaptive
Course Model
Prussia: defense of, 25–28; Moltke as chief
of General Staff of, 29; Pestalozzi and
military education by, 143–45. See also
German military education system

Q-Course (Special Forces Qualification
Course), 128–29, 136–38, 281n13,
282n39, 283nn40–41
questioning thought process, for TDE, 117,
118, 119–20
questions: dumb, in ACMs, 109; Socratic,
107, 147; during TDEs, 160–61

Raising the Bar (Vandergriff), 157, 158, 183,
196, 198
random engagement, TDE design and, 155
rationale for TDE, questioning, 117, 118
readiness assessment, mission essential task
list development and, 61
red teaming, 187
regulations, impeding OBT&E, 140,
283n46
Reiswitz, Georg Heinrich Rudolf von, 170
Reiswitz, Georg Leopold von, 170
reliefs, system of, German staff officers and,
37–38
replacement divisions, 44. See also individual replacement system
reservists, obsolete training for, 65–66
responsibility: Erziehung and, 40; of German officers, 20–21
reverse scenario TDEs, 156
Richards, Chet, 7, 8, 16
rifle marksmanship, teaching, 82–86
road marches: analysis of, 197; BLUFOR,
192; frequency and distance of, 200;
Kriegsakademie and, 33; Q-Course,
137–38
role-playing, TDE design and, 153
Rommel, Erwin, 8, 13, 16, 194–95, 255
Root, Elihu: Army's continued reliance on
theories of, 75; copying the Germans,
271n23; exorcising ghost of, 77; long-
term negative impacts of reforms by,

43, 46, 52; on management science and leader development and, 41–42

Russia, Mellenthin and Balck's campaigns in, 36

safety, skills development and, 99
Saint-Mihel campaign, 45
Sand Castle, combat PT and, 208
sand-table exercises, 176
scenarios: in ACM courses, 110–14, 280n18; formats for training using, 148–49; in German military education system, 144
Scharnhorst, Gerhard von, 22, 28, 143–44, 268n56, 278n34
Schell, Adolf von, 18, 101
School of Advanced Military Science (SAMS), U.S. Army's, 31
school solutions, U.S. military education and, 48, 52
Schoomaker, Peter, 55–56, 63, 90
Schwerin, Field Marshal von, 26
Schwerpunkt (focal point) (point of decision): attacks, character of, 14; commander locating himself at, 39; harmonizing independent actions created through Auftragstaktik, 13; operations planning and, 11; support for, by other commanders, 15
Schwerpunktprinzip (concentration principle), 11
scientific management philosophy, 47–48, 260–61
Scout Leaders Course (SLC), 224–25, 226
Scout Platoon Leaders Course (SPLC), 224
second-generation warfare (2GW) culture, 58, 59, 61
Secretary of the Army Human Dimension Task Force (2011), 75
Seekt, Hans von, 177, 258
seminars, scenarios and, 116
September 11 attacks, Army cultural behaviors and, 64

Shimar, Eitan, 77
Shinseki, Eric, 63
Shoot and Move, combat PT and, 205–6, 207
simplicity, design, TDE design and, 154–55
Simpson, Robert H., 98
simulators, 69, 71–72, 258
Simunition (proprietary non-lethal training ammunition), 188
situational training exercise (canned STX lane), 285n8
situation-based TDEs, 155–56
small unit command, war-gaming and, 175–76
Snow, Daniel P., 54, 67
social Darwinism, 42
Socratic questions, 107, 147
solitaire method, for TDE scenario, 116
solution reaction-based TDEs, 155, 156
Sonstein, Mark, 147, 220, 221–22
Sources of Power (Klein), 7
Special Forces, innovative training of, 62
special operations, difficulty applying TDEs to, 151
Sprey, Pierre, 20
staff exercises, war-gaming and, 174
staff rides: German commanders' development of subordinates and, 23; Germans teaching critical thinking using, 48
student understanding, in ACM courses, 148
students, choosing, for TDE solution presentations, 117, 118
Study on Military Professionalism (1970), 57
subordinates: contract between superior and, 12–13; individuality of, 20; Prussian wars of 1864, 1866, and 1870 and, 29; questioning, Auftragstaktik and, 16; in U.S. Army, goal displacement and, 63; in U.S. Army, indifference to, 53. See also Auftragstaktik
Sun Tzu, 11, 143
superiors: contract between subordinates and, 12–13. See also officers

Swift, Eben, 47, 48, 70, 271n24
symposium-based case studies, ACM and, 92–93
synchronization and synchronization matrix, 68, 69, 256
systems approach to training, 152

tactical decision games (TDGs): ACM and, 92–93, 109; TA certification and, 105
tactical walks, war-gaming and, 175–76
Take a Stroll (tactical movement), combat PT and, 204
task force principle, Woods and, 246
task mastery, OBT&E and, 133
task/conditions/standards (TCS): DePuy's, 61; as training doctrine, 56, 57, 62, 81
Taylor, Fredrick (Taylorism): Army's continued reliance on theories of, 75; competency-based education and, 80–81; exorcising ghost of, 77; individual replacement system and, 43, 45; management theories, 42; reevaluation of Army's use of theories of, 59; scientific management philosophy and, 47; unit-based replacement system and, 44
TDEs (Tactical Decision Exercises): in ACM courses, 114, 116–17; advantages of, 149–51; Brewster on use of, 219; combat PT, 201–2; definition of, 142; design of, 151–57; evaluating decision-making during, 167–68; example tactical questions with, 166–67; Follow Me, 284n12; history of, 142–45; the "how-to" with, 145–49; lesson plan on ambushing (example), 157–62; lesson plan on attacking or withdrawing (example), 162–67; limiting factors, 151; naming, 142; Obstacle, Up and Over, 206–7; personnel benefits from, 149; PT during, 200; Sand Castle, 208; Shoot and Move, 205–6, 207; squad-level casualty evacuation, 202–3; tactical movement (Take a Stroll), 204; team-

level casualty evacuation, 203–4; uses for, 146
teachers: assignments as, 101–2; characteristics of, 101; facilitating techniques, 148; German selection of, 279n2; Kriegsakademie, 33–34; preparation for OBT&E model, 135–36, 282n34; skills necessary for, 143. See also evaluations
teachers of adaptability (TAs): AARS in ACM courses and, 113–14; certification process, 103–6, 280n8; characteristics of, 102–3; scenario development by, 111, 112–13; teaching methods, 106–10, 280nn14–15. See also Adaptive Course Model
team sports, combat PT and, 211
teams, Boyd's advice for, 9–10
technology, late-nineteenth-century European warfare and, 28
terminal learning objectives (TLO), 261
Terrain Board Exercises (TBEs), delivering TDEs with, 149
threat models: Army's assumptions about, 60; Warsaw Pact as, 59
360-degree assessments, 107, 222, 235–36
Thurman, J. W., 224
time limits: in ACM courses, 109; enforcing, for TDE, 117, 118; in Prussian TDEs, 144; for TDE attack/withdraw scenario, 164; TDE design and, 153
TRADOC (Training and Doctrine Command): ACM and, 89, 90–91; Army internal debates on, 61–62; Army Reconnaissance Course and, 225; Asymmetric Warfare Group and, 277n9; competency-based education and, 80–81; drawdown of 1990s and, 62–63, 274n28; intent vs. practice and, 55; as large organization, difficulty of change in, 56–57; learning methodologies of, 3; OBT&E and Auftragstaktik and structure of, 276–77n2; purpose for, 54; reliance on doctrinal

products of, 63–64; reorganization of Continental Army Command and, 57; scientific management of knowledge by, 260–61

training: adapting Auftragstaktik for, 262–64; band of excellence, 273n18; DePuy's personal leadership philosophy and, 58; discouraging thinking and decision-making, 64–65; education compared with, 143; FM 100-5, *Operations* and, 256; German military education and, 24, 35; knowledge and independence fostered in, 39; OBT&E/ASLT&E and, 140–41, 262; systems approach to, 152

training trips, war-gaming and, 174–75

Transforming Command (Shimar), 77

Truppenführung (1933): on joy of taking responsibility, 21; World War II tactics and, 13–16

trust: Army leadership's ownership of, 264; of German officers, 20–21

Tschischwitz, Wilhelm von, 171

Ulmer, Walt, 217

umpires, for war games, 47, 171, 172, 178–79

unit employment, in map exercises, 174

unit manning system: German, 35; individual replacement system and, 44; U.S. Army's attempt at, 43, 270n10

United States: Civil War (1861–65), technology and, 28; French methodical battle in interwar years and, 49–50; misinterpretation of French misunderstanding of German teaching methods by, 48

United States Military Academy (USMA): ACM at, 88–89; evaluations at, 220–21; free-play force-on-force exercises at, 188; French approach to war and, 51; German officer education system compared with, 30, 31, 268n51; objective MOEs supporting outcomes at, 134; TDEs used by, 157

Upton, Emory or Uptonians, 30, 46, 70, 269n4, 270n10

variable modification TDEs, 156–57

Verantwortungsfreudigkeit (joy of taking responsibility), 21–22

Vietnam War, Army culture and, 57

Virtual Battlespace 2 (VBS2), 229

visiting teaching fellowships, for ACM courses, 106

volunteer Army, 57, 58, 63

Voranstalt (cadet preparatory school), German, 30

Wagner, Arthur L., 70

war games (war-gaming): AAR for wrap up of, 183–85; critical thinking using, 48; general course of play, 180–81; German rules for, 172–74, 284n5; German vs. du Vernois' system for, 47–48; history of, 170–72; notes for directors, 176–77; practical example, 181–82; purpose for, 169–70; training value, 177–79; types of, 174–76. *See also* free-play force-on-force exercises

War Made New, 170

warning orders, input vs. outcome example for, 124

Warsaw Pact, 57, 59

Watson, Andrew, 94–95

weapons, in map exercises, 174

West Point. *See* United States Military Academy

Wilcox, Paul, 92, 278n39, 279n6

Wood, John S.: in Eastern France, *244*; 4th AD in Europe and, 250, 251–54, 257, 289n31; 4th AD training and, 241–42; and his officers, 244–49, 288n10, 288n14; relieved for out-thinking seniors, 287n3

World War I: Auftragstaktik during, 35; individual replacement system and, 43–44; lack of U.S. Army commanders and staff officers for, 46; open warfare discarded for combined arms in, 45; U.S. staff officers and commanders training at French schools for, 49

World War II: Army's approach to education since, 68–69; German victories in early years of, 19; officer to enlisted force ratio, 35; *Truppen-führung* (1933) and German tactics during, 13–16; U.S. officer production system and, 168

Wyly, Mike, 261

Yom Kippur War (1973), 57

youth football, ACM training for, 125–26

The Naval Institute Press is the book-publishing arm of the U.S. Naval Institute, a private, nonprofit, membership society for sea service professionals and others who share an interest in naval and maritime affairs. Established in 1873 at the U.S. Naval Academy in Annapolis, Maryland, where its offices remain today, the Naval Institute has members worldwide.

Members of the Naval Institute support the education programs of the society and receive the influential monthly magazine *Proceedings* or the colorful bimonthly magazine *Naval History* and discounts on fine nautical prints and on ship and aircraft photos. They also have access to the transcripts of the Institute's Oral History Program and get discounted admission to any of the Institute-sponsored seminars offered around the country.

The Naval Institute's book-publishing program, begun in 1898 with basic guides to naval practices, has broadened its scope to include books of more general interest. Now the Naval Institute Press publishes about seventy titles each year, ranging from how-to books on boating and navigation to battle histories, biographies, ship and aircraft guides, and novels. Institute members receive significant discounts on the Press' more than eight hundred books in print.

Full-time students are eligible for special half-price membership rates. Life memberships are also available.

For a free catalog describing Naval Institute Press books currently available, and for further information about joining the U.S. Naval Institute, please write to:

Member Services
U.S. Naval Institute
291 Wood Road
Annapolis, MD 21402-5034
Telephone: (800) 233-8764
Fax: (410) 571-1703
Web address: www.usni.org

Donald E. Vandergriff is an expert on mission command, maneuver warfare, and leader development using the latest in learning methodologies. A noted speaker, award-winning author, and teacher, Vandergriff is also the author or editor of six books and more than one hundred articles. He is a former Marine and retired Army officer, having served twenty-four years in uniform and another twelve years as a contractor, both overseas and in the United States. He lives in Woodbridge, Virginia.